INTRODUCTION TO HEALTH PROFESSIONS

Introduction to
HEALTH PROFESSIONS

Edited by

ANNE S. ALLEN, M.A., O.T.R.

Assistant Professor and Assistant Director,
School of Allied Medical Professions,
The Ohio State University,
Columbus, Ohio

THIRD EDITION

Illustrated

The C. V. Mosby Company

ST. LOUIS • TORONTO • LONDON   1980

THIRD EDITION

Copyright © 1980 by The C. V. Mosby Company

All rights reserved. No part of this book may be reproduced in any manner without written permission of the publisher.

Previous editions copyrighted 1972, 1976

Printed in the United States of America

The C. V. Mosby Company
11830 Westline Industrial Drive, St. Louis, Missouri 63141

Library of Congress Cataloging in Publication Data

Main entry under title:

Introduction to health professions.

  Includes bibliographies and index.
  1. Medicine—Vocational guidance. 2. Allied health personnel—Vocational guidance. I. Allen, Anne S., 1923-
R690.I57   1980   610.69   79-26136
ISBN 0-8016-0113-4

C/M/M 9 8 7 6 5 4 3 2 1   05/A/603

CONTRIBUTORS

ANNE S. ALLEN, M.A., O.T.R.

Assistant Professor and Assistant Director, School of Allied Medical Professions, The Ohio State University, Columbus, Ohio

MARTHA WILSON ARRINGTON

Formerly Director of Communications, Association of Physician Assistants, Arlington, Virginia

PHILIP W. BALLINGER, M.S., R.T. (ARRT)

Director, Radiologic Technology Division, School of Allied Medical Professions, The Ohio State University, Columbus, Ohio

MARY ALICE BEETHAM, M.S.P.H.

Assistant Professor, Health Education, and Coordinator, Advisory Committee, Health Education Extension Services, The Ohio State University, Columbus, Ohio

JOHN W. BLACK, Ph.D.

Regents Professor, Speech and Hearing Science, Department of Communication, The Ohio State University, Columbus, Ohio

F. ORIS BLACKWELL, Dr.P.H., R.S.

Professor, Environmental Health, East Carolina University, Greenville, North Carolina

MARJORIE L. BRUNNER, M.S., M.T. (ASCP)

Assistant Professor, Continuing Education, School of Allied Medical Professions, The Ohio State University, Columbus, Ohio

J. ROBERT BULLOCK, R.T. (ARRT)

Director, Radiologic Technology Program, Mt. Carmel Medical Center, Columbus, Ohio

JOHN E. BURKE, Ph.D.

Director, Medical Communications and Medical Illustration Divisions, School of Allied Medical Professions, The Ohio State University, Columbus, Ohio

CLARENCE R. COLE, Ph.D., D.V.M.

Regents Professor and former Dean, College of Veterinary Medicine, The Ohio State University, Columbus, Ohio

JAMES P. DEARING, B.S., C.C.P.

Assistant Professor and Director, Extracorporeal Technology Program and Director, Life Support Services, Medical University Hospital and Veterans Administration Hospital, Charleston, South Carolina

WILLIAM C. DEW, D.D.S.

Associate Dean, Secretary, and Professor, College of Dentistry, The Ohio State University, Columbus, Ohio

F. HERBERT DOUCE, M.S., RRT

Director, Respiratory Therapy Division, School of Allied Medical Professions, The Ohio State University, Columbus, Ohio

GEORGE L. FITE, M.D.

Bethesda, Maryland; formerly Division of Scientific Publications, American Medical Association, Chicago, Illinois

KATHERINE L. KISKER, R.N., M.S.

Instructor, School of Nursing, The Ohio State University, Columbus, Ohio

DAVID A. KNAPP, Ph.D.

Professor, Department of Pharmacy Administration, School of Pharmacy, University of Maryland, Baltimore, Maryland

JAMES R. KREUTZFELD, B.F.A.

Coordinator, Medical Illustration Division, School of Allied Medical Professions, The Ohio State University, Columbus, Ohio

ELIZABETH J. LASCHINGER, M.S.W., ACSW

Lecturer, College of Social Work, The Ohio State University, Columbus, Ohio

BARBARA McCOOL, M.H.A., Ph.D.

Associate Professor, Department of Health Administration, Duke University, Durham, North Carolina

WILLIAM F. MUNSEY, D.P.M.

Clinical Instructor, College of Medicine, The Ohio State University, Columbus, Ohio

JAMES F. NOE, M.A.

Assistant to the Dean and College Secretary, College of Optometry, The Ohio State University, Columbus, Ohio

MELANIE MOERSCH PARISER, M.S., R.R.A.

Director, Medical Records Administration Division, School of Allied Medical Professions, The Ohio State University, Columbus, Ohio

FRANK M. PIERSON, M.A., L.P.T.

Director, Physical Therapy Division, School of Allied Medical Professions, The Ohio State University, Columbus, Ohio

MITZI PROSSER, B.F.A.

Instructor, Medical Illustration Division, School of Allied Medical Professions, The Ohio State University, Columbus, Ohio

NANCY J. REYNOLDS, D.D.S.

Professor and Director, Division of Dental Hygiene, College of Dentistry, The Ohio State University, Columbus, Ohio

MARY BETH SKELTON, R.N.

Director of Paramedic Training, Tulane University, New Orleans, Louisiana

JAMES A. VISCONTI, Ph.D.

Associate Professor, College of Pharmacy, The Ohio State University;
Director, Drug Information Center,
The Ohio State University Hospitals, Columbus, Ohio

BURNESS G. WENBERG, M.S., R.D.

Associate Professor and Coordinator, Undergraduate Dietetic Curriculum,
Department of Food Science and Human Nutrition, College of Human Ecology,
Michigan State University, East Lansing, Michigan

J. SCOTT WORLEY, M.A., O.T.R.

Assistant Professor, Department of Occupational Therapy, School of
Allied Health and Social Professions, East Carolina University,
Greenville, North Carolina

PREFACE

In the course of teaching undergraduate college students about the various health professions, instructors perceived many repeated questions and areas of persistent confusion. To students who have not come from families with personal or professional ties to the health field, it holds a mystery both unwarranted and defeating. To dispel some of this mystery and show the variety of professional pursuits these fields offer, how to prepare for them, and what to expect of them, Burness Wenberg developed the course Introduction to Health Professions at The Ohio State University. This course formed the basis for the first edition of this book.

In their preface to the first edition, Odgers and Wenberg wrote:

> This book is designed to provide education and occupational information for a wide variety of health careers at a time when more and more young people are urgently needed in almost every area of health service. It is intended to show how the health professional functions in his job, what is necessary by way of education and training, and what opportunities for employment are available. It is hoped that it may prove equally useful as a textbook or as a resource for vocational counseling.

It has been my privilege to teach the course to hundreds of students, who have assisted in revisions through their questions, comments, and suggestions. All chapters have been written by practitioners, educators, or planners in health fields. All contributors are closely associated with the problems of attracting competent, motivated persons to the health professions, teaching them, and assisting their plans for effective service. Most authors had trouble dealing with the universal question of salaries and compensation. Some chose to ignore the question; others cited ranges. It should be pointed out that most baccalaureate health practitioners start at similar salaries within a given *geographic location*. There are great variations between locations such as the midwest and the west coast and between urban and rural settings.

Two chapters have been added for the third edition: "Emergency Medical Services" and "Environmental Sanitation." The first was added because of the growing need for specialized emergency skills and knowledge at all levels of health care delivery. The chapter on environmental sanitation, deleted from the second edition just before the current high level of public interest in environmental health showed itself, has been restored. All health occupations could not be included in a book of this size. Those chosen reflect the book's audience, primarily post–high school and college students involved in making vocational decisions. For that same reason I chose to deal with those health careers having significant numbers of educational programs at the postsecondary level, baccalaureate level, and above. Because of its parallel with and impact on human health care, I chose to include veterinary medicine.

The appendixes are designed to give quick information in reference form concerning the length of time necessary to complete training programs, some manpower statistics, and the professional organizations.

Chapter 1 deals with the meaning of "profession" and the responsibilities that accompany that designation and affect the lives of practitioners everywhere. Within each field there is a tendency to subdivide as the knowledge and skills expand. This process gives the responsibility for less demanding operations to people with less training and creates ladders within the field that are useful and attractive for persons wishing to serve in a helping capacity but not wishing to commit themselves to the educational programs and practices of professional service. It is hoped that the lists of related professions carried after the table of contents will be helpful to students seeking these alternative goals.

Grateful acknowledgment is made to Sylvia Upp, J. Hutchinson Williams, and Jon Wills and also to Charles Knouse, Jerry Bailes, and Carl Denbow for their helpful comments and manuscript suggestions. To all the contributing authors and the previous editors, Ruth Odgers and Burness Wenberg, my thanks.

ANNE S. ALLEN

CONTENTS

APPENDIXES

RELATED HEALTH OCCUPATIONS*

The main categories of health careers are shown in boldface type. Related careers that require similar interests and skills are listed under these. Students desiring more information about any of these occupations should find the referent chapter through the index and write to the professional organization cited there.

Dentistry
Dentist
Dental assistant
Dental hygienist
Dental laboratory technician
Dietetics
Dietetic aide
Dietetic assistant
(Food service supervisor)
Dietetic technician
(Food service manager)
(Food service technician)
(Food service assistant)
Dietitian
Nutritionist
Emergency medical services
EMT—ambulance
EMT—paramedic
Health services administrator
Hospital administrator
Health planner
Long-term care administrator
Nursing home administrator
Health information services
Community health educator
Medical communicator

Medical illustrator
Medical librarian
Medical library assistant
Medical photographer
Medical record administrator
Medical record technician
Public health educator
School health educator
Clinical laboratory services
Chemistry technologist
Cytotechnologist
Hematology technologist
Histologic technician
Medical laboratory technician
Medical technologist
Microbiology technologist
Nuclear medical technologist
Pathologist
Medicine
(Allopathic) Physician (M.D.)
Osteopathic physician (D.O.)
Medical specialties
General and/or family practice
Internal medicine
Pediatrics
Dermatology

---

*Adapted from American Society of Allied Health Professions Glossary of health occupation titles, Washington, D.C., 1973, U.S. Department of Health, Education, and Welfare, Bureau of Health Resources Development.

Surgery
Obstetrics and gynecology
Ophthalmology
Otolaryngology
Urology
Anesthesiology
Neurology
Psychiatry
Pathology
Physical medicine and rehabilitation
Radiology
Physician assistant

Medical instrumentation
Cardiopulmonary technician
Circulation technologist (extracorporeal)
Diagnostic medical sonographer
Dialysis technician
Electrocardiograph technician
Electromyograph technician
Electroencephalograph technician
Respiratory therapist
Respiratory therapy technician

Nursing
Nurse
Practical nurse
Registered nurse
Nurse aide
Nurse anesthetist
Nurse midwife
Nurse practitioner
Operating room technician

Pharmacy
Pharmacist
Pharmacy technician

Podiatry
Podiatrist
Podiatry assistant

Radiologic services
Nuclear medicine technologist
Radiation therapy technologist
Radiologic technologist
X-ray technician

Rehabilitation — activities
Art therapist
Dance therapist
Manual arts therapist
Music therapist
Occupational therapist
Occupational therapy assistant
Recreational therapist
Rehabilitation aide
Rehabilitation homemaking specialist

Rehabilitation — physical
Corrective therapist
Orthotist/prosthetist
Orthotist/prosthetist assistant
Physical therapist
Physical therapy assistant

Social services and counseling
Community health worker
Homemaker/home health aide
Medical social worker
Mental health technician
Psychiatric social worker
Rehabilitation counselor
Rehabilitation counselor aide
School health aide

Speech and hearing services
Audiologist
Phoniatrist
Speech and hearing therapist
Speech and hearing therapy aide
Speech pathologist

Vision care
Ophthalmic assistant
Ophthalmic laboratory technician
Ophthalmologist
Optometric assistant
Optometrist
Orthoptist

Veterinary medicine
Laboratory animal specialist
Veterinarian

INTRODUCTION TO HEALTH PROFESSIONS

1

DEVELOPMENT OF THE HEALTH PROFESSIONS

Anne S. Allen

The health professions as they exist today have developed in response to the demands of the technological and population expansions of the first part of the twentieth century. This rapid and enthusiastic growth within the health care family has produced problems that recapitulate those of human families in terms of adolescent turmoil and sibling rivalry. This has been demonstrated by the growing pains of professional organizations and by interdisciplinary quarrels over areas of patient care. That the new professions are showing signs of maturing into responsible components of the health care system is attributable to three factors: the impact of professionalism, the demand of the public for quality care, and the growing legislative support for health care.

IMPACT OF PROFESSIONALISM

Most groups of health practitioners either have already or are proceeding to professionalize their services. The professionalization of an occupation affects career choice through the selection of students. It also affects their education and the focus of their future energies. Professionalization should therefore be examined in terms of its historical development and its benefits and responsibilities.

The practice of medicine has always been identified as a profession and was one of the original three professions established during the rise of the universities in the Middle Ages, the other two being law and theology. There are some today who believe that these three are still the only professions and that others merely aspire to a status that is fundamentally beyond them. In his writings during the early part of this century, Abraham Flexner developed the following criteria for professions. He wrote that professions must be intellectual in their judgmental components, possessing a large body of knowledge unique to their own pursuits; they must be practical in that this knowledge can be applied to real situations; they must possess teachable techniques that can be used for problem solving; they must be organized into associations committed to the regulation, education, and protection of their members; and they must be governed by altruism.

It is probably because of the struggle on the part of so many skilled, helpful, and well-motivated people to professionalize their endeavors that McGlothlin has added a further criterion: a profession must "deal with matters of urgency and significance." Only the purest of academicians today would limit the professions to the original three.

If a group of practitioners establish their credentials according to these criteria and if they are engaged in promoting the state of well-being known as health, they are recognized as health professionals. The concept is broadened significantly by our current disinclination to define health merely as the absence of disease. There is universal acceptance of the World Health Organization's broader concept of health, which defines it as a state of functional well-being having the physical, psychological, and social aspects of the individual in equilibrium.

In any discussion of health professions their debt to the traditional professional model of medicine must be acknowledged. Just as the business and administrative professions owe much to the original profession of law and the teaching professions owe much to theology, so the health professions relate to medicine. From this field they have learned their research techniques, their model of professional organization, and their responsiveness to human need.

It is the adherence to Flexner's criteria for professions that gives rise to many of the problems of the new as well as the more established health professions. Because of their unique bodies of knowledge, these professions must constantly evaluate their bases for practice and revise them through research. Practitioners must teach this information to students and experienced practitioners alike and must further disseminate new knowledge through journals and other publications. The professional organizations that "regulate, educate, and protect" their members require significant amounts of energy and money from their members in order to do their job. They must also at times answer charges of guildism and restraint of trade. Because of their concern with urgent matters of human need, they have worked to design certifying procedures that will protect the public from opportunistic charlatans. In their service to the public they must accept governmental assistance while avoiding governmental control.

Certifying procedures have two components. One component is concerned with establishing, usually by examination, the credentials both of the individual and of his educational institution. The other component deals with what the individual is taught.

Establishing credentials

Professionals who serve the public must demonstrate qualifications to perform that service in such a way that people needing to buy the service can do so with the assurance that they will receive what they are paying for. The professional's ability to serve is evidenced by (1) the quality of the professional school attended and (2) personal knowledge and abilities. The school's qualifications to teach the professional program (whether medicine, occupational therapy, dental hygiene, or another area of health care) are determined through the process of *accreditation*. As part of the accreditation process, a school's curriculum, faculty, and facilities are examined by a committee representing educators and members of the particular profession according to a process set forth by the professional association. Attending an accredited school assures students of the integrity of their preparation. Attending a nonaccredited school makes future employability doubtful. The professional's own personal knowledge and abilities are further attested to by *certification, licensure,* or *registration* within the profession.

In some professions a certificate or diploma from an accredited school makes the graduate eligible for membership in that profession without further examination; others require examination. Certification is granted by the professional organization on the basis of the students' completion of certain qualifying steps. Members of other professions are additionally either licensed or registered. Licensure is a state-controlled process in which professionals sit for an examination that determines their eligibility for a state license to practice. Reciprocity exists among many but not all states.

Registration is usually only procedural. An individual who meets the association's qualification is listed on the official roster, or registry. (Some professions, in the interest both of freer entry into the profession and of career mobility, are allowing persons with equivalent experience to take the qualifying examinations. At this time, it is difficult to establish equivalency.)

A student who wants to enter a professional field must investigate and follow the certification procedures of that field. The procedures have been designed to safeguard the public by ensuring that physicians, nurses, therapists, and other health care practitioners are qualified to

...tice. Further safeguards are being introduced in the form of continu-ing education requirements for continued certification.

Education of health professionals

Important trends in the education of health professionals have in-cluded the shift from hospital-based programs to those established in universities and from apprenticeships to balanced curriculums. This shift took place in part because of the need to have the costs of education paid for by those receiving it. As training programs moved into educa-tional institutions, the responsibility for determining the number and quality of individuals entering the profession fell to the professional schools. As a result, professional schools became actively engaged in student recruitment and admission, and this in turn involved establish-ing criteria for selection. As the selection process evolved, the competi-tion for places in entering classes increased. The inevitable result was that the pressure to make career choices extended downward to ever earlier ages, so that qualifications could be built and the selection criteria met.

The process of professional education in a liberal arts setting has its own confusions. Trade and vocational schools, like many of the early hospital programs that trained nurses and technicians, are quite frankly technical in nature and can provide ''understanding of fundamental principles of technologies and the development of skills and techniques.'' A university, however, is an institution dedicated to the purpose of training minds. Attainment of technical and mechanical skills is secondary to the acquisition of knowledge and mental disci-pline.* A professional school must combine the two philosophies, assisting students to acquire knowledge and discipline while at the same time educating them to understand technological principles and to de-velop skills and techniques for applying theory to practice.

Students who wish to enter a health profession, then, must be able to pursue knowledge and discipline their minds according to the philosophy of liberal arts education, while at the same time acquiring the necessary professional skills and techniques. Needless to say, the two aspects are seldom perfectly balanced in individuals, and fortu-nately so. It is the difference in these abilities that produces the different kinds of professionals—researchers, healers, teachers, clinicians, plan-ners, and so forth.

---

*Discipline may be defined as a branch of knowledge or learning and also as training that develops self-control, character, or orderliness and efficiency.

In contrast to the varying interests and abilities of its students, each profession must maintain basically similar programs that include the essentials of education balanced in such a way that students can acquire the prerequisites during their preprofessional education and pursue their professional studies through a carefully planned mixture of academic and clinical experience. The development of the *essentials,* or standard educational requirements, is the responsibility of the professional organization. The essentials are usually developed by a committee of the association, approved by the entire association, and supervised by a different committee in accordance with given accreditation procedures.

DEMAND OF THE PUBLIC FOR QUALITY CARE

In an address at the convocation of entering medical students at the Ohio State University in 1974, Dr. John Cooper, president of the Association of American Medical Colleges, said, "The increased demand for care comes from the very success of modern scientific medicine in preventing, diagnosing, and curing disease. The public has learned through mass media what is now possible and they want the advances we have achieved. . . ."

The health professions have been responding to the demand for more and better services by increasing student enrollments in order to produce more practitioners. Two further and perhaps more significant responses have been the encouragement of continuing education and the development of the team concept.

Continuing education

Technological advances through research and the development of new techniques and equipment have made many once-trusted medical procedures obsolete. New procedures have been developed. For example, entire wings of hospitals, together with their highly specialized personnel, were restructured and diverted to other needs as the Salk/Sabin polio vaccines virtually eliminated poliomyelitis and the number of such patients was reduced almost to zero. New advances in heart surgery have necessitated the further education of many surgeons and operating room personnel. In addition, people wishing to reenter a health care field after a period of inactivity (for example, women who have been at home for several years with young children) create a demand for short courses and programs that will help them to reacquire lost skills and keep abreast of advancing knowledge.

Opportunities for continuing education are available through universities and other institutions, through conferences and workshops sponsored by professional organizations, sometimes through correspondence courses, and always through professional journals. It is the responsibility of all health professionals to maintain and enhance their own levels of competence. Recertification frequently depends on proof of such continuing education.

Team concept

It is obvious that the ultimate in health care cannot be delivered by one person. In the first place, it would be impossible for one person to know all there is to know about medicine and its related technologies. Second, even if one individual could know it all, there would be neither the time nor the energy to apply this knowledge. Consequently, the concept of the health team has been developed, and it has met with varying degrees of acceptance by health practitioners. In the report of the conference on the interrelationships of educational programs for health professionals, held in October of 1972 at the National Academy of Sciences in Washington, D.C., Pellegrino wrote, "There is no such thing as 'the team' in health care. Instead, there are a *large number* of health teams, dedicated to varying purposes. . . . The purpose of a team approach is to optimize the special contribution in skills and knowledge of the team members so that the needs of the persons served can be met more efficiently, competently, and more considerately than would be possible by independent and individual action."

Pellegrino defines two types of teams, functional and patient centered. Both are transitory and both depend on the problem to be solved, whether individual, family, or community. Functional teams are those whose personnel depend on the nature of the problem (for example, the coronary care team, the nursing team, and the mental health team). Patient-centered teams are made up in terms of closeness of patient contact. Pellegrino further divides the patient-centered teams into three categories.

1. The patient care team is made up of people "who jointly provide needed services that bring them into direct personal and physical contact with the patient and which are part of his personal and individualized program of management. . . . These are the people who lay hands directly on the patient, have the most sustained contact with him as a person, rather than with a part of him, and must experience with him the joy of cure and the burden of failure and death." Doctors, nurses, therapists, and so forth comprise these teams.

2. The medical care team is made up of people who provide "essen-

tial back-up services for the patient care teams . . . not in close continual contact with the patient . . . some deal transiently on a personal
basis with the patient . . . for a short interval. Others do not work with
the patient personally. They deal with a part of the patient—his sputum,
urine, x-rays, medication and so forth.'' These team members are, for
example, pathologists, radiologic technologists, medical technologists,
and pharmacists.

3. The health care team is made up of persons who are the ''most
distantly related to the individual patients and usually have as their concern the entire community. Such teams concentrate on the health of the
aggregate, the delivery of all services, their availability . . . the costs
of care, the distribution of resources . . . the regulation of quality . . .
the production of manpower . . . (this group includes) public health
officers, hospital administrators, health educators, bio-medical engineers, sanitarians, etc.''

If we accept the team concept, we must recognize its changing nature. Teams continually dissolve, and members regroup in order to meet
special problems. Teams are discussed here not only because of their effect on the quality of health care but also because of the influence that
many educators feel they have on the educational process and on a student's choice of a field of health care. (See Fig. 1-1.)

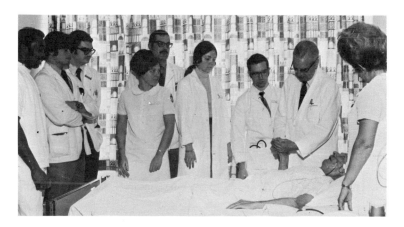

Fig. 1-1. The combined skills of many professionals contribute to modern health
care.

LEGISLATIVE SUPPORT FOR HEALTH CARE

Legislation for health care has contributed to the tremendous growth of the health care industry. The United States Congress has passed laws that have encouraged the health care industry to develop its technologies and manpower in order to prevent disease, to deliver care, and to foster research.

The Cambridge Research Institute in 1975 described the six basic types of governmental programs and regulations that have affected the United States health system.

1. *Those supporting disease prevention and health research.* Control of communicable disease, regulation of food and drugs, occupational safety and health, environmental protection, and atomic energy safeguards are all mandated by legislation. The National Institutes of Health was established to encourage research and presently expends over $1^1/_2$ billion dollars a year.

2. *Those determining the supply of health manpower.* These programs have financed medical and health professional education, first through armed forces and Veterans Administration facilities, then through research grants to medical schools through traineeships and institutional grants. The federal government placed great emphasis on numbers of health professionals during the early 1970s. The 1971 Comprehensive Health Manpower Training Act gave broad loans to medical students and capitation grants to schools. Presently the emphasis is being placed on the development of primary care physicians to reduce the oversupply of specialists and meet the need for primary health services.

3. *Those financing and regulating construction and operation of facilities.* The Hill-Burton Act of 1946 made money available for hospital construction. Health planning within this community was supported by the Comprehensive Health Planning Act. In 1974, reflecting the need for regulation of burgeoning hospital construction and runaway hospital costs, the federal government enacted the National Health Planning and Resources Act. This act imposes regulating controls on the health care system, affecting standards of quality and safety, personnel practices, hospital development, and so forth. New construction can be controlled and superfluous hospitals and agencies can be closed under this act.

4. *Those providing and organizing health services.* The federal government originally organized health care for the armed services and veterans. Next, care was extended to the poor and to children by Social and Rehabilitation Services, and the Maternal and Child Health Act. A

steady stream of enabling legislation followed, so that by 1973, family planning, sickle cell anemia victims, migrant workers, neighborhood and mental health centers, mentally retarded persons, alcohol and narcotic abusers, and emergency medical services were gradually provided for. The Health Maintenance Organization Act (1973) capped this trend by providing a 5-year program of federal subsidies to prepaid group practices, an alternative to the traditional fee-for-service approach to basic health care.

5. *Those financing health care.* In 1965, Medicare and Medicaid were added to the original Social Security Act's workmen's compensation to extend health care benefits to those over 65 years of age and to those under 65 who are medically indigent. Presently several major proposals for National Health Insurance that guarantee payment in various ways for health care for everyone are before the United States Congress.

6. *Those regulating health service costs and utilization.* The Social Security Amendments of 1972 created the Professional Standards Review Organizations, which produce guidelines for medical care, indicating which services are necessary for specific conditions. The states have individually set up public rate-setting agencies, regulating both health and malpractice insurance carriers.

The quality and number of individuals involved in the health professions have increased significantly as a result of this governmental support. The growing public interest in health care for everyone will increase the demand for health manpower that is equitably distributed throughout cities and rural areas, encourage legislation providing payment for services, and create a climate for the increasing regulation of costs, services, certification procedures, research and facility construction. The legislative trend is away from resource allocation and enabling acts, toward cost containment and industry regulation.

SUMMARY

Today's health professions owe much to the traditions of medicine and nursing. The independence of the newer professions has been the logical outcome of their assumption of responsibility for specific areas of patient care, their technological advances, and their organizational responsibility for credentials, standards of practice, and public accountability. The demand for quality health care has fostered continuing education and interdisciplinary cooperation, the team approach. Throughout this development, legislation has played both enabling and regulatory roles.

References

Columbus Tech bulletin 1973-1974, Columbus, Ohio, 1973, Columbus Technical Institute.

McGlothlin, W. J.: The professional schools, New York, 1974, Center for Applied Research in Education.

Pellegrino, E. D.: Interdisciplinary education in the health professions. In Educating for the health team, Washington, D.C., 1972, National Academy of Sciences–National Institute of Medicine.

Suggested readings

Educating for the health team, Washington, D.C., 1972, National Academy of Sciences–National Institute of Medicine.

Hamburg, J., editor: Review of allied health education. I, and II, Lexington, 1974, 1977, The University Press of Kentucky.

Weiss, L. B., and Spence, A. B.: A guide to the health professions, Cambridge, Mass., 1973, Office of Career Services and Off-Campus Learning, Harvard University.

2

DENTAL HYGIENE

Nancy J. Reynolds

Dental hygiene is a profession that is a vital component of the dental profession. The dental hygienist is an extension of the dentist and as such has a responsibility to the patient and the public as well as to the dentist whose patients are served.

The dental hygienist is a licensed health care provider whose functions include both education and clinical treatment. The dental profession in its totality is dedicated to eradicating the disease it treats and to improving the level of oral health of the nation. Accomplishing this is dependent on prevention and control of dental diseases, and it is in this area that dental hygiene functions.

BACKGROUND

Dental hygiene is a new profession when compared with dentistry, medicine, and nursing. Dr. Alfred C. Fones, a dentist, opened the first school for dental hygienists in 1913 in Bridgeport, Connecticut. He was convinced that general health could be improved by good oral health, and his main purpose in educating dental hygienists was to prepare them to work in the public schools in Bridgeport. To this day in the schools, dental hygienists are oral health educators, teaching children proper oral hygiene habits to help them reduce dental decay and improve their oral health.

EDUCATIONAL PROGRAMS

Between 1957 and 1978 the number of accredited dental hygiene programs in the United States increased from 34 to 187. From 1972 to 1977 total enrollment in schools of dental hygiene increased by 20%.*

---

*American Dental Association: Annual report; dental auxiliary education, 1977-1978, Chicago, 1978, The Association.

All dental hygiene programs must meet the standards of the Commission on Accreditation of Dental and Dental Auxiliary Educational Programs. This authority is delegated to the Commission by the United States Office of Education and the Council on Postsecondary Accreditation. The Commission is comprised of 20 commissioners, including representatives of all groups affected by the dental accreditation process: the American Association of Dental Schools, the American Dental Association, the American Association of Dental Examiners, the American Dental Hygienists' Association, the American Dental Assistants' Association, dental laboratory technology, students, specialty groups, and the consumer.

The minimal preadmission requirement is completion of a high school program in an accredited high school. Many require 1 or 2 years of college level study at an accredited university, college, or junior college. This information can be obtained from the American Dental Association. It is usually recommended that prospective students study biology, chemistry, and mathematics in high school. Most schools of dental hygiene that require college credits require biology before admission.

Most schools also require that prospective dental hygiene students take the aptitude test administered by the American Dental Hygienists' Association. The test results are considered in conjunction with the applicant's other qualifications.

Traditionally, dental hygiene curricula were associated with schools of dentistry, but in recent years dental hygiene programs have been offered in 2-year schools as well as in 4-year colleges and universities. Various options are available to the prospective dental hygienist. Two-year junior or community colleges award an associate degree to those who successfully complete the program. Four-year colleges and universities may offer certificates designating as graduate dental hygienists those who successfully complete the 2-year program, or they may award baccalaureate degrees to those who complete the degree requirements plus the requirements for the dental hygiene program. The baccalaureate programs may integrate the university's arts and sciences requirements with an increasing emphasis on dental hygiene courses in each of the succeeding years, or the dental hygiene program may be concentrated in 2 of the 4 years of enrollment.

Some universities offer programs for the graduate dental hygienist leading to a master's degree. These may encompass dental hygiene, health education, public health, education, or the sciences. Among the institutions currently offering such programs are The Ohio State University, Columbus; Southern Illinois University, Carbondale; Columbia University, New York City; the University of Kentucky, Lexington; the University of Michigan, Ann Arbor; the University of Iowa, Iowa City; the University of Missouri–Kansas City School of Dentistry; the University of California, San Francisco; Baylor College of Dentistry, Dallas; and the University of Washington, Seattle.

CURRICULUM

There are some specific requirements for dental hygiene programs, but more general guidelines are outlined by the Commission on Accreditation. In the requirements for curriculum four subject areas must be provided. These include general studies, biomedical sciences, dental sciences, clinical sciences, and practice. General studies must include English, speech, psychology, and sociology. Biomedical sciences include content in general anatomy, microscopic anatomy, physiology, biochemistry, microbiology, pathology, nutrition, and pharmacology. Basic science content, which is essential as a foundation for learning the biomedical sciences, should be prerequisite for the program. Dental sciences include tooth morphology; head, neck, and oral anatomy; oral embryology; and histology. Content in oral physiology and pathology as well as oral therapeutics and dental materials must be provided. Clinical sciences and practice should include periodontics, radiography, ethics, and jurisprudence as well as the actual practicum in which patient care is provided.

Knowledge and practice in oral health education techniques and content in community dental health are included in the basic program. In addition, most schools now include courses that teach functions formerly performed by dentists and only recently delegated to hygienists. Clinical experience is an important part of the dental hygiene curriculum, and courses in which students apply their skills and knowledge provide this experience. (See Fig. 2-1.)

LICENSING

In order to be licensed to practice, most dental hygienists take the written examination administered by the Council on National Board Examination, which is recognized by 51 of the 53 licensing jurisdictions. This includes 48 states (excluding Alabama and Delaware), the District of Columbia, Puerto Rico, and the Virgin Islands of the United States. In addition, most states require that the dental hygienist pass a

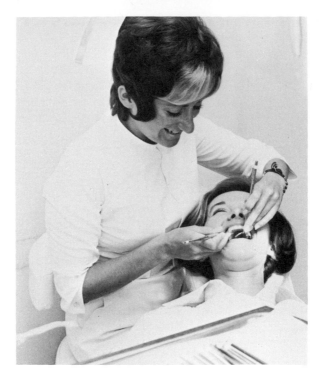

Fig. 2-1. Clinical application of dental hygiene procedures is an important part of the curriculum. A student performs an oral prophylaxis on a patient.

practical examination. Presently regional testing agencies examine dental and dental hygiene graduates. Successful completion of this examination permits the hygienist to apply for licensure in any of the states comprising the region.

FUNCTIONS OF THE DENTAL HYGIENIST AND CAREER OPPORTUNITIES

The dental hygienist is licensed to treat the patient in a private office or clinic by performing oral prophylaxis as well as other services for the patient. Dental hygienists may apply topical fluorides that make the surface of the tooth harder and less vulnerable to disease and may expose and develop radiographs of oral structures. The hygienist also assists the dentist by recognizing and reporting abnormalities of the oral cavity. A most important part of the dental hygienist's work involves educating patients regarding their own individual oral health needs and responsibilities in effectively preventing oral disease.

In many states, laws have been or are now being changed to permit expansion of the duties of this important dental auxiliary. Additional functions may include placing permanent restorative materials (fillings), polishing existing restorations, placing sedative restorations, and taking impressions for making models of the teeth. In some states the dental hygienist may administer anesthetic agents. Effective utilization of dental hygienists extends the services of the dentists by freeing them to perform only those services that require their additional education, experience, and skills.

Dental hygienists who are employed in schools work directly to meet the foremost goal of the profession—education of the public. They are largely responsible for planning and executing that portion of the curriculum pertaining to their special field and for actually performing dental hygiene services if such treatment is provided in the school.

There are opportunities for employment in government institutions and programs, in industrial health programs, in research, in hospitals, and in the United States Army Medical Corps, where dental hygienists serve as commissioned officers. Some positions are available in foreign countries through the Peace Corps, with Project Hope, and with privately sponsored health care projects.

Although most dental hygienists are women, men are also welcome in the profession. Many male dental hygienists serve as health professionals in the armed services. Salaries paid to full-time dental hygienists vary considerably and depend on geographical location and the size and nature of the employing institution or facility as well as on the dental hygienist's training, experience and professional responsibilities. In general, dental hygienists earn a beginning annual salary of $10,000 to $12,000.

PERSONAL QUALIFICATIONS

Those who are interested in the profession of dental hygiene should exhibit traits of personality and character that are consistent with the responsibilities they will assume on entering a health profession— responsibilities to the profession and to the public. Those who are unable or unwilling to give these responsibilities first priority in a professional situation should not enter the field of dental hygiene.

Successful dental hygienists are sympathetic to people and their needs, are meticulous about detail, and are perfectionists in every facet of practice but patient in those instances where perfection cannot be achieved. They regard the profession of dentistry with respect.

PROFESSIONAL ORGANIZATIONS

The professional organization for dental hygienists is the American Dental Hygienists' Association. Affiliated with this organization is a students' counterpart, the Junior American Dental Hygienists' Association. Students are encouraged to join and participate in this organization so that they may learn about the professional organization that governs and protects them. Student members as well as professionals receive the *Journal of the American Dental Hygienists' Association,* the official publication of the organization.

SIGMA PHI ALPHA

Sigma Phi Alpha is the national dental hygiene honor society. Senior dental hygiene students who are outstanding in scholarship, leadership, and professional attitude are candidates for election to the society. The number of students elected annually from each class may not exceed 10% of the total number of students in the graduating class.

SUMMARY

Dental hygiene is an important assistive field to the profession of dentistry. Hygienists are educated to give instruction in the daily care of teeth and gingiva, to perform oral prophylaxis and minor oral treatments, and to take dental x-ray films. They are employed in public schools, public health programs, dentists' offices, and other health care agencies.

Suggested readings

Boundy, S. S., and Reynolds, N. J., editors: Current concepts in dental hygiene, vols. 1 and 2, St. Louis, 1977, 1979, The C. V. Mosby Co.

Motley, W. E.: Ethics, jurisprudence, and history for the dental hygienist, Philadelphia, 1972, Lea & Febiger.

Wilkins, E. M.: Clinical practice of dental hygienist, ed. 3, Philadelphia, 1964, Lea & Febiger.

Professional organizations where further information can be obtained

American Association of Dental Schools
1625 Massachusetts Ave., N.W.
Washington, D.C. 20036
American Dental Association
211 E. Chicago Ave.
Chicago, Ill. 60611

American Dental Hygienists's Association
211 E. Chicago Ave.
Chicago, Ill. 60611

3

DENTISTRY

William C. Dew

Dentistry is the profession concerned with maintaining the teeth and oral tissues in good health, preventing and treating dental diseases, and safeguarding the general health of the individual by detecting symptoms of systemic disease in the oral tissues. It is a challenging profession that offers one the opportunity to use both intellectual abilities and manual skills. Dentistry affords the practitioner an opportunity to be artistic and creative and offers independence, responsibility, authority, and opportunities for public service in a variety of situations.

HISTORY OF THE PROFESSION

The profession of dentistry shares a common origin with medicine. Many of the ancient medical documents and records contain references to dental diseases and their treatment. Egyptian records dating as far back as 3000 BC include sections on the treatment of dental diseases, although there is no mention of the removal of teeth or their replacement. The Phoenicians (1600-687 BC) were the first to devise and record methods of replacing missing teeth and retaining the replacements through the use of soldered gold bands or rivets. Improvements in this art were made by the Etruscans (753-300 BC), who lived in central Italy, and by the Greeks (377-162 BC), the Romans (450-218 BC), and the Arabians (700-1200 AD).

The first records of the separation of dentistry from the profession of medicine date from the thirteenth to the fifteenth centuries. Guy de Chauliac, a great surgeon of the Middle Ages, observed that operations on the teeth were properly the concern only of barbers and "dentatores." He made it clear that the "dentatores" of the fourteenth century were more than mere tooth pullers, for they treated diseases of the teeth and surrounding tissues as well as the scant knowledge of the time permitted. The treatments recommended were taken from the writings of Galen, an anatomist of the second century AD, and from the Arabian writers. The emigration of Greek scholars to Western Europe during this period added much to dental and medical knowledge. Many of the contributors to the science of medicine also contributed much to dentistry—Vesalius, Fallopius, Eustachius, and Paré, to cite a few.

Pierre Fauchard (1690-1761) is considered to be the founder of modern scientific dentistry. His book *Le Chirurgien Dentiste* records the then-current technical aspects of dentistry to which he contributed greatly.

John Hunter (1728-1793), an English physician, also wrote extensively on dentistry. Two of his best-known works are *The Natural History of Human Teeth* and *A Practical Treatise on Diseases of the Teeth.*

Dentistry in the United States had its beginnings in the latter part of the eighteenth century and was based on the dental knowledge of Western Europe. John Boher, an Englishman, was probably the first competent dentist to practice in this country. Another was John Greenwood, who was dentist to George Washington.

Dental education in the United States had its beginning in Bainbridge, Ohio, under the guidance of John Harris, who was preceptor to his brother, Chapin B. Harris, and to James Taylor. These men later formed the first recognized colleges of dentistry in the United States.

The year 1839 is memorable in dental history for the establishment of a dental journal, the organization of a dental society, and the application for a charter to open a school for training dentists. In 1840 the Baltimore College of Dental Surgery, the first of its kind in the world, opened its doors.

Rapid technical advances in dentistry occurred after 1850. Among these were the discovery of vulcanite as a denture base material; the development of gold foil, gold inlays, and amalgam as filling materials; the invention of the dental engine or mechanical drill; and the use of x-ray films and local anesthesia. Two dentists, Drs. Horace Wells and W. G. T. Morton, first used general anesthesia in 1846 and are credited with being among the first to use a general anesthetic agent.

Under the leadership of Dr. G. V. Black (1836-1915), who next to Fauchard is the best-known figure in dentistry, dental education became truly scientific and professional. Dr. Black, who was dean of the dental school at Northwestern University in Chicago, performed brilliant research in anatomy and in the development of dental materials. He invented the foot-driven dental engine, and his classification of cavity preparations as well as many of the technical procedures he developed are still used today.

After World War II, new advances in dental equipment (notably the air rotor), materials, research, and methods of practice made it possible for the dentist to be much more productive than before.

PREDENTAL EDUCATION AND ADMISSION

The length of predental training varies from 2 to 4 years. A very few exceptional students are admitted after only 2 years. About 10% of all incoming students have completed 3 years of undergraduate study and the rest have completed 4 years; nearly all students in this group have baccalaureate degrees. Many colleges have a degree in absentia program in which the enrolled students attend a college of liberal arts for 3 years and earn a baccalaureate degree at the end of their first year in dentistry. Participation in this program makes it possible to earn two degrees in 7 years. Predental students are encouraged to enroll in this type of curriculum if it is available and are often given preference in admissions selection.

Required predental courses are kept at a minimum. These include such areas as the following:
1. English composition and literature
2. Biology, including zoology
3. General chemistry, including qualitative analysis
4. Organic chemistry with laboratory
5. Physics with laboratory

It is usually recommended that predental students pursue a broad educational program that includes the social sciences and humanities rather than overemphasize the basic sciences, because many of these are covered in the professional curriculum.

Because of the nature of the dental curriculum and the physical limitations on the numbers of new students who can be accepted into dental schools, competition for admission is very keen. All students are required to take a dental admissions test given by the Council on Education of the American Dental Association (ADA) at specific times at various testing centers. Admission is based on predental academic performance, dental admission test scores, basic science grades, and a personal interview.

Opportunities in dentistry for women and minorities have greatly improved in recent years, and the number of these students enrolled in dental schools has increased significantly.

DENTAL EDUCATION AND LICENSURE

The objective of dental education is to train a student to be knowledgeable and competent in basic sciences, dental laboratory procedures, clinical dentistry, practice management, and social and preventive dentistry. This is much to accomplish in four academic years; consequently, the program is rigorous and difficult, challenging and demanding. (See Fig. 3-1.)

During the third academic year of the professional curriculum, students are eligible to take the first half of the written examination offered by the National Board of Dental Examiners of the Council on Dental Education of the ADA. Toward the end of the final year, students can take the second part of the examination. In addition, they must pass a clinical examination given by the state dental board of the state in which they desire to practice. On successful completion of this examination,

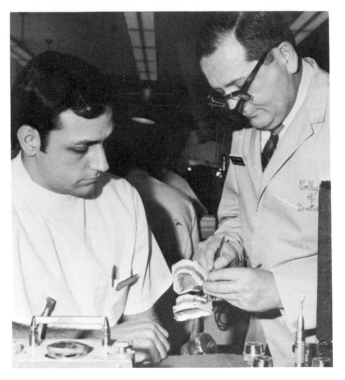

Fig. 3-1. Models of jaws and teeth are used in preclinical study to give students practice in instrument position and techniques.

they are permitted to practice only in that state. However, in some areas, regional examinations offer dentists who qualify a license to practice in each of several cooperating states.

SUPPORTING PROFESSIONALS

Most graduate dentists are engaged in private practice. In this situation a dentist or group of dentists has the responsibility for directing the activities of the office. The physical arrangement and facilities vary with each office, but the trend is toward multiple operating rooms and several auxiliary personnel such as dental hygienists, dental assistants, dental technologists, receptionists, and office secretaries. The dentist who utilizes these additional personnel can be much more productive and provide better service to patients than the dentist who conducts a one-person practice with little or no auxiliary help.

Recent changes in dental practice acts in many states now permit qualified dental hygienists and assistants to perform certain dental procedures that until now have been restricted to licensed dentists. These changes have resulted in increased productivity and efficiency in dental practices.

Training programs for dental hygienists are available at the college level. These professionals are skilled technicians and they may function as teachers in dental health education programs as well. They are becoming increasingly important in reducing dental disease. For the prospective hygienist who plans to work primarily in a private office, there are 2-year professional training programs available, some of which award an associate degree. The profession of dental hygiene is discussed in greater detail in Chapter 2.

For dental laboratory technicians there are vocational school programs at the post–high school level as well as on-the-job training in a dental laboratory. Enrollment in an approved training program provides 2 years of formal training. The tasks of dental laboratory technicians include making and repairing such dental restorations as dentures, inlays, crowns, and bridges. Their objectives are to promote better health, greater comfort, and improved appearance, and they always work from the prescription of a licensed dentist. Salaries for the experienced laboratory technician range from $10,000 to $22,000 annually.

A third type of auxiliary personnel is the dental assistant, who may be employed by an individual dentist or by a group of two or more practitioners. There are increasing employment opportunities for assistants in clinics, hospitals, and other health agencies. Dental assistants are responsible for greeting patients and preparing them for examination, treatment, or surgery. They sterilize instruments, mix fillings, prepare solutions, and help the dentist to practice his skills. The present trend in the profession is to utilize the assistants as part of the dental operating team in a system known as four-handed dentistry. In this capacity dental assistants perform in a manner similar to that of the surgical technician in the medical operating room. In smaller office situations dental assistants may also be responsible for such clerical tasks as making appointments, ordering supplies, sending out statements, keeping patient records, and answering the telephone. Many dentists are willing to select a likely applicant and provide on-the-job training. However, some dental schools, colleges, and junior colleges are offering training for dental assistants. Some programs offer an associate degree. Salaries for these workers range from $8,000 to $12,000 per year, depending on community salary standards, extent of training, and amount of experience.

FUTURE TRENDS IN DENTAL PRACTICE

The emphasis in modern dental practice is increasingly being placed on the prevention of dental disease and the maintenance of oral health. With modern dental knowledge and procedures, it is possible to maintain the entire dentition in good health for a lifetime. There is also growing interest in and concern for the social aspects of dentistry. The goal is comprehensive dental care for all people. There is now such a large backlog of patients with extensive dental problems that it is necessary for the dentist to spend much of his time in the treatment of dental diseases. The mode of dental practice has gradually been changing from individual dental practice to groups of dentists with the same specialty or groups with diverse specialties. Such groups result in increased efficiency. With these changes and currently available preventive measures such as fluoridation, dietary control, preventive treatment by the dentist, and adequate home care, it should be possible to vastly improve the oral health of our citizens.

CAREERS IN DENTISTRY

There are approximately 117,750 licensed dentists in the United States. About 6,900 are on the staffs of federal agencies (Air Force, Army, Navy, Public Health Service, Veterans Administration, Civil Service). Approximately 11,700 are engaged in dental education and research. The remainder are engaged in private practice. There are approximately 5,200 new graduates each year. When retirement and death of members of the profession are taken into account, it is evident that the profession is not likely to be overcrowded in the forseeable future.

Many graduate dentists continue their educational training and become qualified in one of the eight recognized specialties of dentistry.

Endodontics Treatment of diseases of the internal soft tissues of the teeth

Oral pathology Diagnosis of diseases or abnormalities of the oral cavity and associated structures

Oral surgery Treatment of diseases or abnormalities of the oral cavity and associated structures

Orthodontics Treatment of malocclusion and facial deformities

Pedodontics Treatment of dental diseases in children

Periodontics Treatment of diseases of the supporting structures of the teeth

Prosthodontics Restoration of occlusion by replacement of missing teeth

Dental public health Concern with dental epidemiology, biostatistics, and dental public health measures

With the exception of oral surgery, which is a 3-year, hospital-based program, these specialties require from 18 months to 2 years of additional training.

The income of most dentists is well above average. Few dentists become wealthy, but most enjoy a very comfortable life. The 1976 *Facts about States for the Dentist Seeking a Location* shows that the mean net income of all independent dentists for 1974 was $33,587. There is also a certain degree of prestige and respect afforded those dentists who are ethical in practice and have a genuine concern for their patients. According to a 1971 survey by Rotter and Stein in the *Journal of Applied Psychology,* dentistry was ranked third in a listing of twenty selected occupations by the public in terms of trustworthiness, competence, and altruism.

At the present time the energies of the dental profession are directed toward more sophisticated methods of practice, better delivery of dental services, prevention of dental diseases, and the community and social aspects of dentistry.

PERSONAL QUALIFICATIONS

The profession of dentistry is not suitable for everyone. Prospective dental students must have a good background in the basic sciences and the liberal arts. They must be industrious, intelligent, well motivated, and have a high degree of manual skill and artistic ability. They must have a concern for their fellow man and enjoy working with people. They must be competent at business and office management and should have analytical minds and the ability to work well independently. Among the most important attributes are a good character and high moral and ethical standards. It is wise for students who are seriously considering becoming dentists to learn as much as possible about the profession by attending career programs, reading, and visiting dental offices and dental schools. This insight should help them to determine whether dentistry is the profession they should pursue.

The practice of dentistry is confining, demanding, and conducive to tensions. It requires a great deal of self-discipline, but most dentists would consider the rewards well worth these disadvantages. For the person who qualifies to become a successful dentist there can be no more rewarding or satisfying profession.

References

Admission requirements of U.S. and Canadian dental schools, 1978-1979, Washington, D.C., 1977, American Association of Dental Schools.

American dental directory, 1978, Chicago, 1978, American Dental Association.

Annual report on dental education 1977-1978, Chicago, 1978, Council on Dental Education, American Dental Association.

Dalton, V. B.: Genesis of dental education, Columbus, Ohio, 1946, Spahr & Glenn.

Directory of dental educations 1977-1978, Chicago, 1978, American Association of Dental Schools.

Distribution of dentists in the United States by state, region, district, and country 1976, Chicago, 1977, Bureau of Economic Research and Statistics, American Dental Association.

Facts about states for the dentist seeking a location, 1976, Chicago, 1976, Bureau of Economic Research and Statistics, American Dental Association.

Guerini, V.: A history of dentistry, ed. 1, Philadelphia, 1909, Lea & Febiger.

Lufkin, A. W.: A history of dentistry, ed. 2, Philadelphia, 1948, Lea & Febiger.

Prinz, H.: Dental chronology, ed. 1, Philadelphia, 1945, Lea & Febiger.

Rotter, J. B., and Stein, D. K.: Public attitude toward the trustworthiness and altruism of twenty selected occupations, J. Appl. Soc. Psychol. **1:**343, 1971.

Professional organizations where further information can be obtained

American Association of Dental Schools
1625 Massachusetts Av., N.W.
Washington, D.C. 20036

American Dental Association
211 E. Chicago Ave.
Chicago, Ill. 60611

4

DIETETICS

Burness G. Wenberg

Altering a person's nutritional status may affect physical condition, performance, personality, disposition, appearance, and life span. New discoveries are constantly being made in the fields of medicine and nutrition. New and better methods and procedures for preparing and serving food appear almost daily, and new food products on the market have become almost commonplace. As a result, the profession of dietetics continues to change, grow, and expand to serve people better.

The dietitian is commited to improving human nutrition, advancing the science of dietetics and nutrition, and promoting education in these and allied areas. Food is the tool that the dietitian uses in illustrating and promoting good nutrition. Dietitians work with people of all ages in a variety of institutional and agency settings. (See Fig. 4-1.) Hospitals and health care facilities claim the greatest number of dietitians. They are also found in elementary and secondary school, college, and university food services. Others may be employed in business and industry. Teaching at the college level and research in food and nutrition are additional careers for dietitians. An increasing number of dietitians are employed in research settings and are also self-employed as consultants. Many of the new and developing health maintenance organizations have dietitians on their staffs. For those persons interested in working with food and people, a variety of opportunities are available.

HOW DID THE PROFESSION DEVELOP?

Although the profession of dietetics is relatively young, its background reaches into antiquity. The Ebers papyrus, written 1,000 years before Hippocrates, contained what may be the first recorded diet prescription. The famous French scientist Lavoisier made a revolutionary contribution to nutrition in 1794 by making laboratory determinations of the end results of digestive activities. For opening the door

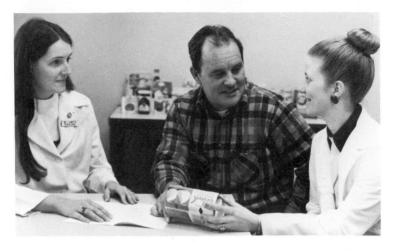

Fig. 4-1. Patients are encouraged to plan their own dietary program with the assistance of the dietitian and the student dietitian.

to scientific research in this field, he is accepted as the father of nutrition.

Continuing inquiry in this century has produced methods that make it possible to measure energy transformation in the body, to determine the exact nutritive values of food materials, and to determine the roles of proteins, minerals, vitamins, and other nutrients in the functioning of the body. Formerly dietitians were associated with the feeding of sick persons and worked almost exclusively in hospitals. As the science of nutrition developed, dietitians have assumed the additional responsibility of applying research findings to the work of feeding groups of people.

The services of dietitians were in great demand during World War I, both in Europe with the armed forces and at home, where they faced the problem of feeding people in institutions despite the limitations imposed by food rationing and food shortages. Expressing a need to share their knowledge and seek better solutions to their problems, a small group of dietitians met in Cleveland, Ohio, in 1917 to organize the American Dietetic Association. The new organization's greatest impact may have resulted from its identification of educational requirements for curricula in dietetics and from its subsequent work with colleges, universities, and hospitals to implement these new standards.

Before 1917 there were a few "student dietitian" programs in hospitals. The applicants' qualifications ranged from a high school diploma to a college degree. By 1935 approximately 60 hospitals and institutions offered programs approved by the American Dietetic Association for the professional education of dietitians. Applicants to these programs were required to present a college degree, with successful completion of courses in foods, nutrition, and chemistry. As the number of dietitians as well as the quality of their training increased, both the profession and the professional organization gained in strength and stature. The professional dietitian achieved recognition as the person skilled in providing quality nutritional care to individuals and groups.

In 1970, with the financial support of the W. K. Kellogg Foundation, the American Dietetic Association charged a study commission with the responsibility for exploring all aspects of dietetic practice, education, and professional organization. The commission's report, published in 1972, included a review of current forces producing change in the field of health services. These findings led to the prediction that dietetic practice in the future would be altered in six ways: (1) there will be increased differentiation in the roles and functions of dietitians; (2) dietitians will become more specialized; (3) new and additional competencies will be required; (4) dietitians will increasingly delegate some of their present tasks and roles to other, less highly trained workers; (5) more dietitians will practice in association with other health professionals; and (6) a greater proportion of dietitians will be self-employed. Only the future will reveal the accuracy of these predictions.

WHAT PARTICULAR QUALITIES ARE NEEDED?

Young men and women should consider careers in dietetics if they (1) find studying the biological and behavioral sciences stimulating, (2) are interested in the nutritional, sociological, and psychological effects of foods on people, (3) enjoy working directly with people, and (4) gain personal satisfaction from using their knowledge to benefit mankind. The ability to be creative and innovative in the preparation and service of food is especially valuable to prospective dietitians. These individuals are entering a highly respected and relevant profession—a profession whose major concern is the welfare of humanity.

WHAT IS THE EDUCATIONAL PREPARATION?

Those who want to become professionally qualified dietitians will find that a variety of pathways lead to their goal. Qualification includes four components: academic course requirements, bachelor's or advanced degree, professional education/experience, and endorsement by a qualified professional. The professional education/experience component is available in a number of different methods and locations. Some are coordinated undergraduate programs, whereas others are postbaccalaureate dietetic internships, approved experiences, or graduate programs. Although some are specialized dietetic programs, the majority are more general. As different programs appeal to different students, they will be described separately.

High school

Preparation for a career in dietetics should begin in high school. College preparatory courses in chemistry, mathematics, biology, and the social sciences are highly recommended.

Academic requirements

A new plan for minimum academic requirements was adopted by the American Dietetic Association in 1972. Rather than specific courses, the requirements are stated in terms of competence to be acquired in specific areas. These include physical and biological sciences, behavioral and social sciences, professional sciences, and communication sciences. In addition, there are advanced competencies for general dietetics plus areas of emphasis in food service management and clinical and community dietetics. In presenting a dietetic curriculum, an accredited college or university selects and/or develops courses that include the stated competencies. These requirements may be incorporated into the curriculum of an undergraduate coordinated dietetic program or into a curriculum that serves as preparation for a postbaccalaureate professional education program. The new requirements are in effect for all applicants January 1, 1980. Students interested in pursuing dietetics at either the undergraduate or graduate level would be well advised to explore whether the college or university of their choice has an American Dietetic Association–approved plan for academic requirements.

Professional education programs

Coordinated undergraduate programs. Established in 1962, the coordinated undergraduate dietetic program is a formalized baccalaureate educational program in dietetics sponsored by an accredited college or university and accredited by the American Dietetic Association. The curriculum is designed to coordinate didactic and supervised clinical experiences to meet the qualifications for practice in the profession of dietetics. This type of program was first offered at The Ohio State University, and now an increasing number of colleges and universities throughout the United States are either offering or planning to offer such a curriculum. A list of currently accredited programs is published annually by the American Dietetic Association. Those who successfully complete such programs are recommended for active membership in the American Dietetic Association concurrently with the awarding of the bachelor's degree.

Clinical or field experience is usually introduced in the junior year and increases in depth and scope with each succeeding term. Some programs focus on general dietetics, whereas others have a food service management, clinical, or community dietetics emphasis. Only those colleges and universities that have access to facilities adequate to provide the curriculum's clinical or field experience can offer this more specialized type of program. The undergraduate coordinated programs have the advantage of orienting students to the typical clinical or field experience setting for the practice of dietetics early in their educational experience.

Dietetic internships. The dietetic internship is a formalized postbaccalaureate educational program in dietetics sponsored and conducted by an organization and accredited by the American Dietetic Association. The curriculum of the program is designed to provide didactic and supervised clinical experience to meet the qualifications for practice in dietetics. The Association annually publishes a listing of currently approved internship programs.

These internships provide an opportunity for the dietetic intern to practice in depth the principles of nutritional care and food service management learned in college. Under the guidance of an experienced staff and faculty, dietetic interns add to their basic knowledge and develop their own professional behavioral style. The dietetic internship has been traditionally viewed as the "fifth year," but since early 1970 there have been many innovations in both existing and developing dietetic internships. Programs that are now offered vary in length from 6 to 8, 9, 10, 12, 15, and 18 months. Accredited dietetic internships are offered in a variety of institutions: hospitals, nutrition clinics, industrial food services, school food services, state institutions, and colleges and universities. Basically, nutritional care in a hospital or an outpatient clinic and food service management in a variety of food service settings are emphasized. After January 1980, all formerly offered dietetic traineeships that continue to offer a program will be accredited as dietetic internships. Successful completion of a dietetic internship qualifies the graduate for active membership in the American Dietetic Association.

Approved preplanned experience. The approved, preplanned experience program is a pathway open to persons who have met the academic requirements and are thus eligible for associate membership in The American Dietetic Association. It is an individualized, post-baccalaureate educational program in dietetics sponsored by an organization and approved by the American Dietetic Association. Each program is designed to provide didactic and supervised clinical experience to meet the qualifications for practice in the profession of dietetics.

In accordance with the concept of an individualized program, the program is developed and arranged between a qualified candidate and the registered dietitians in an organization willing to sponsor such a program. Programs must be at least 24 months in length and may focus on general dietetics or clinical or food service management. Successful completion qualifies the graduate for active membership in the American Dietetic Association. Published policies and procedures for an approved preplanned experience may be obtained from the association.

Graduate study. Membership in the American Dietetic Association can also be obtained by earning a master's degree and experience or a doctoral degree. Recipients of a master's degree in foods, nutrition, food service management, dietetic education, or public health nutrition must satisfactorily complete the equivalent of 6 months of work experience under the supervision of a professionally qualified dietitian. The recipient of a doctoral degree in any of these areas of specialization is eligible for membership. As graduate programs do not require prior approval, documentation of achievement in the curriculum and endorsement by at least one professionally trained dietitian are required when application for active membership in the association is made.

WHO ARE REGISTERED DIETITIANS?

The registered dietitian has successfully completed the examination for registration and meets continuing education requirements. Eligibility requirements to write the registration examination are the same as the active membership requirements of the American Dietetic Association. An American Dietetic Association dietitian is described as a specialist educated for a profession that is responsible for the nutritional care of individuals and groups. This care includes the application of the science and art of human nutrition in helping people to select and obtain food for the primary purpose of nourishing their bodies in health or disease throughout the life cycle. (See Fig. 4-2.) This work may be accomplished through single or combined functions, in food service systems management, in extending knowledge of food and nutrition principles, in teaching the application of these principles according to individual situations, or in dietary counseling.

The concept of professional registration was adopted by the members of the association in 1969. New bylaws were ratified by the association in 1977, creating a separate component of the association, the Commission on Dietetic Registration. Persons meeting eligibility requirements for active membership in the association have the option of applying for active membership or applying to write the registration examination or applying for both options. A major responsibility for the association is providing approved continuing education activities. These are required for the registered dietitian to maintain registration and are usually offered to association members for a lower fee. The abbreviation RD stands for registered dietitian and is a trademark of the association that registered dietitians may use. Registration was adopted with

Fig. 4-2. Using food models and pictures, a dietitian teaches a client how to plan a proper diet.

the goal of maintaining and enhancing the standards of the profession and its individual practitioners.

WHERE DO DIETITIANS WORK?

Many areas of service are available to the dietitian. Many choose to work in hospitals or clinics, while some prefer the atmosphere of nursing homes or extended care facilities. Others find research, community health services, food service management, or teaching especially rewarding. Dietitians may find that they are the only member of their profession employed in a given setting, or they may be a member of a dietetic staff that ranges in size from two to as many as the 25 or 30 professionals found in large teaching hospitals.

Clinical dietitians employed in hospitals or extended care facilities work closely with physicians and other health care personnel in selecting appropriate diets and in providing dietary care. Those working in a nutrition clinic or with groups involved in community health projects will be associated with physicians, social workers, and public health nurses. They may participate in individual counseling and group education. The clinical dietitian may find it helpful or even necessary to visit people in their homes to assist them in the wise purchase, storage, and preparation of foods.

What specifically might the clinical dietitian's job be? Miss Jones is employed by the nutrition services department of a large medical center. She is one of a staff of eight dietitians and is responsible to Miss Webster, the head dietitian of the Service. Miss Jones is assigned to a 90-patient medical unit, and she works with all of the health professionals on that unit. Her working day usually runs from 7:30 AM to 4:30 PM. She begins her day by having a brief meeting with her dietetic team, Mrs. Clark and Miss Miller. Mrs. Clark is a dietetic technician, and Miss Miller is a dietetic assistant. They each have their respective duties, and, under Miss Jones' direction, contribute to the nutritional care of the unit's patients. Miss Miller reports the new admissions and the diet changes that she has just picked up at the nurse's station. She will assume initial responsibility for those patients who have regular and soft diet prescriptions. Responsibility for the other patients will go to Miss Jones and Mrs. Clark. Another focus of their meeting is to ensure that those patients who are being discharged today have appropriate materials and that the needed nutrition clinic appointments for follow-up have been made.

Miss Jones then proceeds to locate and join Dr. Lane, who is on rounds with the current group of medical students and house staff. Participation in these rounds assists Miss Jones in providing needed nutritional care for patients before problems arise. She also contributes to the formulation of the diet prescription for the patients. Following rounds, Miss Jones returns to her office to finish the proposal she has been developing for evaluation of dietetic team productivity. It is to be presented at the dietetic staff meeting tomorrow, and she promised to have it to the typist by noon.

This is Tuesday, the day on which the chief of staff's weekly luncheon conference with medical students, interns, and residents is held. Miss Jones participates in these conferences of patient presentations and contributes her knowledge to the identification and solution of their nutritional problems. From 2:00 to 3:00 PM she participates in daily class activities that the unit presents for all of the patients with diabetes. Today Miss Jones teaches the class on diet. Next on her calendar is a meeting that Mrs. Clark and Miss Miller have arranged with the hospital's medical illustration department. There are two agenda items: themes for the pediatric bulletin board, which they change monthly, and review of the artist's drawings, which he prepared following their last discussion regarding the upcoming National Nutrition Week. Then the three return to Miss Jones' office to recap the day's activities and to plan for tomorrow. That was Tuesday! Wednesday will bring some of the same activities, as well as an entire new set of challenges.

The administrative or food service management dietitian is responsible for planning menus, purchasing the required food and equipment, and organizing and supervising the food service workers who prepare and serve food to the clientele, plus planning budgets and managing the income and expenditure of funds. The clientele may be children in school lunch programs, students who participate in college and university food service programs, employees in industrial cafeterias, customers in commericial cafeterias, or patients in hospitals or extended care facilities. In fact, food service management dietitians can be involved wherever food is served to groups of people.

Let us look at the typical day of a dietitian in a school food service program to gain a better understanding of the work of a food service management dietitian. Miss Smith is the only dietitian employed in the New School District, which operates five elementary schools and a junior and senior high school. The total enrollment is 6,000 students. The kitchen is located in the senior high school, and food prepared there is transported by truck to the other schools. Miss Smith supervises Mrs.

Nood, a dietetic technician, and a staff of 12 food service workers. When she arrives at 7:00 AM, Miss Smith reviews the day's food preparation schedule with Mrs. Nood. The head cook had reported a problem with the milk delivery, which they had resolved. Together they outline the food orders for both lunches and breakfast next week. Mrs. Nood had promised to have them ready for the vendors to pick up by 4:00 PM. Her calendar for today includes a meeting with one of the fifth-grade classes at 10:00 AM to assist the teacher in presenting a nutrition unit. Miss Smith must be available to supervise food distribution to the satellite and the high school cafeteria. At 1:30 PM she meets with the head coach to finalize plans for a spaghetti supper and must attend the superintendent's meeting with all the school district's principals at 3:00 PM to discuss the defeat of the operating tax levy at the previous day's election. As you can see, this food service management dietitian must be able to work with many different types of people, enjoy working with food, and be ready to seek solutions to a variety of problems.

These are just some examples of the dietitian's world of work. Nutrition research, college teaching, and many other opportunities are available to the qualified dietitian.

WHAT IS THE NEED FOR DIETITIANS?

Dietitians are in great demand today, and this demand will continue to increase for many years to come. Presently there are 37,000 members of the American Dietetic Association, approximately 500 of whom are men. The percentage of men entering the field is increasing each year.

It is estimated that 56,000 qualified dietitians will be needed by 1980. In order to satisfy this need, approximately 5,000 persons should be entering the field each year through 1980, but in fact approximately 1,500 join the profession each year.

Because the supply is not meeting the demand, job opportunities available to those entering the field are many and varied. Salaries continue to increase, and fringe benefits become more attractive. The American Dietetic Association has recommended a minimum annual salary of $12,000 for the association dietitian who has just completed educational requirements and is entering the practice of dietetics. The association's recommended minimum salary for the beginning registered dietitian is $13,000.

WHO ARE THE SUPPORTING PROFESSIONALS?

Departments of dietetics in hospitals, extended care facilities, schools, and other institutions employ people who are qualified to assist dietitians in specific areas of food service menagement and nutritional care. These supporting professionals play an important role in the dietetic or food service department. Their major objective is to contribute to the nutritional welfare of the patient or client. Their duties may vary according to the size and type of institution for which they work, but they are always interesting, satisfying, and rewarding.

Dietetic technicians

The dietetic technician is a technically skilled person who has successfully completed an associate degree program that meets the educational standards established by the American Dietetic Association. The successful graduate of such a program is eligible for technician membership in the American Dietetic Association. Graduates of non-ADA approved dietetic technician programs are required to document equivalent education and experience before being approved for membership in the association. The technician, who works under the guidance of a registered or American Dietetic Association dietitian, has responsibilities in assigned areas in food service management, in teaching foods and nutrition principles, and in dietary counseling. To better understand the role of the technician, the following tasks are a sampling of what might be included in a job description. Dietetic technicians plan menus based on established guidelines; maintain and improve standards of sanitation, safety, and security; select, schedule, and conduct orientation and inservice education programs for personnel; obtain, evaluate, and utilize information on dietary history in planning nutritional care; calculate nutrient intake and dietary patterns; and utilize appropriate verbal and written communication and public relation skills, inter- and intradepartmentally.

Dietetic assistants

The dietetic assistant is a skilled person who has successfully completed a high school education or the equivalent and a dietetic assistant's program that meets the standards established by the American Dietetic Association. The assistant, working under the guidance of a registered or American Dietetic Association dietitian or a dietetic technician, has responsibility in assigned areas for food service to individuals and groups. Typically dietetic assistants are responsible for assisting in the standardization of recipes and testing of new products; instructing personnel in the use, care, and maintenance of equipment; assisting in implementing cost control procedures; recommending improvements in facilities and equipment; processing dietary orders, menus, and other directives related to patient care; and helping patients to select menus. Like dietetic technicians, dietetic assistants may be employed in food service departments of health care facilities, educational institutions, or industry.

SUMMARY

Dietetics is one of the well-established health professions that is concerned with both sick and well persons. Food is the tool the dietitian uses to promote nutrition by assisting in the maintenance of good health and in the prevention and treatment of disease. Prospective dietetic students may choose from a variety of educational programs and, depending on their interests and abilities, may select one of a number of available areas for an in-depth study of dietetics. Because food—nutritious food—is essential to life, there will always be a need for dietitians.

References

Allied health manpower, 1950-80, Publication No. 263, Sec. 21, Washington, D.C., 1970, U.S. Department of Health, Education, and Welfare, U.S. Public Health Service.

1979 Directory of dietetic programs, accredited and approved, Chicago, 1979, American Dietetic Association.

Position paper on recommended salaries and employment practices for members of the American Dietetic Association, J. Am. Diet. Assoc. **71:**641, 1977.

Titles, definitions, and responsibilities for the profession of dietetics 1974. Report of the Committee to Develop a Glossary on Terminology for the Association and Profession, J. Am. Diet. Assoc. **64:**661, 1974.

Suggested readings

Kinsinger, R. E., editor: Health technicians, Chicago, 1970, J. G. Ferguson Publishing Co.

The profession of dietetics. Report of the Study Commission of Dietetics, Chicago, 1972, American Dietetic Association.

Student handbook for the profession of dietetics, East Lansing, Michigan State University Press (published yearly).

Professional organization where further information can be obtained

American Dietetic Association
430 N. Michigan Ave.
Chicago, Ill. 60611

5

EMERGENCY MEDICAL SERVICES

Mary Beth Skelton

Emergency medicine is a broad term encompassing individuals who work as physicians in emergency departments, nurses who are specializing in the care of the emergency patient in emergency departments, emergency medical technicians who function in the prehospital phase of care at both the basic and paramedic levels, and first responders such as police and fire personnel who arrive on the scene of an accident and begin first-aid measures for victims of a medical or traumatic emergency.

The addition of the emergency medical technicians to the allied health system is relatively new. The emergency medical technician—ambulance (EMT-A) is trained to provide basic life support skills, such as cardiopulmonary resuscitation (CPR), bandaging, splinting, control of bleeding, and assistance in childbirth in the prehospital phase of care. The more extensively trained emergency medical technician—paramedic (EMT-P) delivers definitive therapy to patients before their arrival in the emergency department. The behavioral skills of the EMT-P include venipuncture and initiation of intravenous fluids, administration of medications, interpretation of electrocardiographic monitoring, defibrillation, and endotracheal intubation. All of these advanced life support skills are performed on the direct orders of a physician via radio communication.

By working from a basic or advanced life support ambulance, these individuals can provide emergency care to critically ill or injured patients before they arrive at an emergency department of a hospital.

HISTORY

Physicians functioning in the emergency departments before the early 1970s had no special preparation or training to deal with the emergency patient as subspecialty. In 1968, the American College of

37

Emergency Physicians was formed and proceeded to define emergency medicine as a specialty and adopt a curriculum for a residency program in emergency medicine.

Nurses also were not prepared by any formal curriculum to deal with the emergency patient. The Emergency Department Nurses' Association was formed in 1971 to help meet the needs of emergency department nurses. Since that time a core curriculum has been developed by the Emergency Department Nurses' Association to prepare nurses in this subspecialty.

In 1966, a white paper titled *Accidental Death and Disability: the Neglected Disease of Modern Society* was published by the Division of Medical Science, National Academy of Sciences. The publication emphasized the deficiency of emergency medical services that resulted in unnecessary loss of life from the time of the incident to the time of arrival of the patient in the emergency department.

In 1970, a curriculum was released by the federal Department of Transportation (DOT) and the National Highway Traffic Safety Administration (NHTSA) for the comprehensive instruction of emergency medical technicians–ambulance. Again in 1976, these two agencies contracted for the development of a standardized EMT-P curriculum that was released in 1977. EMT-Ps had been functioning in various areas of the United States since the late 1960s. Cities such as Seattle, Washington, Jacksonville, Florida, and Los Angeles, California, had found that EMT-Ps could improve death and disability statistics by performing certain procedures in the field rather than wait for definitive care on arrival at a hospital. With the success and visability given to these early programs, many metropolitan and even rural communities began to look at the feasibility of implementing EMT-P services. Not until the release of the DOT-NHTSA curriculum in 1977, however, was there an identified standard of training.

EDUCATIONAL REQUIREMENTS

The EMT-A curriculum released in 1970 by DOT-NHTSA rapidly became the accepted basis for EMT-A training. It consisted of 81 hours of didactic and laboratory experience and included 10 hours of hospital experience. Didactic requirements include instruction in the areas of airway obstruction and respiratory arrest, cardiac arrest, mechanical aids to breathing, bleeding and shock management, wound care, fracture management, chest and abdominal injuries, soft-tissue injuries, medical emergencies, environmental emergencies, emergency

Fig. 5-1. Patient immobilization and extrication is taught in order to treat victims involved in vehicular accidents.

childbirth, extrication from vehicles, medicolegal aspects, and record maintenance and vehicular operations. Laboratory time is required to perfect the behavioral skills including cardiopulmonary resuscitation; the splinting, lifting, and moving of patients; and vehicular extrication. (See Fig. 5-1.) Recommended areas for clinical observation and training include the emergency department, labor and delivery rooms, psychiatric unit, and the intensive care units.

Following the training program, graduates take a certifying examination and must usually work on a basic life support vehicle for 6 months before certification is awarded.

The EMT-P curriculum is much broader in scope than that of the EMT-A. Completion of the training program requires successful attainment of all the didactic and behavioral objectives listed as mandatory. Six-hundred to 1,000 hours are frequently required in order for the students to achieve the didactic and behavioral objectives.

The course of instruction includes three phases. The first phase is divided into 15 modules of instruction. (See Fig. 5-2.) They are:

1. Role and responsibilities
2. Human systems and patient assessment

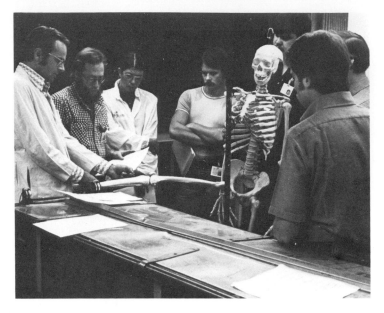

Fig. 5-2. An understanding of anatomy and physiology is essential as the basis of the EMT curriculum.

3. Shock and fluid therapy
4. General pharmacology
5. Respiratory system
6. Cardiovascular system
7. Central nervous system
8. Soft-tissue injuries
9. Musculoskeletal system
10. Medical emergencies
11. Obstetric-gynecological emergencies
12. Pediatrics and neonatal transport
13. Emergency care of the emotionally disturbed
14. Extrication/rescue techniques
15. Telemetry and communications

The second phase is completion of the clinical component. This may be done following all of the didactic instruction or in conjunction with each module of the didactic material. The EMT-P student must perfect such skills as venipuncture, patient assessment, drug administration,

Fig. 5-3. All aspects of the training program are brought together during the field internship when the EMT-P students actually function as members of a paramedic team.

endotracheal intubation, cardiac monitoring, and defibrillation in the clinical areas of the emergency department, intensive care units, pediatrics, labor and delivery units, anesthesia, psychiatric units, and burn units of the hospital. After the first two phases are completed, the EMT-P student enters the third phase, field internship. Here experience as a team member on an advanced life support vehicle (ambulance) is achieved. (See Fig. 5-3.) This vehicle must have telecommunication with a medical command authority for advanced life support. The EMT-P student is supervised by a physician or nurse qualified in emergency medicine or by a state or nationally certified EMT-P. The internship must be within a system that provides advanced life support and evaluates the care provided sufficiently to ensure its quality.

CERTIFICATION AND LICENSING

The National Registry of Emergency Medical Technicians was developed in 1970 in order to standardize instruction, examination, and certification of EMT-A personnel. In 1978 this was expanded to include

EMT-P personnel. A certifying process consisting of a standard written and practical examination is administered for both the EMT-A and the EMT-P by the National Registry or by a designated agency. Upon successful completion of the examination, the EMT-A or EMT-P is given provisional certification. The EMT-A or EMT-P must then demonstrate evidence of employment at the respective levels for a period of 6 months, at which time full certification is awarded.

Nearly 108,000 individuals have been certified at the EMT-A level, and approximately 180 have been certified at the EMT-P level.

The EMT-A and EMT-P are usually also certified or licensed by the state in which they are employed. The state may elect to use the National Registry examination as the certifying process or to develop their own. Currently 18 states use the National Registry examination exclusively in lieu of a state examination.

Evidence of continuing education is required for recertification at both levels. DOT has developed a standard refresher training program for the EMT-A that is incorporated as part of the continuing education criteria adopted by the National Registry for recertification on a biannual basis. To date, a formal refresher training program for the EMT-P does not exist. Specific continuing education criteria varies from state to state at both levels.

CAREER OPPORTUNITIES

The field of emergency medicine has seen rapid growth at all levels over the past few years. Supply has not yet met the demand on the career market. This is especially true for the emergency medical technician as more communities elect to implement emergency medical service systems rather than rely on fragmented ambulance services to provide the prehospital care.

Salaries for the EMT-A range from $7,000 to $10,000 annually. The EMT-P can expect a range of $10,000 to $15,000 annually. This wide variance reflects the differences between training programs and also the mechanism for administering the system. Individuals employed by private enterprise agencies or municipal third service agencies will not receive as high a salary, for example, as a firefighter with 10 years of experience who is trained as an EMT-P in a system administered by the fire service.

Reciprocity among states has been a problem in the past for both the EMT-A and the EMT-P due to the lack of a standard instructional program and certification process. With the adoption of the DOT-NHTSA

81 hours EMT-A curriculum, this problem is diminishing for the EMT-A. The problem still exists for the EMT-P while the new standardized curriculum and certification process are implemented and evaluated.

SUMMARY

The career field of the emergency medical technician offers a new and challenging opportunity for health care delivery. With the rapid growth of the entire field of emergency medicine, the emergency medical technician is being recognized as a vital link in the attainment of early medical care for the emergent patient. The emergency medical technician works in cooperation with physicians and nurses to form a competent team that can provide better care earlier for the patient suffering from a critical illness or injury.

Suggested readings

Accidental death and disability; the neglected disease of modern society, Emergency Health Series A-13, Washington, D.C. 1966, U.S. Government Printing Office.

Course guide, national training course emergency medical technician paramedic, U.S. Department of Transportation, National Highway Traffic Safety Administration, Washington, D.C. 1977, U.S. Government Printing Office.

Course guide, basic training course emergency medical technician, U.S. Department of Transportation, National Highway Traffic Safety Administration, Washington, D.C. 1977, U.S. Government Printing Office.

The EMT Journal, journal of the National Association of Emergency Medical Technicians.

Journal of the American College of Emergency Physicians.

Journal of Emergency Nursing, journal of the Emergency Department Nurses' Association.

Professional organizations where further information can be obtained

American College of Emergency
Physicians
3900 Capitol City Blvd.
Lansing, Mich. 48906

**Emergency Department Nurses
Association**
666 N. Lakeshore Dr.
Suite 1729
Chicago, Ill. 60611

National Association of Emergency
Medical Technicians
P.O. Box 334
Newton Highlands, Mass. 02161

**National Registry of Emergency
Medical Technicians**
1395 East Dublin–Granville Rd.
P.O. Box 29233
Columbus, Ohio 43229

6

ENVIRONMENTAL SANITATION

F. Oris Blackwell

The title "sanitarian" is a time-honored one. At the turn of the century, when the medical profession had very few effective cures for disease, the best weapon was prevention. Environmental factors account for the majority of disease prevention measures. Therefore, the best physicians practiced and taught environmental health in order to prevent disease. These physicians were proud to be called "sanitarians." Today, sanitarians work to reduce health hazards associated both with food and water supplies and with sewage and waste disposal. They are also concerned with atmospheric pollution and, more recently, with radioactive contamination. (See Figs. 6-1 and 6-2.)

HISTORY

Probably the earliest forerunner of our modern sanitarian was a stone-age hominid who decided that the cave was too dirty and did something about it! Down through the ages societies have assigned to persons official duties to look after the general cleanliness and safety of the environment. The Pharaohs of ancient Egypt had highly placed persons in the royal household who kept check on the quality of the stored grain and on the waters of the Nile. The rules regarding cleanliness and isolation of the sick that are found in the Old Testament Book of Leviticus are the first written sanitary codes known. The Romans in 300 BC had aediles—municipal officials who were responsible for public buildings and general cleanliness. The early German cities had "sanitary police" who tried to maintain cleanliness in the market places. In this country environmental health activities developed slowly. Lemuel Shattuck's *Report of the Sanitary Commission of Massachusetts* in 1850 was a milestone set at the first mile. Shattuck made 50 recommendations, most of which dealt with some aspect of what is now called environmental health. These 50 recommendations comprised the bulk of

44

Fig. 6-1. A sanitarian checks a food vending machine.

Fig. 6-2. The sanitarian is using an atomic absorption spectrophotometer to check for trace amounts of a heavy metal in sample.

the 321-page report and could scarcely be summarized here. However, the seventeenth recommendation on p. 153 serves to give the tone: "WE RECOMMEND *that, in laying out new towns and villages, and in extending those already laid out, ample provision be made for a supply, in purity and abundance, of light, air, and water; for drainage and sewerage, for paving and for cleanliness.*" How much better our "towns and villages" would be if we had more carefully heeded Shattuck's advice over the past 140 years.

Of the 50 recommendations, at least 39 have been implemented so far. Shattuck thus laid the foundation for environmental health practice in this country. It was almost 100 years later that environmental health became established as a professional discipline. California passed the first Sanitarian Registration Act in 1945 in which specific educational and experience requirements were defined to designate who could use the title "sanitarian." Forty of the 50 states now have measures that specify qualifications for registration (RS) or licensure. A baccalaureate degree with solid basic science background is the usual minimum requirement, with the ideal preparation being a BS degree from an accredited 4-year environmental health program. As of July 1978, there were 17 such programs distributed throughout the country.* It is estimated that there are about 25,000 persons in the United States working as sanitarians. † Less than half of these have an RS after their name, but the number of fully qualified sanitarians is increasing. As recent as 1950, environmental health sanitarians were almost exclusively men. In 1978 more than 5% of those in the field were women. These women sanitarians are well accepted and are providing equal or better work for equal or better pay. Public recognition of the essential role of the sanitarian in the maintenance of a health promoting environment is growing. Promotion of positive health and the prevention of disease through attention to the environment has received a high priority from government. This also has been the central purpose of sanitarians through the ages.

CAREER LADDER IN ENVIRONMENTAL HEALTH

The entry-level qualification for the professional sanitarian is the baccalaureate degree. However, there is growing realization of the need for and utility of a firm career ladder that bridges preprofessional positions of "sanitarian aide" and "sanitarian technician" to first-level pro-

---

*For a listing see Journal of Environmental Health **41**(1):58, 1978.
†Adapted from Fanning, O.: Opportunities in environmental careers, New York, 1971, Universal Publishing and Distribution Co., p. 206.

fessional sanitarian to the postgraduate sanitarian with master's or doctoral level preparation. Although this career ladder is widely accepted in concept, there are only a few model situations where the concept is in practice. It should be noted, however, that each step of the career ladder need not be represented in any one organization. What is more likely is that career advancement will require a person to be willing to move geographically to better jobs and will perhaps require more education.

SANITARIAN QUALIFICATIONS

As previously noted, the sanitarian with a 4-year degree from an accredited environmental health program is the focal or pivotal point in the career ladder. The accredited curriculum provides effective education in:

Basic sciences and mathematics

Biology
Chemistry
Physics
Microbiology
Mathematics
Epidemiology/biostatistics

Environmental health

Air
Water
Food
Wastes
Shelter
Noise
Radiation
Vectors
Work place
Institution

Communication

Composition (technical writing)
Report writing
Public speaking

Social sciences

Psychology
Sociology
Human relations
Political science

Public health administration and organization
Field Training (recommended)

Structured and supervised work experience

Additional qualifications for anyone entering the environmental health profession should include:

1. Ability to work effectively with people.
2. A strong interest in science and an appreciation of its application and limitations.
3. A commitment to the service-above-self role of a true professional.
4. A true concern for the health and well-being of their fellow man.

The following two statements together give a reasonable definition of a sanitarian:

> Sanitarian: plans, develops, and executes environmental health programs. Organizes and conducts training programs in environmental health practices for schools and other groups. Determines and sets health and sanitation standards and enforces regulations concerned with food processing and serving, collection and disposal of solid wastes, sewage treatment and disposal, plumbing, vector control, recreational areas, hospitals and other institutions, noise, ventilation, air pollution, radiation, and other areas. Confers with government, community, industrial, civil defense, and private organizations to interpret and promote environmental health programs. Collaborates with other health personnel in epidemiological investigations and control. Advises civic and other officials in development of environmental health laws and regulations.*
>
> The sanitarian, qualified by successful completion of an accredited baccalaureate program in environmental health and by creditable field experience, is prepared to plan, organize, manage, execute, and evaluate the many facets of the environmental health program. He is a person whose interest, education, and experience uniquely qualify him to practice in the field of environment for the maintenance of and the promotion of an environment conducive to the optimum well-being of man. He is prepared to perform duties in environmental sanitation and health, including but not limited to scientific investigation, education and counseling.†

---

*Dictionary of occupational titles, ed. 4, Washington, D.C., 1977, U.S. Department of Labor, Employment and Training Administration 079.117-018, p. 64.
†Blackwell, F. O., Adrounie, V. H., and Walker, B., Jr.: Sanitarians examination review book, New York, 1977, Medical Examination Publishing Co., p. 7.

WORK ACTIVITIES

Most sanitarians are employed by public health agencies at the local (that is, city or county), state, or federal level. Entry level sanitarians usually are inspectors who check restaurants, schools, day care centers, hospitals, summer camps, bakeries, and grocery stores. (See Fig. 6-3.) They check individual water supplies, sewage treatment facilities, insect and rodent problems, solid waste disposal and swimming pools. (See Fig. 6-4.) As experience is gained, the sanitarian will become more involved in providing education and consultation in addition to regulation. For example, one service often provided by local health departments is food handlers' training for restaurant operators and food service workers. Experienced sanitarians organize and teach these training programs.

After a few years of responsible work experience, a sanitarian may become a supervisor or director of programs. This advancement will entail administrative duties such as planning, organizing, leading, and evaluating. Graduate studies for the sanitarian, both master's and doctoral degrees, will provide further options for administration, research, and teaching. Also, graduate studies can lead to specialization in such

Fig. 6-3. A restaurant manager discusses food temperatures with a sanitarian.

Fig. 6-4. A sanitarian uses laboratory equipment to help identify insect vectors of disease.

areas as industrial hygiene, institutional hygiene (such as health care facilities), or radiation protection.

The majority of those trained as sanitarians do work in public health agencies as noted earlier, but many other options are available. Industry is increasingly hiring environmental health sanitarians for quality control in food and related industries and health and safety programs. Opportunities are available for private consultation and environmental health related business adventures. Recently sanitarians have beem employed by cruise ship lines to work aboard ships and maintain a healthful environment. International health activities such as HOPE, USAID, VISTA, and the Peace Corps utilize sanitarians.

LEAD-UP POSITIONS: AIDES AND TECHNICIANS

Sanitarian aides are usually high school graduates with on-the-job training in some special area of environmental health. The training and work are under a professional sanitarian and may include such assignments as mixing and distributing baits in an ongoing rodent control program. With experience and 2 years of college (associate degree), a person may work as a *sanitarian technician*. This work might include much that aides do but in addition would require field work in surveys, environmental sampling (air, water, swimming pool), and perhaps initial check and screening of complaints. Associate degree technicians also find employment with industry in plant sanitation programs. Two more years of university work and a degree in environmental health leads to the first-level professional, the sanitarian.

NEED FOR SANITARIANS

There has been over the past 10 years increasing demand for persons with good qualifications to work in environmental health. The increasing cost of curative medicine mandates more effective preventive measures. The public is demanding higher levels of environmental quality. Both factors indicate that the need for sanitarians will accelerate. Current demands are not being met by the number of graduates from accredited programs.

Salaries for sanitarians are competitive with those of persons with comparable educational backgrounds. Although they vary from state to state, starting salaries for first-level professionals range from $9,000 to $13,000 annually in public agencies. Somewhat higher starting salaries may be found with industry. Advancement opportunities have been described earlier, and though some salaries may range up to $50,000 and more annually, the highest paying jobs are limited in number. However, the greatest rewards of the work of the sanitarian lie in the satisfaction of doing a job well that contributes directly and significantly to the vigor of the community and the preservation of a healthful environment.

Suggested reading

Newton, D. F.: Elements of environmental health, Columbus, Ohio, 1974, Charles E. Merrill Publishing Co.

Professional organizations where further information can be obtained

National Accreditation Council for
Environmental Health Curricula
Suite 704
1200 Lincoln St.
Denver, Colo. 80203

National Environmental Health
Association
Suite 704
1200 Lincoln St.
Denver, Colo. 80203

7

EXTRACORPOREAL CIRCULATION TECHNOLOGY

James P. Dearing

Extracorporeal circulation technology is a new addition to the allied health professions. It was conceived and developed during the past decade through the efforts of many people from several disciplines. Medicine and engineering combined skills to develop this new technology in response to a need that had been apparent since the late 1950s.

Extracorporeal circulation technologists play a vital role in caring for patients undergoing heart surgery. They also provide circulatory support for a failing heart or lungs, remove toxic products from the blood stream by means of the artificial kidney, preserve organs for subsequent transplantation, deliver chemotherapeutic agents to the cancer patient, and make possible a variety of diagnostic procedures. Most of these techniques put the patient's circulatory system in direct continuity with instrumentation either for monitoring purposes or for the removal, processing, and subsequent return of the patient's blood to his own circulatory system.

PROFESSIONAL DEVELOPMENT

Since the first successful elective open heart operation supported by cardiopulmonary bypass was performed in 1953, extracorporeal (outside the body) circulation technology has grown remarkably. In 1977 there were more than 100,000 such operations performed in more than 1,000 institutions in which a heart-lung machine was available. (See Fig. 7-1.) Concurrent with the first open heart procedures, hemodialysis (removal of wastes from the blood via the artificial kidney) became an accepted treatment for patients suffering from kidney failure. (See Fig. 7-2.) There are now more than 500 hemodialysis centers registered with the Kidney Disease Control Program of the U.S. Public Health Service.

52

Fig. 7-1. Preparation of the heart-lung machine that is used to provide circulatory support for patients undergoing open heart surgery requires meticulous attention to detail.

Furthermore, organ transplantation has stimulated the development of devices for storing, preserving, and evaluating function in transplantable organs.

During the early developmental days of extracorporeal circulation technology, the devices used were physician developed and physician operated. Gradually these responsibilities have changed hands. Industry, with its technological and engineering expertise, has taken over the development of subsequent devices. The operation of the devices has been assigned to the technologist. The first nonphysician operators of these devices were recruited from the ranks of the other allied health

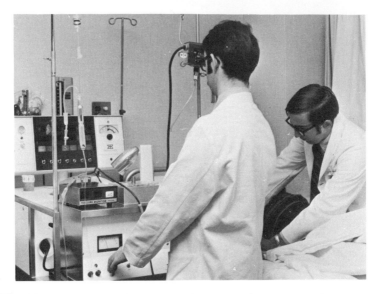

Fig. 7-2. Extracorporeal circulation technology students set up and operate the instrumentation for the hemodialysis of a patient.

professions and trained on the job by the physicians who pioneered the technology.

The separation of the physician from the technology has been intensified during the past decade due to several factors. The technological explosion in the electronics and plastics industries has allowed for the advancement through several generations of extracorporeal circulation devices to the point where the current generation of devices is no longer familiar to the physician inventors. Furthermore, applications of new technologies, such as the augmentation of circulation by means of intra-aortic balloon insertions and long-term respiratory support through membrane oxygenators, have demanded time commitments not possible for the practicing physician. Today, intensive training in extracorporeal circulation is no longer part of the residency requirements for physicians.

Over the past 2 decades two points have become clear. First, utilization of nurses or other allied health professionals to operate extracorporeal circulation devices was taking professionals from areas where they are sorely needed. Second, the technology has become so complex and specialized that training in other allied medical areas was not sufficient for safe and effective utilization of this technology. A new allied health professional was needed with specialized education and training in this technology.

Because of the lack of well-defined criteria for training and qualification, a concentrated effort was launched in the late 1960s to identify and define the practitioners in this technology as a new allied health profession. The approach was twofold: first, to develop curricula and standards for the education of those specialists and second, to qualify the existing technologists.

A variety of training programs have been developed in extracorporeal circulation technology since the pioneering effort took place at The Ohio State University in 1968. The length of programs ranges from 1 to 2 years. Two programs, those in schools of allied health where there are two preprofessional and two professional years, terminate in baccalaureate degrees. Several programs offer associate degrees, and several provide postbaccalaureate certification. A listing of these programs is available from the American Board of Cardiovascular Perfusion, P.O. Box 20345, Houston, Texas 77025.

Concurrent with the development of educational programs, an effort to identify and qualify the technologists already practicing in the field was launched through an examination program developed by the technical society representing most of the practitioners.

EDUCATIONAL REQUIREMENTS

In November of 1974, the American Society of Extracorporeal technology established minimum standards for training programs in extracorporeal circulation technology. These criteria were established to encompass all of the training programs currently in existence. The criteria establish the administrative and faculty requirements for schools and define minimal curricular requirements. The elements of the required curriculum are:

Course area	Clock hours
Anatomy and pathology	36
Physiology	36
Pharmacology	36
Extracorporeal circulation technology	48

Extracorporeal circulation technology represents a complex field of study, drawing upon the fields of biology, engineering, pharmacology, physiology, and related sciences. (See Fig. 7-3.)

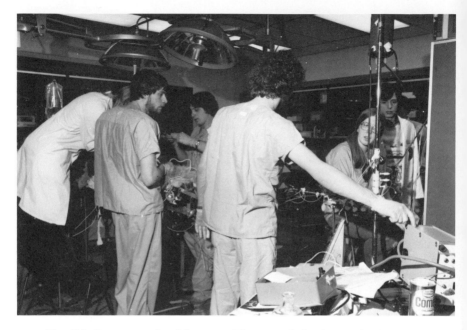

Fig. 7-3. Instrumentation laboratory. Elements of circulatory physiology and electrical engineering combine to form the knowledge base for this assignment where students monitor oxygen and other blood gases in the interrupted circulatory system of an animal in surgery.

In addition to the didactic requirements there is a clinical experience requirement of a minimum of 50 clinical cases. This requirement may be met in an internship program in an approved clinical institution if the institution offering the program does not have the clinical case load. On completion of an approved program, graduates must be employed in this field for 6 months before they are eligible to take the certification examination administered by the American Board of Cardiovascular Perfusion.

The examinations were developed through the process of examining only those technologists that meet two requirements: a minimum of 2 years in the field and a minimum of 100 unsupervised clinical cases. It was felt that these technologists had stood the test of time, and thus their skills level could be used to standardize the certification examination for new entrants in the field. To date approximately 1,000 technologists have been certified through this examination process.

CAREER OPPORTUNITIES

Due to the rapid growth of medical practice that has required the support of extracorporeal circulation, technologists find an open career market. Although most technologists are employed by large medical centers, some have developed their own private groups that provide service to several hospitals on a fee-for-service basis. Others have gone into practice with a medical group. With the rapid growth of clinic dialysis, many career opportunities exist in privately operated clinics that specialize in ambulatory patient hemodialysis. Finally, there is a demand for well-educated and trained personnel in industry.

The salary range is broad. Annual starting salaries for new graduates range between $12,000 and $20,000. This wide range reflects both the differences among training programs and the types of jobs available. The higher salaries are commanded by those graduates with extensive knowledge in all areas of the technology and who are given the responsibility of developing and coordinating efforts in all of these areas.

SUMMARY

Extracorporeal circulation technology is a new, exciting, and demanding profession that offers the practitioner a challenging career at the leading edge of medical and technological advance. The profession deals with the use of artificial organs to sustain life and with the development of new and better techniques for performing this task. The emergence of this technology into a profession offers an enticing opportunity for those who enjoy applying new technologies to the solution of biological problems.

Suggested Readings

Bailey, G. L.: Hemodialysis; principles and practice, New York, 1972, Academic Press, Inc.

Norman, J. C.: Cardiac surgery, ed. 2, New York, 1972, Appleton-Century-Crofts.

Professional organizations where further information can be obtained

American Board of Cardiovascular Perfusion
P.O. Box 20345
Houston, Tex. 77025

American Society of Extracorporeal Technology
Reston International Center
Suite 322
11800 Sunrise Valley Dr.
Reston, Va. 22091

8

HEALTH EDUCATION

Mary Alice Beetham

Health education is one of the oldest health professions to deal with the transmission of knowledge and of the skills to apply that knowledge. In March of 1973, the latest report of the Joint Committee on Health Education Terminology* officially defined health education as ''a process with intellectual, psychological, and social dimensions relating to activities which increase the abilities of people to make informed decisions affecting their personal, family, and community well being. This process, based on scientific principles, facilitates learning and behavioral change in both health personnel and consumers, including children and youth.''

Health educators are identified professionally as school health, public health, or community health educators. The trend has been to recruit school and community health educators at the baccalaureate level. *School health* educators have received a teaching certificate and are respected members of public school systems with expertise in an identifiable subject area. Opportunities for employment outside the classroom encouraged the extension of teacher training programs so that professional preparation became available for *community health* educators. The *public health* educator is predominantly educated at a school of public health and earns a master's degree. Public health educators have long been respected members of the public health team in agencies where the team concept is revered. A high commitment of all health educators is to education for ''wellness.''

---

*This committee consists of representatives of the American Academy of Pediatrics; American Association of Health, Physical Education, and Recreation; American College Health Association; American Public Health Association; American School Health Association; and Society of Public Health Education, Inc.

SCOPE OF HEALTH EDUCATION

In R. M. Titmuss' terms, health education is a social service activity that is intended for the well-being of the population. In the terms of the Joint Economic Committee of the United States Congress, health education contributes to the development of human resources. Scott Simonds, Professor of health education at the University of Michigan school of public health, states that individual behaviors have a great deal to do with health outcomes and that a considerable reduction in morbidity and mortality rates could be achieved by informed and "health-activated" citizens. To compound existing societal problems, a recent study by Smith and associates showed that 5% of all television time in a metropolitan area was allocated to transmitting inaccurate or misleading health information. During the 1974 Federal Focus on Health Education Conference in Atlanta, Dr. Charles Edwards, assistant secretary for health, United States Department of Health, Education, and Welfare, called for health education "not for education's sake but for its impact on total health." He cited lowered morbidity and mortality rates as a measure of health education. Successful programs are demonstrated by "each and every segment of society working toward a common objective measured in human terms" with each individual possessing a sense of responsibility for (his) own health, as well as that of the community."

According to the Report of the President's Committee on Health Education, there are 25,000 professional health educators in the nation—persons with bachelor's, master's, or doctoral degrees in either school or community health education.

School health education reaches 55 million children in the United States (one fourth of the entire population). The first 10 years of life are cited by many experts as being the most crucial in terms of physical and psychological development, yet school health education is often not given much emphasis in the curriculum until the senior high school level. Hopefully, new federal comprehensive health education legislation will be forthcoming. Meanwhile, groups such as parent-teacher associations and medical auxiliaries are actively championing comprehensive health education. The State Planning Committee for Health Education did pioneering work in a legislative committee to achieve cooperation between official state agencies and health-related organizations in order to move health education from a paper priority to an action priority.

Community health education reaches out to the adult population

Fig. 8-1. Health education. Children and youth project. (Courtesy Children's Hospital, Columbus, Ohio.)

primarily through programs at places of business (40% of the population is employed) and through television and other public media. Insurance companies, such as Blue Cross and Blue Shield, are introducing health education messages and programs into the schools, community, and the workplace. Some examples are: the nutrition program for schools— "eat right to your heart's delight", jogger clinics and "runs" in the community, and plans for smoking withdrawal clinics and other strategies to encourage a healthier life-style in the workplace. (See Fig. 8-1.)

PERSONAL QUALIFICATIONS

A school health educator needs basically the same qualifications as any other certified teacher, because these educators are concerned primarily with classroom teaching. Socrates said, "Example is not *one* method of teaching but the *only* method." A health teacher should embody positive physical, mental, and social health. Identification and imagery are very important, particularly to the elementary student. Love and respect for self and others is paramount. A sound informational base is required, but a teacher who enjoys teaching and who believes fundamentally that learning can be fun is assured of success. Skill as a facilitator of learning is a professional asset.

A community health/public health educator also must have a sound informational base but needs more preparation in communications and group process skills, since much education will be accomplished through committee teamwork and community organization. The educational focus is on the nonschool community. The public health educator holds the philosophy that if you teach one person who in turn teaches another, the "multiplier effect" is seen, whether the teaching is through intermediaries, personal instruction, or mass media. A good community health educator must be interested in working with people. An extroverted personality is helpful but not essential. The positive health image is essential because a community health educator is in public view. It is difficult to "sell" trimness when one is fat or the dangers of smoking while one is lighting a cigarette.

EDUCATIONAL PREPARATION

The school health educator receives a bachelor's degree in education and meets the basic requirements for any teacher certification program. This includes a student teaching requirement. Preparation in health education may be as a major or minor field.

The community health educator is a graduate of a bachelor's degree program that may or may not include a period of student teaching. The usual substitution for student teaching is supervised field work. The program may be based in a college of education or school of allied health professions.

The public health educator is a master's degree recipient (MPH or MSPH) from a school of public health. A list of accredited schools may be obtained from the American Public Health Association (APHA). Also, universities such as the University of Tennessee that are accredited in community health education have a master's degree program following a school health education program as well as an APHA-accredited master of science degree. Doctoral degrees are offered in both health education and public health education.

CAREER OPPORTUNITIES

Health educators are not licensed. There are tremendous varieties of employment possibilities available. School health educators are usually found in public school settings; with graduate degrees, they may teach in colleges or universities. Many voluntary health agencies utilize persons experienced in this discipline as program directors. Official agencies such as city and state health departments add them to the health team within the agency and also in program areas. Another viable option is the clinic setting.

Community health educators are sought by official and voluntary agencies and recently have joined the staffs of health planning programs, neighborhood health centers, community mental health centers, hospitals, clinics, industries, and other community projects.

Public health educators are able to satisfy requirements for consultative positions (federal, state, and local), administrative positions in health-related fields, and occasionally collegiate appointments in addition to opportunities in community health. (See Fig. 8-2.) Growing

Fig. 8-2. Student viewing health education exhibit in the student health clinic of a major university. (Courtesy Dept. of Photography and Cinema, The Ohio State University.)

numbers of public health educators work as "patient health educators" in the provision of health care services. As health maintenance organizations gain visibility and as the criteria are established for health education as a benefit reimbursable through health insurance programs, this role is becoming more established. Hospitals are now being encouraged to expand their services to include patient education. Some form of national health insurance is imminent, and prevention of illness through health education will be stressed. There are four basic criteria for judging the effectiveness of any national health program or facility: (1) accessibility, (2) availability, (3) acceptability, (4) accountability. Without health education, accountability would not be possible within our economic restrictions. Health educators will help to ensure the acceptability of health care programs through the application of communicating and listening skills.

SUMMARY

Health education is a profession that bridges the gap between health information (what one knows) and health practices (what one does). It must start at the level of the learner. The responsibility of individuals for their own health has always been of paramount importance to the school health educator, although collectively these same individuals are the primary targets of community-wide health education.

Health educators must encourage the productive effort of health education by all—the health team (governmental, voluntary, and private agencies) and the general public joining hands, so to speak. Many prominent health educators believe that optimal health for all is an attainable goal. They define health holistically. The potential for all children to be born healthy and wanted depends on health education that reaches the parents of our nation's children before conception and therefore contributes to a better quality of life. Attitudes and behavior reflect values and decision making. A sense of responsibility for individual and community health is essential.

References

Joint Economic Committee, United States Congress, Subcommittee on Economic Progress: Federal programs for the development of human resources, Washington, D.C., 1966, U.S. Government Printing Office.

Proceedings of the Federal Focus on Health Education Conference, Washington, D.C., 1974, U.S. Department of Health, Education and Welfare.

Report of the President's Committee on Health Education, Health Services, and Mental Health Administration, Washington, D.C., 1973, U.S. Government Printing Office.

Smith, F. A., and others: Health information during a week of television, N. Eng. J. Med. **286:**516, 1972.

Titmuss, R. M.: Commitment to welfare, New York, 1968, Pantheon Books, Inc.

Professional organizations where further information can be obtained

American Association for Health, Physical Education, and Recreation
1201 Sixteenth St., N.W.
Washington, D.C. 20036
American College Health Association, Health Education Section
2807 Central St.
Evanston, Ill. 60201
American Public Health Association, Public Health Education Section, School Health Section
1015 Eighteenth St., N.W.
Washington, D.C. 20036

American School Health Association
P.O. Box 708
Kent, Ohio 44240
Society for Public Health Education, Inc.
655 Sutter St.
San Francisco, Calif. 94102

9

HOSPITAL AND HEALTH SERVICES ADMINISTRATION

Barbara McCool

Health services administrators manage complex organizations such as hospitals, public health agencies, health maintenance organizations, and other health-related facilities. Their main role is to marshal and coordinate the resources necessary for the delivery of health care, accomplish organizational goals, and motivate others toward optimal performance.

Within single institutions (such as a community hospital) the health care administrator is directly responsible to a board of trustees, a group of civic-minded community leaders who determine broad policies and objectives. The administrator directs the day-to-day activities of the institution and assumes a major role in planning and promoting the development of health care services (See Fig. 9-1.) In larger institutions this may involve supervising and coordinating the activities of more than 30 highly specialized departments that perform administrative, professional, or maintenance and operational services.

Within multiple hospital systems (many hospitals under one corporation), the administrator at the unit level represents the system to the local board and medical staff and acts as the coordinating agent between the hospital and corporate office.

Health care administrators act to ensure that the health care facility operates efficiently as a unit; they see that necessary facilities, equipment, and services are available; they help to coordinate the development of educational programs for nurses, physicians, technologists, and other personnel; and they oversee the facility's contributions to preventive medicine and to improving the health of the people the facility serves. Besides providing the optimum internal environment, the administrator represents the health institution in the community, in the

65

Fig. 9-1. Hospital administrators plan future health services.

state through membership in state associations, and nationally through participation in the work of associations that represent such special interest groups as the American Hospital Association, the American Public Health Association, and the Association of Mental Health Administrators.

HISTORY OF THE PROFESSION

The institutionalization of health care in the United States began in 1752 when Benjamin Franklin and Dr. Thomas Bond established the Pennsylvania Hospital in Philadelphia. The early hospitals were viewed as boardinghouses for the poor and terminally ill. As advances in medical science were made, the hospital became the focal point of care and continued to grow in importance and complexity. There are approximately 7,000 hospitals in the United States today.

Parallel to the development of the modern hospital has been the evolution of the profession of hospital and health services administration. The early hospitals were managed on a part-time basis by a physician or nurse whose primary responsibility was to act as the custodian of property and equipment. As medical care became more complex and as governmental, legislative, and community factors grew in influence, administrative responsibilities also grew.

Hospital and health services administration became a profession with the formation of the American College of Hospital Administrators in 1933 and the beginnings of graduate education in health services administration in 1934. The goal of the American College of Hospital Administrators was to develop standards of performance and education. Concomitantly, the first graduate program in hospital and health services administration was started in 1934 at the University of Chicago. Other graduate programs were developed to prepare professional administrators, and today there are approximately 70 programs offering the master's degree.

EDUCATIONAL PREPARATION

The usual preparation for a career in hospital and health services administration takes place at the graduate level. Students receiving a master's degree in health administration exhibit an advanced level of management competency, which becomes the basis for entry into both middle- and upper-level administrative positions.

Programs in hospital and health services administration provide students with theoretical and experiential grounding in health care management and stress the importance of analyzing, synthesizing, and evaluating large quantities of information.

The curricula of the various programs that offer graduate study reflect the particular emphasis of the university department of which they are a part, such as medicine, business, or public health. Some programs require two academic years on campus with summer work experience in a health facility, whereas others require 1 year on campus in academic work and a second year in an administrative residency at a health services institution.

On completion of their formal education, new graduates usually start their professional careers as administrative assistants in a hospital, insurance firm, public health agency, or health maintenance organization.

Undergraduate programs are a new development in education for hospital and health services administration. At the present time, 22 institutions offer a baccalaureate degree for persons who wish to become middle managers in large health institutions or administrators of extended care facilities or other less complex health agencies.

An undergraduate health services administration degree is not the best preparation for a graduate degree in the field. A number of graduate programs prefer students who have completed a broad liberal arts education.

PERSONAL QUALITIES NEEDED

A future health care administrator should possess (1) a commitment to serving others, (2) above-average intelligence, (3) the ability to get along with many different kinds of people, (4) the ability to work under pressure, and (5) adequate physical and emotional stamina.

RELATED PROFESSIONALS

The hospital and health services administrator works with physicians, community and business leaders, government officials, and a wide variety of health professionals to organize and coordinate health care delivery for a defined population. Within the health care institution the administrator creates an environment in which highly skilled health professionals can apply their knowledge and skills to the care of the patient.

• • •

A profile of a day in the life of a hospital administrator illustrates the challenges facing this health professional. Richard Cramer is the administrator of Northfield Community Hospital, a 400-bed, general acute care institution operated by a nonprofit corporation in a midwestern city with a population of 500,000. It offers medical, surgical, pediatric, obstetrical, and psychiatric care programs, has modern diagnostic and therapeutic facilities, and cooperates with other hospitals in the area in operating a comprehensive outpatient clinic. It is fully accredited by the Joint Commission on Accreditation of Hospitals and sponsors several medical and allied health educational programs. Mr. Cramer has been the administrator of Northfield for 3 years. He is active in the American College of Hospital Administrators, serves as a delegate to the American Hospital Association, and is president of the State Hospital Association. He has three assistant administrators, all of whom are active in the civic life of the community.

8:00 Mr. Cramer arrives at the hospital parking lot and is stopped by Dr. Kenneth Stone, chief of the medical staff. Dr. Stone arranges a meeting with Mr. Cramer for 1:30 that afternoon to review the applications of physicians who have applied for medical staff privileges.

8:15 As he approaches the entrance to the hospital, Mr. Cramer meets Mrs. Evans, a member of the hospital's board of trustees. Mr. Evans is currently a patient at Northfield, and Mr. Cramer is pleased to learn that Mr. Evans is recuperating from his surgery and will be going home in a few days.

8:25 When Mr. Cramer arrives at his office, his secretary, Miss Rolfe, hands him his appointment schedule for the day, a folder of correspondence, and a list of several phone calls that must be returned. Mr. Cramer glances quickly through his mail, which includes a letter from the Blue Cross Association concerning a revised reimbursement schedule, several thank you notes from patients who have been discharged from the hospital, a letter from the hospital's attorney explaining the institution's legal position in a pending liability case, bids from contractors for construction of a new facility, a letter of resignation from a department head, and confirmation of his reservation for the upcoming annual meeting of the American College of Hospital Administrators.

8:30 Mr. Cramer's three assistants and the director of nursing services arrive for their daily meeting. Mrs. Smiley presents the patient census for the day and reports on events that occurred on the night shift and on the condition of critical patients. Mr. Pace distributes copies of the pharmacy reorganization plans that will be presented at the meeting of department heads later in the day. He also announces that he will be representing the hospital at the certificate of need hearing with the comprehensive health planning agency. Mr. Brooks reports that the parking lot construction will be slowed down by a delay in the delivery of entrance gates and that representatives of the housekeeping employees' union have approached him about negotiations for a new union contract. Mr. Parks mentions that he and Dr. Summerfield will be leaving the next day to recruit interns and residents for the following year. Mr. Cramer announces that the revised wage and salary program will be discussed at an administration meeting to be held the following day. During a discussion of plans for a new coronary unit, the hospital's architect arrives with drawings to be submitted to the board of trustees for approval. During the meeting, Miss Rolfe is busy answering telephone calls and arranging appointments. The meeting ends abruptly as the administrator is summoned to the emergency room, where the town's mayor has just been brought in following an automobile accident. Mr. Cramer instructs Miss Rolfe concerning notification of the press.

10:00 The president of the board of trustees arrives to discuss the agenda for the board meeting to be held that evening.

11:30 Mr. Cramer addresses a luncheon meeting of the Kiwanis Club on the subject of national health insurance.

1:30 Dr. Stone arrives to review applications for medical staff privileges. The physician wants Mr. Cramer's recommendations before a meeting of the credentials committee that is scheduled for the following week. A problem that has arisen in the anesthesiology department is discussed and resolved.

3:00 Mr. Cramer attends the meeting of department heads and gives a report on the new management training program.

4:00 In a meeting with the hospital comptroller, the director of nursing, and the personnel director, Mr. Cramer discusses the nursing service budget.

6:00 Mr. Cramer attends a dinner meeting of the executive committee of the board of trustees and discusses long-range development plans to be presented later at a meeting of the full Board.

10:00 Following the executive committee meeting, Mr. Cramer returns briefly to the hospital to check on the mayor's condition. He is relieved to find him resting comfortably and to learn that his injuries are not serious.

NEED FOR HOSPITAL ADMINISTRATORS

The rapidly expanding demand for comprehensive health care has intensified the need for competent hospital and health care administrators. This has become one of the critical issues facing the American health care system today, and the shortage of administrators will become more severe with the increased emphasis on extended care facilities, community mental health centers, expanded general hospitals, and area-wide planning agencies. Newly graduated hospital administrators may earn from $17,000 to $19,000 annually. Depending on the size of the facility, experience, and competence, an administrator may eventually earn from $40,000 to $100,000 a year.

SUMMARY

Today's health care delivery system is undergoing critical reexamination. Hospital and health services administrators are restructuring health care delivery systems so that all segments of the population may have equal access to comprehensive health services at costs lower than at present. The health care arena is characterized by change in virtually every area of its operation. In this dynamic milieu the hospital and health services administrator is faced with changing financial requirements, quality control systems, new mergers, government regulations, and other pending changes in national health policy. Those responding effectively to these challenges receive both the material rewards of high status and salaries and the many intangible rewards associated with human service.

Suggested readings

Education for health administration. Report of the Commission on Education for Health Administration, Ann Arbor, 1974, University of Michigan Health Administration Press.

Hospital administrators, SRA Occupational Brief No. 235, Chicago, 1972, Science Research Associates, Inc.

Kirk W. R.: Your career in hospital administration, Chicago, 1972, American College of Hospital Administrators Press.

Quatrano, L., editor: Health administration education for 1979, Washington, D.C., 1978, Association of University Programs in Health Administration.

Professional organizations where further information can be obtained

American College of Hospital Administrators
840 N. Lake Shore Dr.
Chicago, Ill. 60611

The Association of University Programs in Health Administration
#1 Dupont Circle, N. W. Suite 420
Washington, D.C. 20036

10

MEDICAL COMMUNICATIONS

John E. Burke

The field of medical communications has evolved in the last several years as a result of a strong interdisciplinary challenge. As the demand for greater numbers of better-trained health professionals and improved health information systems became more urgent, there was clearly a need for communications specialists and researchers with a variety of skills. As communications technologies became more sophisticated, their applications in clinical and educational areas were explored by professionals with widely varying backgrounds in media, education, engineering, health, and the computer, behavioral, and social sciences.

Increases in population and information, together with advances in technology, brought communications specialists into a new relationship with many health professionals. (See Fig. 10-1.) This relationship, which began as consultation, has grown broader as communication problems have been recognized in every sector of biomedical education and indeed at every level of health care delivery. What has emerged is a new type of health professional with special background and skills in communication and an understanding of the needs and priorities of the health professions.

The importance of communication in the health care system has increased dramatically in recent years. The effective dissemination of health information is critical in controlling disease. Practitioners as well as scientists need current research information, teachers need better ways of transmitting an increasing volume of knowledge to larger numbers of students, and the consumers of health services need to know what services are available and where and how they may be obtained. Most important, the public needs to know how to stay well.

Much of the material for this chapter is based on the chapter prepared by Kathryn Schoen for the first edition of this book.

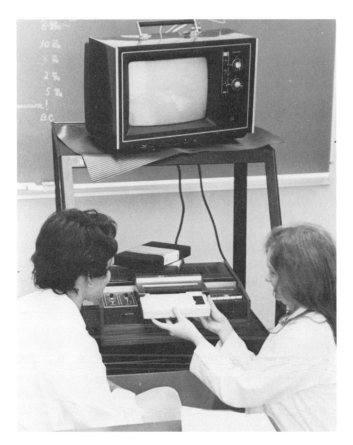

Fig. 10-1. Medical communications specialists work with many different health professionals in a variety of settings to improve communication effectiveness.

In order that patient care may be improved, the health care system must strengthen itself internally. Here again, communication is increasingly significant. Members of the health care team must learn better methods of communicating with each other as well as with their patients. They must understand their respective roles, cooperate in the development of hospital and public health information systems, and work together to find solutions to the many communications problems peculiar to the health professions. As Walker has pointed out, if the health care system is to continue to increase its efficiency, it must learn to cope with the new patterns and methods of communication.

Although a global definition of biomedical communication is still being refined, its basic components are clear. Whether it be in formal education in the health sciences, postgraduate education, in-service training, public information, clinical support systems, or research and development, the role of medical communications is to improve information transfer, processing, retention, and utilization. This implies a knowledge of behavioral change in its many forms, especially as it affects the health care delivery system. Although many professionals with special communications skills can be found in the health sciences, few practitioners have been trained specifically for this aspect of their work. Those such as medical illustrators, biomedical photographers, and medical librarians, who have received special training, usually work in highly specialized areas and are rarely involved in solving communications problems outside their special areas of expertise. It is extremely difficult to find professionals trained in communications in the broader sense who also know the language and environment of the health sciences. Generalists as well as specialists are needed to solve the many complex communication problems in modern health care. Programs have therefore been developed to train the professional medical communicator.

HISTORICAL DEVELOPMENT

Communications media and concern for the communication process are not new to the health professions. Indeed, written communication combined with aural and visual reinforcement is as old as medical science itself. Examples include the writings of Hippocrates, the anatomical drawings of Leonardo da Vinci, and the functional operating theaters of the late nineteenth century that were designed for the effective "audiovisual" orientation of young surgeons. The most dramatic communications advances, however, have come in this century. Progress in electronic technology, photography, and other media forms, combined with a better understanding of human communication, has led to exciting experimentation in medical education and communication. New learning systems are being introduced into medical education in an effort to meet the challenge for more and better-trained health professionals. The quality of the presentation of content (the instructional message) and the choice of proper media (film, audio, television, computers, slides, and so forth) are fast becoming an important part of the repertoire of every educator in the health professions. Microwave interconnection, satellite transmission, closed-circuit telemedicine, and computerized information systems are all examples of advanced technologies being used today to help solve health care problems in a complex society.

Before the more revolutionary advances in communications technology such as television and the computer, other media were used to improve medical education and clinical services. Books, drawings, models, specimens, audio tapes, films, and so forth continue to be important tools of the medical communications specialist. With the introduction of television in the 1940s, however, medical communications became a more significant force in both educational and clinical settings. The expense and complexity of television and later the computer prompted biomedical and communications professionals to share ideas regarding the use of these new media. In 1953 the Audiovisual Conference of Medical and Allied Sciences was organized to further audiovisual education. If these early efforts did not solve the communication problems in the health sciences, they at least brought them into focus.

The first training programs in biomedical communications, organized in the 1960s, emphasized the technological and managerial rather than the social and behavioral aspects of communication. The objective of these educational programs was to harness the new technologies for the improvement of medical education. Trainees were drawn from professional schools or doctoral programs and exposed to various types of media applications and management systems, principally in large medical centers. One such training program was initiated by the National Medical Audiovisual Center in cooperation with Tulane and other universities. Other programs were sponsored by the National Library of Medicine to prepare specialists to manage the automated and information storage and retrieval networks that have been designed to improve the flow of biomedical information.

EDUCATIONAL PREPARATION
Undergraduate programs

In recent years several undergraduate as well as postbaccalaureate and graduate programs have evolved in an attempt to meet the growing demand for communications specialists in the health sciences. Early academic programs at the baccalaureate level emphasized such areas as biological photography or instructional media. More recently, however, the trend has been toward a more flexible, generalist approach to undergraduate education.

The first generalist program in medical communications at the undergraduate level was initiated at The Ohio State University in 1969. With its philosophical foundations in the behavioral and health sciences and the parent disciplines of communication and education, the medical communications program was developed in much the same way as baccalaureate degree programs in other allied health disciplines. The program was designed to prepare entry-level professionals whose knowledge of communication theory and biomedical science would be sufficiently broad to consider various types of communication-based problems in health areas and whose skills training would be sufficiently strong to provide an operational base from which to begin. With these objectives established, a problem-solving approach emerged as the foundation for the professional curriculum, which begins in the junior year. Before entering the professional curriculum, prospective medical communicators must meet basic university requirements in liberal arts and develop an interdisciplinary approach to communications theory and skills. The schedule in the preprofessional program provides maximum exposure to disciplines related to medical communications and includes courses in photography and cinematography, television and audiovisual production, communication theories and models, biology, psychology, and sociology.

Potential students are screened carefully by the faculty before admission, as student selection is an extremely critical determinant of program success. Students are selected on the basis of interest in the field and academic performance during the first 2 years, with emphasis placed on aptitude and interest in the behavioral and communications sciences.

Having been admitted to the program in their third year, students begin their orientation to health sciences communication. As allied health students, they interact with other health science students and professionals both in and out of class and begin to develop a professional identity. The professional curriculum includes courses in communication, education, human anatomy, medical science, management and statistics, writing and editing, followed by more specialized courses in advanced media production in biomedical communication, design and evaluation of instructional systems, and biomedical computer systems application. Students attend special seminars in the psychosocial aspects of disease and in organizational development. The curriculum relies heavily on the resources of the College of Medicine and the medical center. This provides the student with the opportunity to gain "real world'' experience while still in training in such areas as the Medical Audiovisual and Television Center, the Center for Continuing Medical Education, the Computer-Assisted Instruction Regional Education Network, the Nisonger Center for Mental Retardation, University Hospitals, and the Patient Education Network as well as other departments and divisions within the College of Medicine. Students have the opportunity for independent study in such areas as patient and health personnel interaction, medical language, mediated teaching and learning, and teleconsultation and diagnosis. They learn to select the media or means of communication most appropriate for their own designs. Working and studying in a medical environment provide the medical communications student with the opportunity to develop a strong professional identity and the confidence to relate to other health professionals as equals. These experiences are essential to the development of a stable biomedical communications curriculum at any level.

During the fourth year in the baccalaureate program, students are required to spend 15 or more hours weekly during each of two quarters in ''clinical'' or field experiences. The students are assigned to ''preceptors,'' or supervisors, who act as both teachers and models to the students. They may be assigned to such diverse areas as an inner-city health center, colleges of veterinary medicine or dentistry, community hospitals, or the drug crisis center. Students have done part of their internship in the information offices of the National Institutes of Health, research centers, and volunteer organizations such as the American Lung Association and the American Heart Association. In the clinics, students are required to focus their unique interdisciplinary background, media skills, and knowledge of the medical and behavioral sciences on problems and projects assigned by their preceptors. They are responsible for the total design, implementation, and evaluation of their projects subject to the same constraints of time, space, and money as any other staff professional. Students also meet in class to discuss their problems and progress. Experience has shown that preceptor and internship programs are very valuable elements in the training of medical communicators.

Graduate programs

Medical communications specialists may continue their formal education at the graduate level. Building on knowledge and skills acquired at the undergraduate level, medical communicators may move from the role of generalist to that of specialist through graduate study. Programs with highly structured curricula exist to produce biomedical computer and information specialists, instructional development specialists, educators, managers, and research and development specialists. Schools such as the University of Nebraska, The Ohio State University, and the University of Texas at Houston and Dallas have developed graduate programs with a variety of professional emphases in biomedical communications.

CAREER OPPORTUNITIES

The multidisciplinary nature of their profession requires medical communicators to be generalists. They must learn to work effectively with all types of health professionals and consumers of health care in a constantly changing environment with its incessant priorities. Thus medical communications graduates must be sensitive to change, work comfortably with it, and indeed, often serve as its agent. With respect to the celerity of change within the field as well as the environment in which it is developing, it is important that medical communications professionals avoid what Edgar Dale has referred to as "frozen perspectives," that is, inflexible definitions or attitudes in an emerging profession. They must be eclectics who are prepared to use many specialties to coordinate and improve communication and instruction in the health sciences. Their approach must be creative and dynamic, and they must be ready to change with the needs and priorities of the health care system. With their academic foundation firmly fixed in communication, education, and the health sciences, medical communicators should take an integrative, humanistic, and holistic approach to both clinical and educational problem solving. As process consultants, they must be sensitive to the human as well as the professional needs of their clients as they analyze, evaluate, organize, coordinate, and activate any new system or project. (See Fig. 10-2.)

Graduates of baccalaureate programs may serve as communications consultants or media specialists in large teaching hospitals or smaller community hospitals. They may coordinate educational media programs, participate in the design and implementation of communications research in the medical environment, or assist health agencies, professional organizations, and educators to communicate with either lay or professional audiences. They may assist in the planning and development of instructional aids or work in publishing or public relations. Whatever their role in the health care system, medical communicators continually evaluate all related communication efforts in order to im-

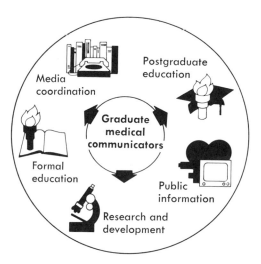

Fig. 10-2. Medical communications graduates work in a variety of areas in the health care environment.

prove their effectiveness. They are allied health professionals capable of conceptualizing and designing action-oriented programs to coordinate health needs, communication principles, media, and people.

Graduates of baccalaureate programs have accepted positions in health care centers such as the Cleveland Clinic, government settings such as the National Institutes of Health or the South Carolina Medical Television Network, teaching institutions such as the Columbia University School of Nursing, the University of Arizona Colleges of Medicine and Nursing, and the Indiana University College of Medicine, pharmaceutical firms, cancer research programs, computer centers, volunteer health organizations, and mental retardation centers. They have such titles as instructional resource specialist, instructional programmer, public relations specialist, coordinator of media services, hospital personnel director, director of training, and research assistant. Their unique interdisciplinary background prepares medical communicators for a wide variety of new and existing career opportunities in the health care system.

SUPPORTING PROFESSIONALS

The broad area of medical communications draws on the expertise of many contributing professionals and technical personnel to meet its goals and objectives. The graduate medical communicator relies on such specialists as medical photographers, medical librarians, educational developers and researchers, computer programmers, electronics engineers and technicians, and medical illustrators, the visual communicators of the health professions. These specialists must also be both versatile and exacting in their contributions to the field of medical communications.

The graduate medical communicator recognizes the importance of the many specialized contributors who help to meet the demand for improved communication services in the health field. The needs are too far-reaching and the goals are too important to work in isolation.

SUMMARY

Medical communications is concerned generally with facilitating the transfer of information for the improvement of health care, both directly or indirectly. Medical communicators, still fresh on the professional scene, use their unique interdisciplinary training in communications theory and media and their knowledge of the medical, social, and behavioral sciences to disseminate information for the improvement of patient care. They select and evaluate techniques to enhance biomedical education and to facilitate communication patterns in all areas of an increasingly complex health care system.

References

Burke, J. E.: Medical communications as a health science discipline. Paper presented at the sixteenth annual meeting of the Health Science Communications Association, Denver, Colo., 1974.

Dale, E.: Personal communication, 1973.

Walker, H. L.: Communication and the American health care problem, Commun. **23:**349, 1973.

Professional organizations where further information can be obtained

Health Education Media Association
P.O. Box 5744
Bethesda, Md. 20014

Health Sciences Communications Association
P.O.Box 79
Millbrae, Calif. 94030

11
MEDICAL ILLUSTRATION

Mitzi Prosser and James R. Kreutzfeld

Medical illustrators are health professionals who design, illustrate and graphically represent biomedical facts, research data, surgical procedures, pathological studies, and anatomical plates. As an important member of the health care team, the illustrator works with physicians, research scientists, allied health professionals, and educators to visually record the constantly changing knowledge and skills of the ever-expanding medical profession.

HISTORY OF MEDICAL ILLUSTRATION

Medical illustration is as old as civilization, as indicated by the primitive anatomical drawings done on the walls of cave dwellings during the Stone Age. Leonardo da Vinci (1442-1519) made a lasting contribution to the science of anatomy. He combined curiosity, acute observation, and artistic talent to produce remarkable sketches that can still be used as teaching aids today.

During the 1500s several factors influenced the growth of medical illustration. Woodblock carving was developed early in this period to help meet the demand for multiple copies of graphic art as well as written material. This led to the production of books, the first available mass-produced materials. Raffaello Santi's accurate depiction of the human body leads us to believe that his sketches were based on the direct observation, dissection, and investigation of cadavers. Jan Stephan Kalkar illustrated the anatomical works of Andreas Vesalius. Together they used woodcuts to produce the anatomical atlases *De Humani Corporis Fabrica*. From the expanded use of woodcuts to the development of copper engraving, the variety of visual aids used in educating people was increasing.

The introduction of the printing press, the invention of the process of lithography, and advances in photographic technique opened the way to more efficient methods of producing finished material. These processes were less expensive and required less time. The artists of the late eighteenth century were obviously influential in developing new and better methods for the reproduction of printed and graphic materials.

The early twentieth century saw the establishment of teaching centers where students could acquire the knowledge and skills necessary for a career in medical illustration. A leader in this area was Max Brödel (1870-1946), the man who has had perhaps the greatest influence in the field of medical illustration. Brödel established the first school of medical illustration at The Johns Hopkins University in 1910. He still remains the preeminent figure in medical illustration and has come to be known as the father of medical art.

EDUCATIONAL REQUIREMENTS

Students interested in the profession may choose one of seven recognized schools of medical illustration. There are variations in entrance requirements as well as in the professional curricula. Some schools offer baccalaureate programs, whereas others offer programs leading to a

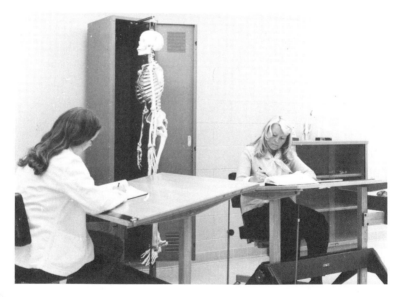

Fig. 11-1. Students perfect their drawing ability while learning various illustration techniques.

graduate degree. For specific information concerning these programs, write to the individual schools or the Association of Medical Illustrators. Regardless of entrance requirements, students learn to adapt their artistic skills to the requirements of medical illustration and visual communication, acquiring at the same time a thorough background in the biological sciences.

Students in the professional programs develop skills in line, continuous tone, and color drawing techniques. Studies in biomedical photography, design, advertising, education, and management are an important part of the curriculum, as is training in the preparation of charts, graphs, and diagrams. Students are also required to take anatomy courses covering general and gross human anatomy, embryology, and histology. The acquired knowledge and developed skills are combined and integrated in the production of videotapes, films, and slide shows and in the preparation of exhibits, three-dimensional models, and prosthetics. (See Fig. 11-1.)

PROFESSIONAL MEDICAL ILLUSTRATION

Medical illustrators may receive assignments from a physician, researcher, or educator. For example, a surgeon may need a series of sketches of a particular operation. He calls on the medical illustrator, and together they review the operation before the scheduled surgery. During the operative procedure the medical illustrator may make sketches, take photographs, or both. (See Fig. 11-2.) Medical illustrators use these sketches or photographs and collaborate further with the surgeon in preparing the final renderings. Educational programs in medical illustration prepare students to execute finished illustrations of pertinent surgical, anatomical, and pathological aspects for use in medical textbooks, journals, and other media. These teaching aids are used not only for the education of medical students, interns, residents, attending staff, and allied health professionals but also for practitioners on a national and international level. They may also be used directly to educate patients regarding their own health care needs.

CAREER OPPORTUNITIES

Medical illustrators work in universities, medical or research hospitals and centers, scientific institutions, museums, pharmaceutical houses, publishing firms, and commercial art studios, or they may work on a free-lance basis for any of these agencies or for private physicians.

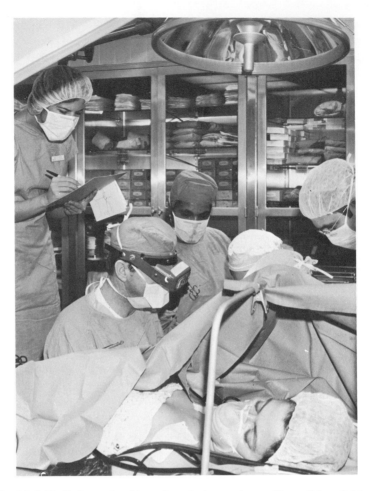

Fig. 11-2. Preliminary sketching of surgical procedures will result in a finished illustration to be included in a forthcoming textbook.

The beginning salaries in the field range from $12,000 to $14,000 annually, depending on the abilities and responsibilities of the illustrator and on the needs of the employer.

If medical illustrators wish to pursue their education at the graduate level, there are programs available that offer the opportunity to structure an interdisciplinary approach to an illustrator's specific problems and needs. Such a program may broaden concepts and strengthen skills in teaching, administration, communication, and research.

SUMMARY

Professional medical illustrators prepare visual materials for publications, exhibits, and teaching aids. The work requires artistic talent and scientific knowledge combined with accuracy, attention to minute detail, and technical versatility in each of the communications media. Medical illustrators use a wide variety of visual media such as drawing, painting, sculpture, and photography; the illustrations may be either realistic, diagrammatic, or representational. Some illustrators concentrate on work within one of the medical specialities. A medical illustrator is a highly trained artist who can conceive, design, illustrate, and produce visual material to inform and to educate members of the health professions as well as the entire community.

References

Bethke, E. G.: Basic drawing for biology students, Springfield, Ill., 1969, Charles C Thomas, Publisher.

Clarke, C. D.: Illustration—its technique and application to the sciences, Baltimore, 1939, John D. Lucas Co., Publishers

Vesalius, A., and Kalkar, J. S. De humani corporis fabrica, Cleveland, 1950, Cleveland World Publications.

Suggested readings

McLarty, M. C.: Illustrating medicine and surgery, Baltimore, 1960, The Williams & Wilkins Co.

Price, F.: Medical illustration (do-it-yourself basis), Proc. R. Soc. Med. **62:**815, 1969.

Waters, L. B.: The mechanics of medical and dental visualization, Springfield, Ill., 1963, Charles C Thomas, Publisher.

Zollinger, R. M., and Howe, C. T.: The illustration of medical lectures, vol. 14 (No. 3), London, 1964, British Medical Association.

Professional organization where further information can be obtained

Association of Medical Illustrators
6022 W. Toby St.
Chicago, Ill. 60648

12

MEDICAL RECORD ADMINISTRATION

Melanie Moersch Pariser

The medical record administration profession is concerned with the design, implementation, and management of health information systems. The profession combines knowledge of health care, information management, and administration to meet the demands of today's health care industry. Health information is used for research, education, medicolegal matters, accreditation and licensing requirements, and most important, the provision of health care. Demands for health information require that the information be readily accessible, manipulable, and credible. The allied health professional responsible for assuring that the demands and requirements for health information are met is the medical record administrator.

HISTORICAL PERSPECTIVE

Medical records are not a new concept. Information of a medical nature was recorded as far back as 25,000 BC. Early cave drawings and relics relate the fact that ancient men of medicine understood the importance of keeping information on medical achievements. The recording of health information in history served physicians of old as the medical record serves the physician of today. As medicine advanced thoughout the ages, so did the need for better documentation and storage of health information. It became increasingly important for health information to be written in a manner that would be usable for patient care and education. Early hospitals initially recorded patients' health information in log books; however, hospitals gradually began to record all patient information in one place, a patient's medical record.

Techniques for recording, storing, and retrieving medical records were developed early in the twentieth century. Medical schools and teaching hospitals recognized the need for better methods of recording health information. Thus, by the turn of the century, physicians were pressing for standardization and quality in medical record keeping. The endeavors of these health professionals were instrumental in the development of the medical record profession.

Individuals responsible for the custodial care of medical records were brought together in 1928 and formed the American Medical Record Association. The objective of the new association was to strive for higher standards of patient care through better quality medical records. The medical record profession continues to strive for this objective while changing to meet the rapidly increasing demands of health care technology.

HEALTH INFORMATION SYSTEM AND
THE MEDICAL RECORD

The term "health information system" denotes a network of interacting, interrelating communications channels found in any health care institution or organization that deals with the generation, storage, and retrieval of health information. The end product of information flow in some institutions such as hospitals is the medical record. The medical record tells the who, what, where, when, and how of an individual's experience in a given health care facility or health care delivery system. Any individual who presents himself either for an illness or for preventive health care, such as an annual physical examination, will have a medical record generated for him. The contents of the medical record may include a history, results of a physical examination, observations, findings, orders, diagnostic tests, and treatment plans.

The type of information found within a medical record will vary according to the type of health care facility involved. These facilities may include general and psychiatric hospitals; long-term care facilities (nursing homes); neighborhood health, mental health, ambulatory care, and rehabilitation centers; health maintenance organizations; and doctors' offices. The term "medical record" may also vary according to the facility. Records are sometimes called health, clinic, outpatient, psychiatric, nursing home, and long-term care records.

Why should health care facilities generate and store medical records? Huffman summarizes the purposes of medical records as follows:
1. Provides a means of communication between the physicians and other professionals contributing to the patient's care.
2. Serves as a basis for planning individual patient care.

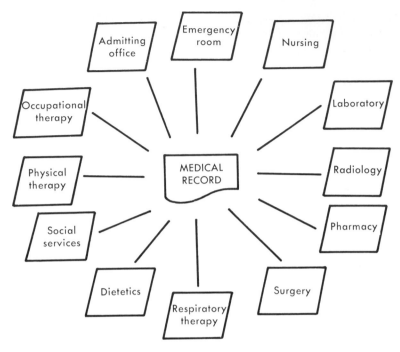

Fig. 12-1. The medical record is made up of information from several health care services.

3. Furnishes documentary evidence of the course of the patient's illness and treatment during each term of care.
4. Serves as a basis for analysis, study, and evaluation of the quality of care rendered to the patient.
5. Assists in protecting the legal interests of the patient, facility, and health care professional.
6. Provides clinical data for use in research and education.

The medical record is a communication link between all services within a health care facility. (See Fig. 12-1.) Health professionals use the medical record to record observations, findings, and treatments relative to an individual's illness. The medical record provides an up-to-date picture of what has happened to the individual since the last visit made by the health professional. As an additional means of communication, the medical record represents evidence of the quality of medical care received by an individual. Reimbursement of health care costs through government programs such as Medicare and Medicaid requires that health care facilities evaluate and review the type of health care services offered and medical care given to individuals treated within a facility. The medical record has become the best evaluation instrument for quality review of medical care. The medical record also serves as evidence in cases of litigation. A properly documented medical record will help protect the legal interest of the individual, health care facility, and the health professional.

Medical records are a major source of information for medical researchers and educators. Prospective, concurrent, and retrospective studies are conducted utilizing information gleaned from medical records. Results of such studies provide information for the development of new technologies in the prevention and treatment of diseases. Public health departments rely on the medical record to find clues in their research for incidence or trends in community diseases or health needs.

In order to ensure that the medical record is available and fulfills the purposes as stated by Huffman, an arrangement for generating, storing, retrieving and using medical records must be established. This arrangement represents a health information system within a given health care facility. However, health information systems also exist in numerous other types of organizations.

An example of a nonmedical organization with a health information system is an insurance company offering health insurance policies. Although the insurance company may not generate medical records as found in facilities like hospitals, the insurance company does receive health information about individuals it insures. This information may be in the form of an insurance physical or medical checkoff list. As an individual applies for health insurance, the information he supplies the insurance company is stored in a record. As the individual goes through life and uses his health insurance for whatever reason, the insurance company adds to the individual's record. Thus, the insurance company has established a health information system. The information gathered by the insurance company may be used to reimburse providers of health care, raise premiums, deny benefits, and so forth.

Computer technology has played a significant role in the establishment of health information systems. Health information systems found within health care facilities may be totally or partially computerized. Portions of the medical record may have been generated from information fed into computers. In organizations like the previously mentioned insurance company, the entire health information system is usually computerized. Computer technology plays an important role in the management of medical records and health information systems. The health care industry has generally been slow to use computers; however, health care is quickly moving toward the use of more sophisticated means of storing and retrieving information as commerce has done for years.

RESPONSIBILITIES OF THE MEDICAL RECORD ADMINISTRATOR

The medical record administrator is responsible for the design, implementation, and management of health information systems as found in direct care institutions, health care agencies and groups, and commerce. In direct care institutions, such as hospitals, the medical record administrator is the manager of the medical record department. As manager of the department, the medical record administrator coordinates all departmental functions with the administrative, medical, ethical, and legal requirements of the facility. Managerial responsibilities include the supervision of departmental personnel and control of all budgetary, equipment, and supply needs.

The medical record administrator oversees the entire health information system. The administrator is aware of all information needs of health professionals and service departments within the facility. The administrator assists health professionals in evaluating medical care and in reviewing professional services within the facility by developing criteria and methods for evaluating medical records. Health professionals rely on the medical record administrator for interpreting and explaining facility requirements regarding the recording of health information in the medical record as well as the reporting requirements for such government programs as Medicare and Medicaid. (See Fig. 12-2.) The medical record administrator is also responsible for developing and controlling the privacy and confidentiality of health information. This responsibility entails the development of procedures and policies on the release of information regarding individuals treated within the facility. In addition, these policies and procedures include the processing of the medical record for litigation purposes.

Overall, the medical record administrator may play several roles in fulfilling job responsibilities. These roles include manager, consultant, researcher, and educator.

Health care agencies and groups along with commerce utilize the expertise of the medical record administrator in a variety of ways. These

Fig. 12-2. A major responsibility of the medical record administrator is to explain reporting requirements to health professionals.

types of organizations vary in their information needs; thus, the responsibilities of the medical record administrator vary. In addition to managerial duties, the medical record administrator may be engaged in research or consultative services. However, these organizations, as well as the direct care institutions, rely heavily on the mangerial skills of the medical record administrator. These skills include the ability to make decisions and solve problems in order to facilitate the most efficient means of generating, storing, retrieving, and utilizing health information.

For example, a medical record administrator may investigate the current system of a manual patient index and decide that the manual index should be changed to a computerized system in order to better accommodate the demands on the system. Management skills would be used in assessing the old systems as well as in planning and implementing the new. The new system may require that the administrator (1) design the format of information that will go on the computer, (2) assist the computer specialists in developing procedures for putting the information in the computer, (3) train personnel in the new procedures, and (4) develop a backup system for times when the computer is down. In the process of change, the medical record administrator acts as liaison

Fig. 12-3. The physician and medical record administrator refer to the computer for needed health information.

between the people involved, such as data processing personnel and the medical staff.

As an educator, the medical record administrator may be engaged in training and development programs for facility personnel or instructing 2- or 4-year college students in medical record technology or administration. In the college-level program, responsibilities of the medical record administrator may include program directorship, teaching, research, and publication.

The trend in medical record administration is toward increased emphasis on information systems and how these systems are managed. (See Fig. 12-3.) Computer technology is part of this trend, as demonstrated by such components as computerized patient and disease indexes. As manager or director of a health information system the medical record administrator must keep abreast of new technologies. The administrator must be willing to change and expand present knowledge and skills to accommodate new discoveries of the future.

PROGRAMS IN MEDICAL RECORD ADMINISTRATION

An individual wishing to pursue a career in medical record administration must successfully complete a baccalaureate degree or postbaccalaureate degree certificate program in medical record administration. The medical record administration program must be a program that has been accredited by the Committee on Allied Health Education and Accreditation of the American Medical Association in collaboration with the American Medical Record Association. Programs of this nature may be found in colleges and universities throughout the United States. However, not all colleges or universities have such a program. Successful completion of an accredited program qualifies an individual to sit for the American Medical Record Association's national certification examination for medical record administrators. If the individual successfully completes the examination, he assumes the title of registered record administrator (RRA).

The educational requirements of a medical record administrator may consist of proprofessional and professional course work. Preprofessional course work consists of basic educational requirements in the humanities and the behavioral, biological, and physical sciences. Science requirements may entail study in general biology, chemistry, microbiology, a laboratory course in anatomy and physiology, and once within the professional curriculum, the study of diseases in man or medical science. Professional course work may vary from program to program; however, curricula usually include the following areas of study:

Medical record science
Record content and analysis
Standards for documentation
Classification, indexing, and registry systems
Medical care evaluation techniques and procedures

Management
Quality assurance techniques
Utilization and control of financial resources and budgets
Selection, utilization, and control of space, supplies, and equipment
Personnel administration
Wage and salary administration
Labor relations/unions
Professional communication skills

Information systems
Systems design and analysis
Information storage and retrieval techniques
Computer science: programming, hardware
Computer application in medical care

Legal aspects
Federal, state, and local laws and regulations
Moral and ethical control of health information
Privacy and confidentiality issues and procedures
Security of computerized health information

Health care delivery
Accreditation and licensure standards for health care facilities
Philosophy and objectives for governmental and community health care
    programs
Organizational patterns of a health care institution and agencies
Principles and practices of public health, local, state, and federal
    agencies
Current trends in health care delivery
Role and interrelationships of health care practitioners
Changing role of the health care provider

Statistics
Research methodology
Statistical techniques

Clinical experience

QUALITIES OF THE MEDICAL RECORD ADMINISTRATOR

As health professionals, medical record administrators are responsible for (1) conducting themselves in an ethical manner at all times; (2) changing with the profession as new technologies and opportunities face them; (3) utilizing appropriate written, verbal, and nonverbal communication skills; and (4) displaying insight, understanding and feeling toward themselves, others, the health care system, and their profession. These responsibilities require that such individuals possess certain qualities in order to effectively carry out the stated responsibilities. They must be honest, reliable, flexible, responsible, and open. In addition, the qualities of motivation, organization, assertiveness, confidence, and sensitivity are essential. Last, as managers, medical record administrators must be creative and innovative in their approach to the rapidly changing technologies of the medical record profession.

SUPPORT PERSONNEL

The American Medical Record Association recognizes a second level of professional: the medical record technician. The medical record technician is trained in the technical skills of medical record technology. These skills encompass coding and indexing health information, analyzing medical records for completeness, compiling health and administrative statistics, handling the release of medical record information, abstracting information for storage and retrieval purposes, and maintaining files, indexes, and registry systems. Employment opportunities for the technician are as varied as those for the medical record administrator. The technician may find employment in direct care institutions, health care agencies and groups, and commerce. The job responsibilities of the technician vary according to the employment setting. The technician may be classified as a staff employee, supervisor, or assistant to the medical record administrator. In smaller hospitals and some long-term care facilities, the technician may be the director of the medical record department.

The technician's education consists of attending an approved 2-year community or technical college program in medical record technology or enrolling in the American Medical Record Association's independent study program in medical record technology. Enrollment in the independent study program requires that an individual be employed in a health care facility under the guidance of a medical record administrator for a minimum of 20 hours per week. After April 1980, the American Medical Record Association will require an individual to obtain a minimum of 30 semester hours of academic credit, in addition to successfully completing the independent study program. Successful completion of the 2-year community or technical college medical record technology program or the independent study program entitles an individual to sit for the national certification examination for medical record technicians. Upon passing this examination, an individual is credentialed as an accredited record technician (ART). Once an individual receives credentialing as an ART, he or she may wish to progress to the level of RRA. To do so, the ART should contact the American Medical Record Association for information and guidelines on progression.

JOB OPPORTUNITIES

Job opportunities for the medical record administrator exist in direct care institutions, health care agencies and groups, commerce, government, and education. In direct care institutions, the medical record administrator may find employment in hospitals, neighborhood health centers, mental health centers, long-term care facilities, and ambulatory care services. Recent health care legislation has opened more job opportunities to the medical record administrator in the areas of quality assurance and medical care evaluation departments. The medical record administrator may be employed as the manager of a quality assurance department, as a utilization review coordinator, or as a medical audit specialist. Health care agencies and groups such as professional health care organizations, planning agencies, and world health organizations employ the medical record administrator in various capacities. Employment opportunities are available on the local, state, and federal government level. The medical record administrator may be employed as a consultant or director of a health information system in state health departments, Veterans' Administration hospitals, or the United States Public Health Service.

Medical record administrators interested in education may teach at the 2- or 4-year college level. Medical record technology and administration programs are in great need of qualified medical record administrators who will assume program directorship and faculty appointments. Commerce offers jobs to the medical record administrator in insurance, computer, and dictating equipment, data abstracting, and management consulting firms. Industry has begun to hire the medical record administrator to manage its employee health information systems. A medical record administrator may choose to be self-employed and offer consulting services to long-term care facilities, small hospitals, physicians' offices, and other health care facilities or organizations that do not require the services of a full-time medical record administrator. Overall, the skills of a medical record administrator may be utilized by an organization or facility handling health information.

Salaries for the medical record administrator tend to vary according to the size, type, and location of the employment setting. Salaries are usually higher in metropolitan areas. However, many rural areas offer comparable compensation. Average annual salaries range from $13,000 to $20,000, and with experience salaries may exceed $30,000 per year. The employment outlook for the medical record administrator is excellent. As more emphasis is placed on health information and quality of health care, more employment opportunities are available.

SUMMARY

Medical record administration is a challenging profession in which the medical record administrator plays an important role as a member of the health care team. The need for properly documented health information has been demonstrated throughout the history of medicine. Recording of health information has progressed from etchings on cave walls to written medical records. These records tell a story of the patient's problem, care, and treatment and at times serve to ensure that the patient receives quality health care. The responsibility of the medical record administrator is to design, implement, and manage a health information system. This responsibility may include the organization and administration of a medical record department. Increasing demands to ensure quality of patient care are placing more emphasis on the uses of medical records and the role of the medical record administrator. Medical record administration offers an individual a part in health care delivery and in a profession growing daily in terms of new technologies and excellent employment opportunities.

References

Committee on Allied Health Education and Accreditation in collaboration with the American Medical Record Association: Essentials of an accredited educational program for medical record administrators, Chicago, 1974, American Medical Record Association.

History of medical record science; from hieroglyphics to . . . electronic data processing, Med. Rec. News **40**:20, 1969.

Huffman, E. K.: Medical record management, ed. 6, Chicago, 1974, Physicians' Record Co.

Mosier, A.: Medical record technology, Indianapolis, 1975, The Bobbs-Merrill Co., Inc.

Task force on the future role of the medical record administrator; final report, April 9, 1974, Med. Rec. News **45**:66, 1974.

U. S. Department of Labor, Bureau of Labor Statistics: Employment outlook for medical record administrators, medical record technicians, and clerks, Washington, D.C., 1974, U.S. Government Printing Office.

Professional organization where further information can be obtained

American Medical Record Association
Suite 1850, John Hancock Center
875 N. Michigan Ave.
Chicago, Ill. 60611

13

MEDICAL TECHNOLOGY

Marjorie L. Brunner

Medical technology is one of the rapidly growing professions associated with modern advances in medical science. Medical technologists work in clinical pathology laboratories performing the scientific tests that track down the cause and cure of disease. Some diseases, diabetes and leukemia, for example, can be positively identified by laboratory methods alone. The presence of other suspected diseases can be confirmed by laboratory examination.

Medical technologists are prepared to function not only as laboratory workers but also as supervisors, instructors of supportive laboratory personnel, and researchers. They are educated and technically trained to perform the various chemical, microscopic, bacteriological, and other medical laboratory procedures used in the diagnosis, study, and treatment of disease. Medical technologists work under the supervision of a pathologist, a physician who specializes in laboratory medicine.

HOW DID MEDICAL TECHNOLOGY DEVELOP?

In the early days of clinical laboratory science, pathologists, who were just beginning to receive recognition as necessary and important medical specialists in their own right, performed their own laboratory tests. As the field of laboratory medicine developed and broadened, pathologists found it necessary to train assistants to help perform the simpler tests. The profession of medical technology thus came into being in the early part of this century.

In those years, high school graduates interested in medical technology commonly became apprentices in medical laboratories. Then a few commercial schools were established, but the training they offered was often inadequate, and their fees were usually exorbitant. Realizing that laboratory medicine was developing rapidly and that standards had to be established for the training of laboratory assistants, the American Soci-

98

ety of Clinical Pathologists (ASCP) established the Board of Registry of Medical Technologists (ASCP) in 1928 and elected six pathologists to serve on the board. The registry administered the national certification examination to prospective medical technologists after they completed all educational requirements. The first certificates were issued in 1930.

The American Society for Medical Technology (ASMT) was organized in 1933. Membership was restricted to medical technologists certified by the Board of Registry. The present ASMT membership totals approximately 31,000. Today the Board of Registry of Medical Technologists (ASCP) consists of physicians, laboratory personnel, and consumers.

A second registry became available to medical techologists in 1978. It is administered by an autonomous agency called the National Certification Agency for Clincal Laboratory Personnel (NCA). Certification is for 4 years, after which one must show evidence of continued competency. The first examinations were given by this agency in July 1978. Individuals successfully completing the examination are given the title clinical laboratory scientist.

In 1949 the ASCP formed a standing committee, the Board of Schools, to handle the accreditation of medical laboratory programs. The Board of Schools functioned until October 1973, when the National Accrediting Agency for Clinical Laboratory Sciences (NAACLS) was created and co-sponsored by ASMT and ASCP. It assumed all the accreditation and transcript evaluation functions fomerly held by the Board of Schools. NAACLS is composed of three medical technology educators active in ASMT, three clinical pathologist educators who are fellows of ASCP, two supportive-level practitioners, and six individuals elected by the above. By gradually elevating educational standards and improving the quality of technical training, both the Board of Registry and NAACLS have done much to raise the status of medical laboratory workers to a professional level.

WHERE DO MEDICAL TECHNOLOGISTS WORK? WHAT ARE THEIR CONTRIBUTIONS TO HEALTH CARE?

Clinical pathology laboratories, where most medical technologists are employed, include a variety of specialized areas. In microbiology the greatest amount of work involves bacteria. The technologists grow and identify bacteria present in biological specimens obtained from patients and do tests to help determine which antibiotics will be most effective in subduing the organism causing the infection. (See Fig. 13-1.)

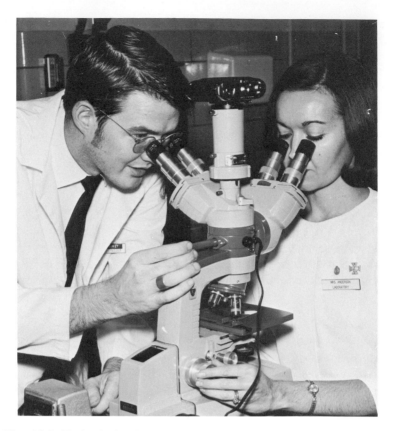

Fig. 13-1. Technologists in a microbiology laboratory examine a patient's specimen for the presence of bacteria.

Problems in parasitology center on the search for and identification of parasites—the small animals living inside the body. These may be tapeworms or pinworms, or they may be tiny one-celled animals, such as the parasite that causes malaria.

A knowledge of chemistry is used in many ways in medical laboratories. Technologists determine the presence and quantity of chemical substances in blood and other body fluids obtained from patients. Comparisons of the chemical constituents of patient specimens with normal values established in specimens from healthy individuals provide useful guides for the physician in the diagnosis and control of disease.

Toxicology is a special area of clinical chemistry in which medical technologists determine the presence and quantity of drugs in blood and urine samples. This is useful in monitoring drug therapy and in determining the cause and extent of drug overdoses.

In immunology the medical technologist uses standardized techniques to demonstrate the presence and amount of antibodies or antibodylike substances in body fluids such as serum, plasma, spinal fluid, and urine. In many instances the production of these substances by the body has been stimulated by an infection or by immunization. The Widal test, for example, is used to demonstrate the presence of serum antibodies to *Salmonella typhosa,* which is the causative agent of typhoid fever.

Immunohematology is a special area within immunology. Here, the medical technologist's knowledge and skill in matching blood samples are crucial. In addition to the familiar testing for blood groups and Rh factors, verifying that the patient's sample is compatible with the donor's blood can require many highly sensitive and specific determinations.

Analyses of urine samples are beneficial in diagnosing or controlling illnesses caused by malfunction of the kidneys. Examination of urine specimens gives clues to such diseases as nephritis and diabetes. A potential new application for these tests is emerging through research into the biochemical conditions that are related to mental disorders.

In hematology, tests are conducted to detect conditions that primarily affect the blood, such as anemia (a deficiency of red blood cells, commonly known as tired blood), hemophilia (a disease in which the blood clotting mechanism is defective), and leukemia (a type of cancer involving an abnormal increase in the number of white blood cells). (See Fig. 13-2.)

Work in a medical laboratory requires the use of a wide array of intricate precision equipment—microscopes, automatic analyzers that permit an increased number of patient fluid samples to be chemically analyzed with greater speed and accuracy, and electronic counters used for the enumeration of red and white blood cells. Specialized procedures such as electrophoresis and gas chromatography are used to isolate compounds present in body fluids so they may be identified and quantitated. New instruments and methods of analysis are constantly being developed, so that medical technologists are involved in an atmosphere of continuous learning, evaluation, and progress.

The types of positions available to the medical technologist are as varied as the many tests they perform. Laboratory work is being done in

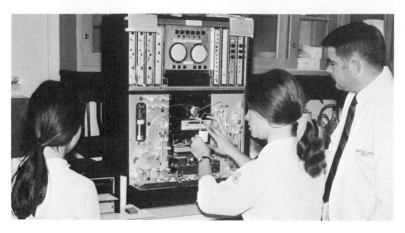

Fig. 13-2. Precision instruments are used to increase the accuracy and speed of blood counts performed in the hematology laboratory.

hospitals, clinics, doctors' offices, public health departments, and private research institutes as well as in industry. Those who prefer to watch the results of their work as it affects the health of specific individuals would probably prefer a position in a small hospital, clinic, or physician's office, where they have an opportunity to get acquainted with the people they help. Other technologists may choose to work in research or industry, where their contributions may one day have a far-reaching effect on the health of many people.

Research positions that involve primarily routine laboratory techniques are often filled by supporting laboratory personnel such as medical laboratory technicians (associate degree) and medical laboratory technicians (certificate). However, research positions involving the development of new laboratory methods, the adaptation of existing methods to new equipment, and the evaluation of technical problems are available to experienced technologists in many clinical laboratories. Occasionally experienced technologists or those with advanced education work in basic research, an area that requires a good deal of initiative and independent thinking. They work closely with consultant pathologists or specialists in a related scientific field.

The following case study illustrates the contribution a medical technologist might make to the study, diagnosis, and treatment of a patient.

A 34-year-old expectant mother was seen by an obstetrician for prenatal care. Her medical history revealed that this was her fourth pregnancy. Her blood type was recorded as A, Rh negative, and her husband's blood type was O, Rh positive. Her first pregnancy had occurred when she was 23 years of age, and her baby was delivered after a full term of 40 weeks' gestation. The baby's blood type was O, Rh positive, and he was unaffected by the incompatibility of his parents' Rh factors. During the patient's second pregnancy, when she was 26 years of age, Rh antibodies present in her blood passed through the placenta into the baby's circulatory system, where they reacted with and destroyed some of the baby's red blood cells. The infant was delivered after 40 week's gestation and was given an exchange blood transfusion to replace his damaged red blood cells. He responded well to this treatment. The patient's third pregnancy occurred at the age of 29 years. An Rh incompatibility was again apparent; however, this time the baby died in utero from anemia caused by the mother's Rh antibodies.

With this background information the obstetrician began to study his patient's condition. He requested that a medical technologist obtain blood samples from the patient and her husband to confirm their blood types. The medical technologist in the blood bank determined the patient's type as A, Rh negative, and the husband's type as O, Rh positive. The technologist also detected the presence of antibodies against the Rh factor in the patient's blood and determined further that the antibody level was significant.

At 24 weeks' gestation the obstetrician collected a specimen of the amniotic fluid in which the baby was floating. This specimen was sent to the clinical laboratory, where another medical technologist performed a test that indicated the amount of red blood cell destruction present in the baby. A second test was done to determine the maturity of the infant's lungs. This aided the obstetrician in deciding when the baby would be old enough to breathe alone and therefore could be delivered safely. The tests on the amniotic fluid were repeated at 26 weeks of gestation and again at 27 weeks because it seemed that the baby's condition was deteriorating. During the twenty-eighth week of gestation the obstetrician and pathologist decided that laboratory results of the amniotic fluid tests indicated the need for an intrauterine transfusion, which would supply the red blood cells needed to sustain life until it was safe for the baby to be delivered. Compatible blood was found and cross-matched by the medical technologist. The baby received a total of three transfusions in utero at 28, 30, and 32 weeks' gestation. Amniotic fluid was collected just before each transfusion. Part of this fluid was sent to the clinical bacteriology laboratory, where the medical technologist inoculated it onto media that would enhance the growth of any microorganisms present. Fortunately there were no indications of intrauterine infection.

At 36 weeks' gestation, labor was induced, and when the baby was delivered, blood samples were immediately collected from his umbilical cord and sent to the clinical laboratory. The medical technologist in the hematology laboratory performed blood cell counts and hemoglobin measurements to determine the degree of anemia present, and the medical technologist in the clinical chemistry laboratory made repeated measurements of the amount of bilirubin present in the blood. This is a compound produced by red blood cell destruction, and it can cause brain damage in the newborn infant if it is present in the blood in large quantities. Results of these tests showed dangerously high levels of bilirubin, and exchange transfusions were needed to correct this problem. The baby responded well to this treatment and was released in good condition 2 weeks later.

WHAT ARE THE EDUCATIONAL REQUIREMENTS?

Educational requirements for medical technology include a minimum of 3 years of college plus 12 months of clinical training in one of the 667 hospital laboratory schools of medical technology accredited by the Council of Medical Education of the AMA. Since January 1, 1962, the pretechnical educational requirements for admission to an approved school of medical technology have been 3 years (90 semester hours or 135 quarter hours) of course work in any accredited college or university. The student's program must include the following credits.

1. A minimum of 16 semester hours (24 quarter hours) of chemistry are required. Organic chemistry or biological chemistry must be included. Quantitative analysis and physical chemistry are recommended.
2. A minimum of 16 semester hours (24 quarter hours) of biological science are required. Microbiology and immunology must be included. Genetics, physiology, and anatomy are recommended.
3. A minimum of one semester or quarter of college-level mathematics is required. Courses in statistics and physics are strongly recommended.

The college or university should accept this course work toward the first 3 years of a baccalaureate program in medical technology. Some of the approved schools of medical technology have their own specific course requirements in addition to those mentioned.

After earning the necessary college credits, students must satisfactorily complete a course of instruction in all phases of medical technology at an approved school. Major topics of instruction include hematology, urinalysis, clinical microbiology, immunology, immunohematology, and clinical chemistry. After completing these professional education requirements, students must be eligible for a baccalaureate degree.

In order to become registered medical technologists MT(ASCP)—students must pass the examination administered by the Board of Registry of Medical Technologists (ASCP).

There are also advanced educational programs for medical technologists who wish to obtain categorical certification in one particular field. For example, the certification program of the American Association of Blood Banks is designed to train specialists in blood banking. This program is offered only by institutions that have been approved by the association and consists of 1 year of training. This program includes both didactic study and practical experience and is designed to provide a comprehensive education in all aspects of the modern-day blood bank. After completing the course, all candidates for certification must take the examination that is given once each year by the Board of Registry of Medical Technologists (ASCP) in cooperation with the Committee on Education of the American Association of Blood Banks. The examination consists of written and practical portions, and both must be passed in the same year. The technologist then becomes a certified blood bank specialist—MT(ASCP)BB. There are also certification programs in chemistry, microbiology, and hematology. Since these specialists are expected to have a wide range of competence and a thorough understanding of their particular fields, they often become supervisors or work in advanced research projects or special reference laboratories.

Students planning a career in medical technology should consider the possibility of pursuing a graduate degree. Graduate education is assuming increasing importance as necessary preparation for the more interesting job opportunities. Specialist certification in hematology, microbiology, or chemistry is available by examination for those with a master's or doctoral degree in the specialty and/or the required years of experience. Information concerning graduate programs in medical technology is available through the NAACLS.

WHAT PARTICULAR QUALITIES ARE NEEDED?

A list of qualifications for a career in medical technology might include an interest in and aptitude for science, an active curiosity, the ability to work under pressure, manual dexterity, and a general desire to help mankind. Self-discipline, a spirit of cooperation, and thorough moral and intellectual integrity are essential in the practice of this profession. The laboratory findings obtained by medical technologists are used in making vital decisions concerning human lives. Therefore procedures must be performed with accuracy and the results evaluated with the utmost integrity.

WHO ARE THE SUPPORTING PROFESSIONALS IN MEDICAL LABORATORIES?

There are many workers in medical laboratories whose educational backgrounds are more limited than those of medical technologists. Nonetheless, they are trained to perform necessary and valuable services in the laboratory. Medical laboratory technicians (certificate) are capable of handling a variety of procedures under the supervision of a medical technologist. Their tasks may range from collecting blood specimens to operating modern and complex equipment. Educational requirements for medical laboratory technicians (certificate) include a diploma from an accredited high school plus 12 months of training in one of the 116 AMA-approved hospital schools for medical laboratory technicians. Training includes lectures and applied laboratory training, and students who complete the program are eligible to take the national examination given by the Board of Registry of Medical Technologists (ASCP). Those who pass the examination become medical laboratory technicians (certificate)—MLT(certificate)(ASCP). Proficiency examinations for clinical laboratory personnel or basic military medical laboratory courses and appropriate experience may replace the training programs just described.

A second supporting professional in a medical laboratory is the cytotechnologist. Cytotechnologists are concerned with cytology, the science of cells, and are trained to recognize those minute abnormalities in the size, shape, and color of cell substances that may signal the presence of cancer. Their main tool is the microscope, and a variety of special stains are used to accentuate cell patterns. Cytotechnologists must complete two years of college, including 14 semester hours in biology, plus 12 months of training at one of nearly 100 schools of cytotechnology approved by the AMA. After candidates pass the examination given by the Board of Registry of Medical Technologists (ASCP), they become cytotechnologists—CT(ASCP).

Histologic technicians are also members of the medical laboratory team. They prepare portions of selected body tissues for microscopic examination. Tissue preparation involves freezing and cutting tissue samples into ultrathin slices, mounting them on slides, and staining them with special dyes to make cell details more clearly visible under the microscope. Histologic technicians must have a high school diploma plus 1 year of supervised training in a qualified pathology laboratory or graduation from one of the 32 programs of histologic technique approved by the AMA. After certification through examination by the Board of Registry of Medical Technologists, histologic technicians are given the designation HT(ASCP).

Medical laboratory technicians (associate degree) are the most recently established category of supporting professionals in a medical laboratory. The level of responsibility that can be assumed by the medical laboratory technician (associate degree) lies between that of the medical laboratory technician (certificate) and the medical technologist. Two-year programs lead to an associate degree for medical laboratory technicians. Sixty-four such programs have been approved by the AMA. Certification as medical laboratory technicians (associate degree)—MLT(associate degree)(ASCP)—is available to those who successfully complete the certification examination given by the Board of Registry (ASCP).

Nuclear medical technologists assist the physician in the operation of scanning devices using radioisotopes. The educational and experience requirements for acceptance to take the registry examination are varied and may be obtained from the Board of Registry of Medical Technologists (ASCP).

WHAT CAN LABORATORY PERSONNEL EXPECT TO EARN?

Starting salaries earned by laboratory personnel vary according to the level of their training and performance and are also determined in part by the size of the employing facility and its geographical location. According to a 1977 national compensation survey, newly graduated medical technologists could expect to earn an annual salary of $9,500 to $12,000. Entry-level medical laboratory technicians (associate degree) earned an annual salary of $7,500 to $10,000, and the annual salary of entry-level medical laboratory technicians (certificate) ranged from $7,000 to $8,500.

WHAT IS THE DEMAND FOR MEDICAL TECHNOLOGISTS?

A career in medical technology is both stimulating and rewarding. Although a majority of the approximately 80,000 ASCP-registered medical technologists are women, the number of men entering the profession is increasing rapidly. The growing dependence on laboratory tests in the diagnosis and treatment of disease as well as the construction of more hospital and medical facilities have increased the demand for medical technologists. Registered medical technologists will find opportunities for employment in every part of the country.

References

Allied health education directory, Chicago, 1978, American Medical Association.

The registry of medical technologists of the American society of clinical pathologists, Chicago, 1969, Board of Registry of Medical Technologists, American Society of Clinical Pathologists.

What kind of a career could I have in a medical laboratory? Chicago (no date), Board of Registry of Medical Technologists, American Society of Clinical Pathologists.

Suggested Reading

ASMT Position paper; differentiation among MT, MLT, and CLA expected capabilities at career entry, Am. J. Med. Tech. **39**(9):362, 1973.

Williams, M. R.: Introduction to medical technology, Philadelphia, 1971, Lea & Febiger.

Professional organizations where further information can be obtained

American Society of Clinical Pathologists
2100 W. Harrison St.
Chicago, Ill. 60612
American Society for Medical Technology
Suite 200
5555 West Loop South
Bellaire, Tex. 77401
National Accrediting Agency for Clinical Laboratory Sciences
Suite 1512
222 S. Riverside Plaza
Chicago, Ill. 60606

National Certification Agency for Clinical Laboratory Personnel
Suite 726
1625 Eye St.
Washington, D.C. 20006
Registry of Medical Technologists of ASCP
2100 W. Harrison St.
Chicago, Ill. 60612

14

MEDICINE

George L. Fite

THE VARIETIES OF MEDICAL PRACTICE

The profession of medicine as we know it today has developed from early practices rooted in magic and superstition, herbalism, bloodletting, and folk medicine. Nurtured by the knowledge of the early European universities, supported by practices rooted in cultural biases, and divided by differing beliefs regarding the basic functions of the human organism, the profession of medicine has managed to evolve as both a healing art and an essential science.

Remnants of the early differences of opinion still survive, resulting in sectarianism in medicine, specifically homeopathic, osteopathic, and allopathic. No realist can expect these forces to be wholly extinguished, but their histories have shown a steady departure from their origins into union with the majority to form an eclectic discipline.

Homeopathy as taught by the German-born Samuel Hahnemann at one time enjoyed a large following. According to this discipline, all diseases were to be treated by the administration of minute doses of drugs that would produce the symptoms of the particular disease if the particular drug were given to a healthy person. Hahnemann Medical College and Hospital was founded in 1848 and still flourishes in Philadelphia. Although token recognition is given to the homeopathic philosophy, the school now is a standard medical educational institution.

Osteopathic medicine tends to merge similarly with standard academic medicine but has resisted attempts at organizational merger and remains a practice differentiated by its underlying emphasis on the importance of the musculoskeletal system in the body's efforts to resist and overcome disease. Its basic scientific knowledge and its system of medical education have indeed moved toward the standard practice in diagnostic, preventive, and therapeutic procedures, but its practitioners always maintain their focus on the musculoskeletal system and its effect on neurophysiologic processes. Osteopathic physicians, who are awarded the DO degree, maintain a separate organizational identity and tend to be involved in general practice more than in the specialties.

Allopathic medicine is the most widespread branch of modern medicine. Originally, the allopathic physician (MD) treated disease by giving relatively large doses of drugs that produced effects opposite to the symptoms from which the patient suffered. This dominant medical discipline has evolved into a system based on the premise that a disease process can be altered by action against the causative agent. An example of this would be the reduction of bacterial infection through the action of penicillin. Most DOs would use this same treatment but might also use manipulative therapy to speed up the body's own recovery mechanisms.

The practice of modern medicine not only derives from these different approaches but also is affected by new interests such as that presently appearing in North America in the practice of acupuncture, which to some holds great promise. This ancient technology, new to our culture, has become interwoven with modern technology and exemplifies the way in which the outer reaches of medical practice invite scientific investigation to produce imaginative proposals for the prevention or cure of all disease.

Primary physicians

Home-visiting physicians have disappeared from our cities and most of our country, as have their turn-of-the-century buckboards and little black bags. Neither hitching posts nor automobile parking spaces are available for them today. The problem of primary care is better described as a problem in logistic medicine, the delivery of health care to the patient. It is medicine's business to support health in the community before signs and symptoms appear; hence the primary physician may fill this role, and that primary physician may today be an internist, a pediatrician, or an obstetrician and gynecologist, as well as a family physician. This person can guide the patient to advanced inquiry and treatment, if the physician alone cannot provide it. Primary physicians are badly needed in many sparsely settled and low-income communities. Their incomes may be smaller than those of their specialist colleagues, and their work may be hard and their hours long. Approximately 33% of today's medical school graduates and 75% of the graduates of osteopathic colleges enter primary care. The federal government is encouraging more graduates each year to point their career development in that direction.

Family physicians. The principal primary physican is the family physician. Internships (residencies) are today offered in family medicine. The existence of an Academy of Family Medicine and a recognized specialty certification board in family medicine have done much to enhance the image of this most vital specialty in health care delivery. In this field where patients are in need of much examination that does not demand the physician's skills, the physician assistant emerges as a force in the delivery of health care (see p. 169).

Specialties

Among students who wish to enter a specialty, only a few make their decision early. A thorough general knowledge of medicine is believed to be a desirable foundation for specialty training. In the last academic years and in internships, electives help specialty-bound physicians to find their field. The specialties* are themselves highly organized, and they require examination before their boards prior to admission. Although some have charged specialty groups with similarity to the guilds of western Europe during the Middle Ages, the standards they set are high. Few hospitals, clinics, or group practices will accept specialists who either have not passed MD or DO board examinations in their specialty or are eligible to become so certified.

Group practice

The gathering together of specialists into a unit capable of handling most medical problems has developed naturally from its predecessor, the hospital outpatient department. The advantages of group practice to both patient and physician usually include the all-important availability of hospital beds when needed. Indeed, some hospitals have originated and developed from the needs prescribed by group practices.

As small businessmen, many physicians finds themselves involved in things for which they have no real taste. These include the purchase of expensive equipment, office rentals, finding secretarial-receptionist help and nursing aides, and problems with taxation, insurance, and fee collection. The larger private clinic or group practice can enjoy an administrative staff, freeing the physician from nonmedical duties. Partnership in group practice usually includes retirement provisions and

---

*Specialties are listed on pp. xv-xvi.

vacation coverage. Possible disadvantages are that the group practitioner will lose some of his or her individuality and freedom for personalized behavior.

Military and government service

The armed forces and the United States Public Health Service offer career positions to physicians as commissioned officers. Several thousands of physicians find this service helpful in repaying the heavy debts acquired during their educations. The extensive hospital system of the Veterans' Administration is a large employer of physicians. These large institutions relieve physicians of their role as family counselor, giving them more time to follow personal medical interests. State and county health societies employ many physicians, not always on a full-time basis, as do insurance companies.

Foundation medicine

The largest research organization in the world is the National Institutes of Health (NIH) in Bethesda, Maryland. It is federally owned and operated by the Department of Health, Education, and Welfare. The NIH is a massive laboratory of investigative medicine and employs hundreds of chemists, physicists, and scientists knowledgeable in all fields of biology and medicine. Other examples of research institutions are the Communicable Disease Center in Atlanta, the Rockefeller University (formerly the Rockefeller Institute of Medical Research) in New York City, and the American Cancer Society, which channels funds from both public and private sources into the support of advances in research, patient care, and treatment throughout the country. Scores of other foundations attack many individual diseases, and commercial firms also support private research along the lines of their own interests.

HUMAN VALUES IN MEDICINE

Hippocrates, often called the father of medicine, enjoyed a flourishing general practice on the island of Cos following his study in Athens. This was 400 years before the birth of Christ and 2,000 years before the beginnings of a correct understanding of physiology. The Hippocratic oath, probably written some years after his death, reflects the importance of impeccable behavior on the part of the physician toward medical colleagues as well as patients. Somewhat pious in tone, its concept of the ''good physician'' remains essentially unchanged today, so much so that the oath is commonly recited at medical school graduation exercises as a declaration of moral fiber and as a recognition of the human responsibilities of the physician. Revisions have been suggested to adapt the oath to the modern scene, while articles about the "good physician" still appear in medical journals, and relicensure of physicians and continuing medical education are demanded.

The ethical dilemma of modern medicine is that the endeavor to save one life often involves human judgments concerning other lives and other values. This conflict is seen in the kidney transplant candidate

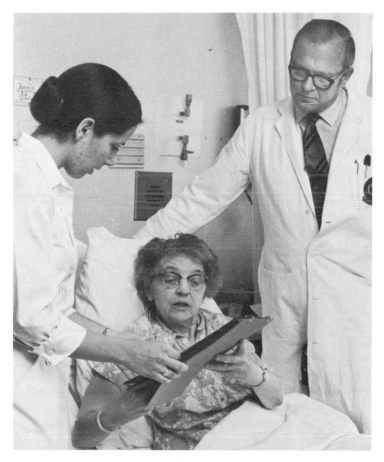

Fig. 14-1. Physicians develop treatment plans in conference with other members of the health care team, in this case a dietitian and the patient.

waiting for a suitable cadaver kidney, in the woman seeking an abortion, in the mechanical prolongation of life where meaning and humanness have ceased.

Medical knowledge acquired during the past 20 years exceeds *in quantity* all that was acquired earlier. What sort of resolutions will the physicians of today and tomorrow find for the dilemmas that have already begun to occur at the interface of technology and human values? (See Fig. 14-1.)

MEDICAL EDUCATION

America's first allopathic medical school opened its doors 200 years ago. The oldest osteopathic college is less than 90 years old. Medical education in the United States developed slowly during its first 100 years and was greatly influenced by European medicine throughout the nineteenth century. Only after World War I did medical education in the United States come to occupy a position of leadership.

Teaching programs in United States medical schools vary only slightly from school to school. The 50-year standard has been the study of basic sciences during the first 2 years, with clinical medicine and bedside experience the focus of the second 2 years. This division has permitted the existence of the 2-year school, which offered only the subjects standard to the first half of the process, sometimes because resources were not great enough to meet the demands of clinical education.

The basic sciences commonly taught in the first year of medical school are gross and microscopic anatomy, human physiology, biological chemistry, and pharmacology. During the second year students are introduced to the disease process. They will experience prolonged classroom and laboratory instruction in microbiology, including bacteriology, virology, the study of fungi, parasites, and all related agencies of infectious disease. In addition, in pathology they will be taught both the gross and microscopic anatomy of disease processes and will learn their epidemiological and genetic backgrounds and applications in sanitation, public health, and practical immunology.

During these 2 years their interest in medicine and its practice will be steadily stimulated by some introduction to and exhibition of the clinical process, but they will have little direct involvement in this aspect. They will be hard put to absorb and retain what they have been taught.

After these 2 years students are eligible to take the first part of either the MD or DO National Board examinations and will probably do so at this time when their knowledge of the subject is freshest.

Teaching the basic sciences has been a subject for considerable academic debate. Obviously, the student who is to become a psychiatrist or ophthalmologist will have spent many hours learning things that will seem forever useless. Potential cardiologists may easily lament time given to the study of tropical diseases, cases of which they will never see. Fifteen years ago, therefore, some schools relaxed their teachings of basic sciences, introducing clinical medicine as a replacement. The results were not altogether happy; too many students even from the best medical schools were unable to pass their National Board examinations. The tide has recently reversed, and the basic sciences have been reinstated. To say that the problem has been resolved is false. Behind the problem lies the enormous fund of information to be assimilated as well as the difficulty of presenting the material in ways appropriate to individual needs.

Within the past 5 years, nearly a third of the medical schools have introduced accelerated curriculums. These changes have frequently redesigned the basic and introductory clinical sciences of the traditional first 2 years so as to follow body systems in presentation. To reduce the amount of time spent in academic preparation, vacations have virtually been eliminated for students who complete the total MD requirements in 3 years. Many programs have added some flexibility in time and a few have introduced innovative independent study programs that allow for considerable variation in self-pacing through the basic sciences.

In order to accelerate medical education even more than is possible with the 3-year curriculum, several allopathic colleges have started programs requiring only a high school diploma for admission. These schools have a 6-year curriculum and have been somewhat controversial within the MD profession. No such program exists at any of the osteopathic colleges, because the American Osteopathic Association requires a minimum of 3 years of premedical work. Partially as a result of these differences in American Medical Association and American Osteopathic Association requirements, about 90% of allopathic students have bachelor's degrees compared with 97% of osteopathic students.

During their third year many schools require medical students to spend much time in the outpatient clinic, within many or all of its divisions. Under supervision they will examine many patients, working together with a few colleagues in comparatively small groups. They will still be students, even though their white coats, stethoscopes, and pocketsful of throat sticks give them the appearance of physicians.

Students will be introduced to most of the specialties, perhaps all of them. In addition, they will be intensely lectured to, both didactically and with amphitheater demonstration, and will have difficulty in keeping up with as much as they could wish. They will begin to discover the fields that interest them most, surely giving more time to these at the expense of others.

In their fourth year, students will enter the hospital wards, spending much time in many of the byways of the hospital, its laboratories, its meetings, its ward rounds, its surgeries, its radiologic areas. They will take the ward patient histories, be mercilessly scouted by the residents, and be put through what may well turn out to have been the most fascinating year of their lives.

Then they will receive the degree of doctor of medicine or doctor of osteopathy and be permitted to take the second part of the National Board examinations. But they cannot yet practice medicine. Some states require service of 1 or 2 years in hospital internship or residency as a requisite to licensure. Thus, armed with their degrees, physicians are still many months away from independent practice.

Licensure to practice medicine is required by all states, and all demand examination of the candidate. All but two states have now joined the FLEX group and use an identical examination given at the same time each year. Questions for this examination are chosen from the National Board pool, and the grading is weighted so that basic sciences count one sixth, clinical sciences count one third, and clinical problem-solving questions count one half in final grade computation. Reciprocity, better termed *licensure by endorsement,* is facilitated and made more uniform by this cooperative testing mechanism. However, it should be noted that each state maintains its own individual passing score for licensure. In some states, scores from the National Board examinations are accepted in lieu of individual state or FLEX examinations.

PREREQUISITES FOR MEDICAL SCHOOL ADMISSION

Fifty years ago many educators thought the entering medical student should have a broad background in literature, language, and the fine arts. They wanted the students with a proved aptitude and capacity for learning—"We'll teach them the rest."

Medical schools still want the student with aptitude and zeal, but the prerequisites for the basic science portion of the curriculum are too many and too essential for the school to accept a candidate without them.

Prospective physicians must start to acquire the prerequisites 2 to 3 years before applying to medical school. Whether or not they eventually enter medicine, their decision to prepare cannot wait, and their eligibility for entry to medical school will drop progressively if they procrastinate. Today's medical school asks that the entering student be prepared for the maximum course load, and it has come as a substantial shock to many beginners to discover that what they considered a heavy load in college was only recreation. If medical school candidates were not sufficiently motivated to have started early, their handicap becomes evident. Potential dropouts are costly risks to the school, and they are mercilessly screened out, especially because the demand for entry far exceeds available places.

Premedical preparatory courses cannot be specifically listed. Because microbiology is emphasized in medical school, a limited course in college bacteriology would not be important. A reading knowledge of French and German means less today than a grasp of calculus, and without a solid background in physics, organic chemistry, and genetic biology, medical students are behind in their capacity to absorb what is offered them and to produce what is demanded.

There is no trend back to "The Doctor" as portrayed by Sir Luke Fildes, copied in a 1947 United States postage stamp, in which the doctor sits with chin on hand studying a sick child. An irreverent medical student has commented, "He can't figure the kid out, and is waiting for the rescue squad to take over." The compassionately correct approach is not enough. The demands of the practice of medicine also apply to premedical preparation.

FOREIGN MEDICAL SCHOOLS

Of the several thousand annual disappointed applicants to medical schools in the United States, many hundreds seek admission to foreign medical schools, especially those in France and Mexico. Although their qualifications may not be as high as those of the accepted applicants, many of the better applicants are as eligible as some of those accepted and are wholly competent to become physicians. Among the better, success is the rule. The road is rough, expensive, and long.

At one time tuition fees in foreign schools were low, but they have risen. In Mexico, United States students pay fees much higher than those assessed their Mexican classmates, and the total costs will be comparable to those of expensive schools at home, perhaps higher. The language problem has not been an obstacle, except as regards the time required to learn the foreign tongue.

The major stumbling block has been that foreign medical schools do not provide clinical training demanded of United States returnees after graduation from a foreign medical school. Before being permitted to practice in the United States, graduates of foreign medical schools must pass an examination given by the Educational Council for Foreign Medical Graduates (ECFMG). They must have a foreign license. To obtain a license in Mexico, graduates must give a year to a Mexican internship and another to Mexico's social service. They may succeed in bypassing some of this, but foreign medical graduates have not always been welcome as interns in United States teaching hospitals because of lack of experience in direct patient care. Alternate pathways, serving as an assistant to a practicing physician, for example, have not yet become real possibilities.

Still it is something of a tribute to the determination and the character of these students that a great many do catch up with their United States-educated colleagues, achieving full equality. The cost is high in money and in time.

Many foreign medical schools, aware of all this and wishing to promote the best in medicine, have raised admissions standards, thereby reducing the percentage of dropouts. They seek to expand teaching in clinical medicine, although facilities are painfully inadequate. The ECFMG examinations emphasize knowledge in clinical medicine.

Meanwhile, the rising number of United States medical schools and their increasing numbers of students will increase the supply of physicians, supplemented as at the moment by numerous native graduates from many foreign countries. In the end, United States medical schools should supply adequate numbers of physicians, for the present number of qualified applicants to medical schools is large enough to provide the physicians needed. The decline of applicants to United States medical schools in the late 1970s (a function of the decline in 22-year-olds in the population) has already reached the number of highly qualified applicants forced to go abroad. The certification of United States graduates of foreign medical schools will soon be a problem only in individuals, rather than to the many now affected.

MEDICAL MISTAKES AND THE PHYSICIAN'S DILEMMA

Today's physician-surgeons are beset with legal problems. They are legally obligated to practice the skills normal to the procedure they perform, whether surgical, pharmacological, or other. They may make an honest mistake without penalty, provided that they have used all the medical skill inherent and common to the art or the surgery they have practiced. Determination of what may reasonably be expected of them is arguable, and determination of penalty in case of fault is a decision made by a jury subjected to emotional as well as medical demands. "Malpractice" is a current multimillion dollar football game, with lawyers the offensive coaches and doctors the defensive players.

Protective insurance, once available at an annual cost of $4,500 to the practitioner, has doubled or tripled. A recent news item told of the retirement of an active orthopedist when he was required to pay a $14,000 annual fee for malpractice insurance. A major company refuses to insure except against claims filed within the insurance year, but many claims arise many months or years after the fact. Still another major insurer against malpractice has retired from the field altogether.

Currently a number of state medical societies have formed captive insurance companies for the purpose of making available malpractice insurance at reasonable rates to their members. An example of one such company that has been highly successful in its 2 years of existence is the Physicians' Insurance Company of Ohio, a stock company formed by the Ohio State Medical Association. A leveling of premium rates for malpractice insurance in general has come about pursuant to, and perhaps as a result of, the formation of these companies.

The future of this moderately insane situation will be substantially affected by the increasing involvement of the federal government in medicine. Will a national health insurance act additionally insure the physician against malpractice judgments? An honest physician doing his or her best can today be made bankrupt by a judgment in the hundreds of thousands of dollars, more than most physicians earn in a lifetime. Not even the best in competence and utmost in caution can rid the physician of this dilemma. Current physician self-improvement regulations (PSROs) enacted by the government have not eased the problem and may not ever be sufficient in and of themselves for this task.

Big malpractice awards have grown enormously, as have suits. Newly graduated physicians can expect to be sued once or twice in their careers. Hospitals do not escape, nor do manufacturers of devices that have failed or caused injury. In the end the malpractice judgment is charged back to the patient in higher fees, but not to the same patient. Group practices and medical societies succeed in averaging things out, but the incongruous problem persists.

WOMEN PHYSICIANS

The steady increase in the number of women physicians and in the number of women entering medical schools suggests that in the 1990s at least a fifth of the physicians practicing in the United States will be women. Almost one fourth of the new admissions to United States medical schools are now women, and the increase continues. The ratio is still far below that in the Soviet Union, however, where every other physician is a woman.

Prejudices against "lady doctors" and "henmedics" have changed, but the lion that wears the mane still likes to roar. His voice, now a growl, has not yielded to equal rights movements or feminism but to the obvious realization that a woman who can be a capable mother, secretary, nurse, or administrator, qualifies similarly as a physician. Prejudice against women arises occasionally in the argument that women cannot effectively examine and treat male patients for venereal disease, however effective they may be as pediatricians. These same prejudices have not been voiced regarding obstetricians and gynecologists.

In practice, the woman physician's difficulties in patient relationships dissolve quickly in the light of competence and understanding. In the end, the effectiveness of the prescription counts, not the handwriting thereof.

MINORITY PHYSICIANS

Medical schools in the United States, working together in The Group on Student Affairs of the Association of American Medical Colleges, set as a goal for the 1970s the achievement of minority student representation in medical schools similar to the proportion of these minorities in the population in general. The early 1970s saw a significant rise in the percentage of minority applicants and entrants, but by mid decade this had leveled off and actually declined slightly. Continued efforts are needed to correct this still distressing imbalance in the profession as it relates to the population at large. Continued efforts must be made at the primary and secondary educational levels to stimulate young people from minority backgrounds to achieve the excellence necessary to achieve a place in medical school.

SUMMARY

The prospective medical student has many fields of practice from which to choose. The years of study and clinical training require careful preparation and single-minded concentration, demanding at the same time an awareness of human values and the development of the young physician's own values together with clinical skills.

Suggested readings

Howe, H. F., editor: The physician's career, Chicago, 1967, American Medical Association.

Journal of the American Osteopathic Association, Education Annual **72**(suppl.): entire issue, 1973.

Knight, J. A.: Medical student, doctor in the making, Des Moines, Iowa, 1973, Meredith Corp.

Lipkin, M.: The care of patients, concepts and tactics, New York, 1974, Oxford University Press, Inc.

Medical school admissions requirements, Washington, D.C., 1978, Association of American Medical Colleges.

Professional organizations where further information can be obtained

American Medical Association
535 N. Dearborn St.
Chicago, Ill. 60610

American Osteopathic Association
212 E. Ohio St.
Chicago, Ill. 60611

15

NURSING

Katherine L. Kisker

HISTORICAL PERSPECTIVE

The real beginnings of nursing, contrary to popular belief, can be traced far beyond the mid nineteenth century, because nursing is a profession that is almost as old as civilization. There are references to nursing in writings of the ancient Egyptians, Greeks, and Persians. In India, for example, there were training programs for nurses as early as 300 BC. The word "nurse" is derived from the Latin word *nutrio,* which means to nourish and nurture, and these seem to have been the principal activities of nurses at that time.

Very little was done to improve the quality of nursing until the "Nightingale era" in the mid 1850s. In fact, in the early 1800s, nurses in European countries often had an unfavorable reputation and seem to have been concerned primarily with their own personal gain. Few had any real education. Florence Nightingale was a well-educated woman, although she had received only a few weeks of formal training in nursing. Deeply concerned with social and health reforms in England, she endowed a training school for nurses in that country and was instrumental in planning the curriculum and selecting the students. The influence of her successful program spread throughout England and eventually to the United States, where in 1872 the first class of trained nurses was graduated from the New England Hospital for Women and Children in Boston. Nursing education began to move into the university setting in 1909, when the first collegiate school was established at the University of Minnesota.

Many social changes have occurred since the first nursing programs were developed in the United States, and these changes continue to have a great influence on both nursing practice and nursing education.

NURSES' CONTRIBUTIONS TO HEALTH CARE

Nursing practice involves several essential areas of patient care. Nurses are most frequently associated with physical care, because they provide or supervise the care that patients need because of illness or disability. This includes supplying what is necessary for the patient's safety and comfort as well as helping to prevent complications that may occur as a result of illness or measures used in treating it.

Another essential contribution is the provision of emotional support. The nurse helps patients to acknowledge, express, and understand their feelings about their illness and what implications the illness may have for their life-style. This understanding may strongly contribute to rehabilitation and recovery.

The education and experience of registered nurses enable them to make observations and assessments of patient states that are invaluable to patient care. Many baccalaureate nursing curricula prepare students in areas of health assessment that were once thought to be only in the realm of other health care providers (such as taking a patient history and doing a physical examination). Nurses are generally the only health professionals who have contact with patients on a 24-hour-a-day basis. Their ability to observe, assess, and note pertinent data regarding a patient's state; to act on the basis of this information; and to communicate their observations to appropriate persons on the health team are crucial to optimal patient care. (See Fig. 15-1.)

Nurses are responsible for executing treatments that have been ordered by the physician. This requires a combination of technical skills and knowledge of the procedure, together with an understanding of its expected results.

Teaching patients and their families about an illness and the therapeutic measures used to treat it involves another essential aspect of nursing. The instruction, whether planned or incidental, must be based on a sound knowledge base and on the learner's previous experiences and readiness to learn. The nurse must be sensitive to the most appropriate time for giving such information as well as the approach that would be most successful with a given individual.

Nurses also confer and collaborate with other health team members, patients, and their families so that all patient services can be coordinated. This ensures that those who are involved will be working toward the same ultimate goal. Because nurses observe and interact with the patient in an ongoing manner (Fig. 15-2), they often have gathered information other health team members need in order to make their most ef-

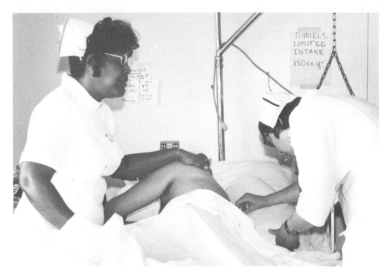

Fig. 15-1. Turning patients regularly and checking skin for pressure sores are essential parts of nursing care for patients who are unable to turn themselves.

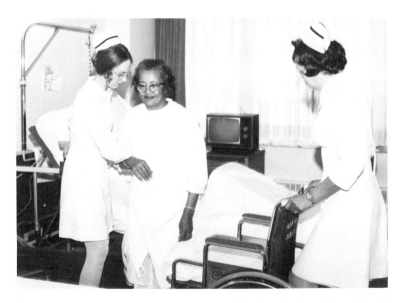

Fig. 15-2. Nurses help a surgical patient transfer from bed to chair so that she may go to another floor for therapy.

fective contribution to the patient's care. Collaborative efforts such as this assure the patient's attainment of his optimal state of health.

A last important function of nursing practice lies in the area of health promotion and maintenance. This positive approach to health care is receiving a greater emphasis in the health care system of today and is often a key component of nursing curricula.

EDUCATIONAL REQUIREMENTS FOR THE REGISTERED NURSE

Three types of programs prepare students to become registered nurses: the diploma program, the baccalaureate degree program, and the associate degree program. The oldest form of preparation is the diploma program, which is sponsored by and situated within a hospital. Diploma programs are generally 3 years in length. In some instances, they are affiliated with colleges where the students take basic science and liberal arts courses, whereas in other instances all instruction is given at the hospital school. These programs emphasize instruction and related clinical experience that focus on the care of hospitalized patients. Part of the cost of a diploma school education may be borne by the sponsoring hospital itself. In recent years a large number of diploma programs have been phased out, and additional baccalaureate and associate degree programs have been developed in areas where diploma schools were once in operation. This trend away from diploma school education will continue into the 1980s.

The second type of program is the baccalaureate program, which most commonly offers a bachelor of science degree in nursing. Graduates of these programs are prepared as professional nurses and assume job responsibilities in a wide variety of health care delivery systems. Baccalaureate programs are designed to give the student a wide variety of educational experiences as well as the knowledge and skills specific to nursing. In most baccalaureate curricula, nursing courses and related supporting courses (for example, anatomy and physiology) account for somewhat more than half of the total credit hours required for graduation. The remaining credits needed for graduation are drawn from related biological, physical, and social sciences, the humanities, and electives. Many baccalaureate programs are based on a theoretical framework. They approach the study of nursing through a nursing model that utilizes a well-defined process in the approach to nursing care. (See Fig. 15-3.) The programs vary in length from 4 to 5 academic years.

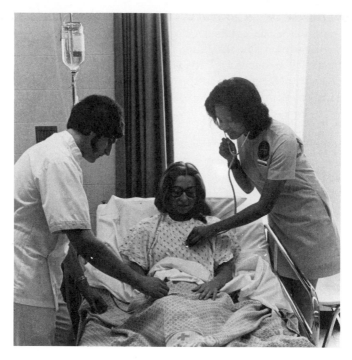

Fig. 15-3. Two student nurses check a newly admitted patient. (Courtesy The Ohio State University.)

The third type of program is the associate degree program, which may be offered through a community college, a technical institute, or a university. The graduate of this program is prepared as a technical nurse and may find a narrower range of job opportunities than the graduate of a baccalaureate program. Associate degree programs are generally 2 years in length and provide the student with basic courses in the physical, biological, and social sciences and the humanities along with nursing courses that provide nursing theory and practice experiences.

Today nursing education emphasizes programs that operate under the auspices of degree-granting institutions, that is, nursing programs that award associate or baccalaureate degrees at their conclusion. As diploma programs have been phased out, a number of associate degree or baccalaureate programs have been developed in similar localities.

There is some degree of concern in nursing circles about the articulation of association degree and diploma programs with baccalaureate degree programs for those individuals who wish to achieve a baccalaureate degree in nursing after they have become qualified as nurses through one of the other programs. A few baccalaureate programs have developed their curricula in a manner that helps previously prepared nurses to enter degree programs. Some systems (for example, the University of the State of New York Regents External Degree) have developed a series of proficiency examinations that allow candidates to demonstrate the knowledge level they have acquired from previous work or educational preparation. Many other programs, however, are still studying the situation and do not make full allowance for the learning experiences the registered nurse seeking a higher level of education might have had.

Admission requirements to schools of nursing vary. Many schools require college preparatory work in high school. It is highly advisable to contact specific schools to determine their requirements. The costs of programs vary greatly, depending on the nature of the institution and the length of the program.

The graduates of all three types of programs qualify to take the State Board Test Pool Examination. Successful performance on this examination leads to licensure as a registered nurse. The requirements for licensure are determined by each state and are administered through the State Board of Nursing. At the present time, all states use the same examination, although this practice may change in the future, especially once minimum levels of practice are established and agreed on for baccalaureate degree (professional) and associate degree and diploma (technical) graduates.

Preparation for positions in nurse education, nursing administration, and clinical specialty are available at the master's degree level. Graduates of diploma and associate degree programs must earn a baccalaureate degree in nursing before pursuing a master's degree in nursing. Educational preparation in nursing is developing at the doctoral level. Nineteen programs were in existence in 1978, and more are now in the planning phases. Nurses prepared at the doctoral level make important contributions to nursing research and nursing education in the collegiate setting.

A listing of the programs accredited by the National League for Nursing (NLN) can be obtained by writing to the league at 10 Columbus Circle, New York, New York 10019. This listing is also published periodically in the organization's journal, *Nursing Outlook*.

JOB OPPORTUNITIES

Graduates of the three types of programs have a variety of employment opportunities. The extent to which nurses are able to assess a patient's condition and needs, carry out nursing care, and function with other health professionals is determined by their own abilities, preferences, motivation, educational background, experience, and the policies of the employing agency.

Nurses are employed in a wide variety of settings. Perhaps the setting most often associated with nursing is the general hospital. Hospitals employ the largest number of nurses. Within this setting nurses may work in the emergency room; operating room; coronary and intensive care units; delivery room; newborn, premature, and intensive care nurseries; medical or surgical patient care units; or a number of other settings where nursing care is needed. The type of care and the responsibilities of nurses will vary with the area of the hospital in which they work, the size and location of the hospital, and its policies and procedures.

Nurses may also work in extended care facilities, outpatient departments, clinics, physicians' offices, psychiatric care settings, rehabilitation centers, schools, industries, public health agencies, and numerous other settings where health and health care are areas of concern. If nurses choose to be self-employed, they may work as private duty nurses or independent nurse practitioners.

A few areas of nursing practice are highlighted to provide an idea of the diversity of fields available in nursing, the nature of the field, and the skills needed for practice in them.

Psychiatric nursing, sometimes called psychiatric-mental health nursing, provides nurses with the opportunity to contribute to the care of mentally ill people and the promotion of mental health. The setting may be a mental health clinic, a psychiatric hospital, or a psychiatric unit within a general hospital. Communication and interpersonal skills are of prime importance in this area because the nurse must be able to recognize and deal with the complexities of relationships between individuals and within groups. Nurses, psychiatrists, social workers, and others often work in a team effort to help the mentally ill patient. Psychiatric nurses build on their basic nursing education by adding clinical experiences and by participating in various forms of continuing education experiences to become increasingly expert in this field.

Community health nursing, often referred to as public health nursing, is part of the community's effort to meet the health needs of large groups of people. This area of nursing practice helps in meeting the health needs of individuals and families in their normal environment, for example, the home, school, or place of employment. The goal of this area of nursing is common to all nursing in that the community health nurse strives to help people maintain the highest possible level of health. This is achieved by promoting and teaching good health habits, working to prevent disease, and caring for and assisting in the rehabilitation of the sick and disabled. Many times the community health nurse works in cooperation with the family in securing services from or acting as a liaison with other professionals in health, education, and social work. There are a number of programs for advanced preparation as well as numerous workshops and conferences that pertain to the specific needs of public health nurses to better prepare them to handle the responsibilities of this field.

Rehabilitation nursing involves working with patients who have sustained a physical disability. The nurse works very closely with other health team members (physicians, physical therapists, occupational therapists, speech therapists, social workers, and so forth) to assist the patient in making the most of the functional abilities he has remaining to him. The nurses assist the patient in coping with the magnitude of the disability. Nurses also participate in a planned teaching program for both the patient and his family. This includes information about the nature of the disability, the care he needs, the prevention of complications, and ways in which the patient can reach his highest level of independence in the activities of daily living. The nurse provides for continuity of care by formally referring the patient and his family to the local community health nursing agency when he is discharged from the rehabilitation center.

A relatively new and exciting field in nursing is the *independent nurse practitioner*. These nurses acquire advanced skills, especially in physical assessment, and generally have a master's degree in nursing. They establish their own practice in a community and provide health care for clients who contract for this service. They participate in areas such as health teaching, health assessment, and physical care within the realm of nursing practice. They generally relate closely to a specific physician for the purpose of patient referral and follow-up after medical care has been initiated.

Some fields of nursing require the individual to complete a structured program of advanced preparation before being qualified to practice in that area. Two of these fields are nurse anesthesia and nurse midwifery.

Nurse anesthetists have completed an advanced program that has qualified them to administer anesthesia to surgical and obstetrical patients. They work in the presence of and in accordance with the directions of either the surgeon in charge or the anesthesiologist. Their responsibility includes an obligation to the patient, the surgeon, and to the operating team. The length of the program to prepare a registered nurse to be a nurse anesthetist is generally a minimum of 24 months. Classroom instruction, clinical instruction, and involvement with many clinical cases are central to the program. (See fig. 15-4.) On completion of

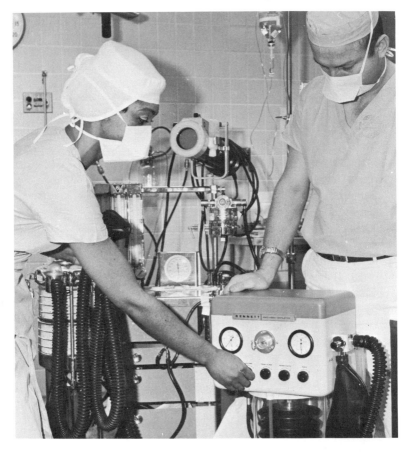

Fig. 15-4. It is important that all equipment be carefully prepared and checked before an anesthetic is administered to the patient. A student nurse anesthetist, under the watchful eye of a supervisor, prepares instruments to be used during neurosurgery.

the program, the individual takes the qualification examination, which is given in a number of different locations in this country. The 1976 starting salaries for these specialists who are employed by hospitals range from approximately $12,000 to $19,000, with the average about $15,000.

The *nurse midwife* is a registered nurse who has either completed a certificate training program or a master's degree program in midwifery. Both programs present theory and clinical experience covering the entire maternity cycle. The current trend, however, seems to favor the establishment of the master's degree program. After completion of either program, the registered nurse is eligible to take a national certifying examination given by the American College of Nurse Midwives.

The nurse midwife's focus of care is on the maintenance of health and well-being of mother and child before, during, and after birth, including the newborn and infancy periods. The nurse midwife cares for clients whose condition is defined as normal. Clients whose conditions are judged to be complicated or abnormal are referred to physicians.

Nurse midwives function in a number of health care settings that offer services to women, infants, and families during the maternity cycle. They may be found working in the community, in hospitals, or in educational settings. Nurse midwives may follow normal clients on an independent basis for the periods both preceding and following the infant's birth. In hospitals, the nurse midwife manages uncomplicated labor and delivers the infant and provides follow-up care to mothers and newborns during hospitalization. The nurse midwife also provides information and instruction regarding family planning and infant and child care. Salaries for these specialists vary with education, experience, and geographical locale.

It has been noted throughout this chapter that nurses work with many other health professionals. These include such personnel as occupational therapists, physical therapists, pharmacists, dietitians, and medical technologists. In circumstances where some of these professionals are not available and patients have need of their services, nurses may be expected to expand their technical skills to fill the void. The only health team member with whom the nurse collaborates constantly is the physician. As health care becomes more and more complex, the nurse is becoming increasingly responsible for decisions that directly influence the well-being of patients.

The registered nurse not only works with people from other health fields but also directs members of the nursing team who assist in giving direct patient care. These team members include *practical nurses* and *nursing attendants*. The practical nurse is also referred to as a licensed practical nurse or licensed vocational nurse. These individuals complete a training program approximately 1 year in length that qualifies them to take the licensing exam as prescribed by the state in which they wish to practice. Nursing attendants are often referred to as aides and orderlies and receive their training on an inservice basis from the institution that employs them. This training ranges from an introduction to the tasks they are expected to perform to a multiweek program where they must successfully pass an examination on the knowledge they are expected to acquire before they are assigned job responsibilities.

Continuing education is essential for nurses who wish to maintain a high degree of proficiency in their field. With the rapid expansion of knowledge in the health fields, nurses need to update and maintain their level of understanding through such activities as reading current nursing literature and enrolling in workshops and conferences. Continuing education units may be awarded for participation in programs if approved by the State Nurses' Association. For nurses who have not worked for a period of time (usually due to personal or family obligations), refresher courses are available in many areas and prepare individuals to return to active employment in nursing.

EMPLOYMENT STATUS OF NURSES

The need for health care professionals is expanding. Nurses are no exception. Approximately half of all professional people in health care occupations today are nurses. In 1976, a total of 961,000 nurses were actively employed in the United States as compared with 778,470 in 1972 and 689,000 in 1968. The Division of Nursing of the Public Health Service projects 1,100,000 nurses will be needed by 1980. It is also projected that the need for educational preparation at the baccalaureate or advanced level is becoming increasingly important as the complexity of health care needs and services increases.

The ratio of nurses to national population has been increasing dramatically. In 1976, there were 449 employed registered nurses per 100,000 population. This is an increase from 366 per 100,000 in 1971 and 319 per 100,000 in 1966. These figures not only represent an increase in the number of nurses but also reflect the fact that there is a substantial increase in the number of nurses remaining in the labor force. This is probably due to a marked rise in registered nurses' salaries, the impact of the women's movement, and general economic conditions.

There may be marked shortages of nurses in some geographical areas and an adequate supply in others.

The salary scale for registered nurses varies according to geographical location, educational background, and the type of employing agency. In 1976, most beginning practitioners who were employed by a hospital earned an initial salary ranging from $8,500 to $15,000 per year, with an average annual salary of above $10,500.

The field of nursing offers a flexible far-reaching career for both men and women. It allows one to serve others in a variety of ways and settings. There is a high degree of job security because of continued need. Work opportunities continue to be available in most geographical locations.

References

Blumberg, J. E., and Drummond, E. E.: Nursing care of the long-term patient, New York, 1963, Springer Publishing Co., Inc.

Cutter, I. S., and Viets, H. R.: A short history of mid-wifery, Philadelphia, 1964, W. B. Saunders Co.

Dietz, L. D., and Lehosky, A. R.: History and modern nursing, Philadelphia, 1967, F. A. Davis Co.

Facts about nursing '76 '77, Kansas City, Mo., 1977, American Nurses' Association.

National Commission for the Study of Nursing and Nursing Education: An abstract for action, New York, 1970, McGraw-Hill Book Co.

National Commission for the Study of Nursing and Nursing Education: From abstract into action, New York, 1973, McGraw-Hill Book Co.

Regenie, S. J.: The new definition of nursing in relation to nurse midwifery, J. N. Y. State Nurs. Assoc. **4:**1, 1973.

Swenson, N.: The role of the nurse midwife on the health team as viewed by the family, Bull. Am. Col. Nurs. Midwives **13:**125, 1968.

The training and responsibilities of the midwife, New York, 1967, Josiah Macy, Jr., Foundation.

Professional organizations where further information can be obtained

American Association of Nurse Anesthetists
Suite 929
111 E. Wacker Dr.
Chicago, Ill. 60601
American College of Nurse Midwives
1000 Vermont Ave., N.W.
Washington, D.C. 20005

American Nurses' Association
2420 Pershing Rd.
Kansas City, Mo. 64108
National League for Nursing
10 Columbus Circle
New York, N.Y. 10019

16

OCCUPATIONAL THERAPY

J. Scott Worley

The goals of occupational therapy are to promote health, prevent disability, evaluate behavior, and treat or teach individuals with psychosocial or physical dysfunction. Occupational therapy enables people to improve their ability to function in their daily lives and contributes to their sense of worth. It uses the individual's ability to accomplish tasks that are important and meaningful both as a means of evaluating abilities and of promoting active client participation in his health or recovery. Two essential features of occupational therapy are the therapist's analytical selection of the task to meet specific health needs of the client and the client's active participation. (See Fig. 16-1.)

DEVELOPMENT OF THE PROFESSION

The beneficial effects of physical and mental activity (occupation) have long been recognized. It was not until this century, however, that selected activities were used to reduce the effects of illness by meeting the specific needs of an individual patient. During World War I, occupational therapists trained in the United States were sent to assist soldiers who had been wounded and were convalescing in Europe. This was the beginning of occupational therapy as it is known today. The many soldiers wounded or otherwise disabled as a result of World War II required more skilled assistance, as the advanced surgical and other lifesaving techniques meant that a great number of physically and emotionally disabled soldiers were in need of advanced rehabilitation techniques. This demand provided additional stimulus for the growth of occupational therapy. The early hospital-based training programs gave way to baccalaureate education in colleges and universities. More programs developed at the graduate level to meet the increased need for therapists with specialty skills. At present the profession is establishing

134

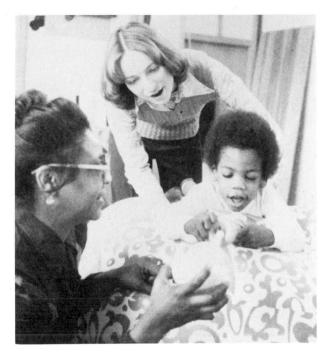

Fig. 16-1. A mother learns that she can help her child use his arms and play more effectively by first properly positioning him.

itself as a community-based service through its emphasis on preventing dysfunction and maintaining health throughout an individual's life span.

PROFESSIONAL FUNCTIONS

Occupational therapy is a profession concerned with the client's optimal development of physical, emotional, and social abilities, permitting him to function effectively in all aspects of his life. In their work, occupational therapists evaluate each patient's particular physical and psychological needs and capacities and then develop an appropriate treatment program. They determine the therapeutic activities and procedures necessary to achieve the desired improvement. An understanding of health, pathological conditions, and human behavior, keen and perceptive observation, and recognition of individual needs make it possible for an occupational therapist to build a cooperative relationship in which both therapist and patient strive to attain the patient's highest level of performance. Therapists must discover which of the patient's specific physical and emotional needs are amenable to treatment through specifically structured purposeful activity, and they must understand the meaning and dynamics of specific tasks from the cultural standpoint as well as from the perspective of the individual patient. These tasks are frequently those that are a part of the patient's normal daily life. (See Fig. 16-2.)

The occupational therapist works with patients individually and in groups, using a variety of creative, educational, industrial, manual, musical, prevocational, and recreational activities to enhance motor

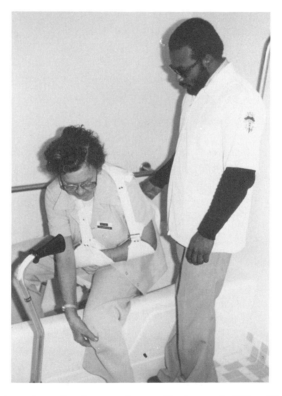

Fig. 16-2. A stroke patient learns safe use of bathroom facilities. The therapist will visit her home to suggest changes that will permit her independence and safety.

function and promote psychological, social, and economic adjustment. Teaching patients to regain daily living skills through the use of artificial limbs, assistive devices, or special equipment is an additional responsibility of the therapist.

The occupational therapist collaborates and works cooperatively with a variety of health professionals and with others significant in the client's life in order that services for him be most effective. The patients may be of any age and may suffer from cardiac or neurological impairment, arthritis, physical injury, mental retardation, emotional disturbance, or may be at risk of developing conditions that may result in their ineffective function within their environment. Occupational therapists work in a variety of settings, including children's hospitals, general hospitals, rehabilitation centers, psychiatric clinics, schools, sheltered workshops, home health services, and other community agencies. (See Fig. 16-3.) Some therapists, working in conjunction with qualified pro-

Fig. 16-3. Exploration of work-related abilities begins for this disabled patient before he leaves the rehabilitation center.

fessionals, establish their own practices. The following case studies illustrate some of the contributions an occupational therapist can make to health care.

Bobby is 11 years old and in a special class for exceptional children because of problems with perceptual motor coordination and mental retardation at the educable level. Two months ago he was referred to the occupational therapist because he was not learning at the expected level. He was behind classmates of comparable intelligence, both in learning and in play. Referral was precipitated by his increasing refusal to attempt tasks and his declining self-esteem.

The occupational therapist closely observed Bobby's performance in a series of tasks designed to evaluate the specific factors interfering with coordination and also tested his sensory and motor functions associated with incoordination and learning problems.

Bobby was found to be poor in using touch and kinesthetic sensations to help him guide his movements. This and a vestibular dysfunction could be interfering with his academic learning and his ability to play successfully. His teacher and mother had described him as being afraid of heights and climbing and, in recent months, as being more irritable, angry, and less willing to participate in activities.

The therapist worked with Bobby twice a week for 8 weeks. He was involved in tasks selected to improve his ability to interpret his sensations and integrate them with his motions. Bobby enjoyed this program because from his perspective it was play, but play at which he was successful and challenged to do more.

The immediate results were best summed up by a comment of his father "It's the first time I've seen him able to roughhouse and have fun with his younger brothers in the yard." The therapist expects that within 2 more months improvements in his abilities will begin showing themselves in Bobby's academic work.

Vivian, a 32-year-old alcoholic, was found to have diabetes. Her erratic diet and activity level resulting from the alcoholism made it virtually impossible for her to adjust to the necessary medicine. As a result, she went into shock several times and had to be rushed to the emergency room of the local hospital. She was hospitalized each time to stabilize her medication with only temporary success.

Under the guidance of the occupational therapist on the last hospitalization, she began a program that required a consistent level of activity designed to help her begin to deal with the emotional problems that prevented her from adequately caring for herself. The occupational therapist also helped her to plan for her life after discharge from the hospital.

Upon discharge, she continued occupational therapy in a local sheltered workshop where her employment skills and potential were explored. She was helped to set goals for eventual employment. Under this guidance Vivian's work habits, attitudes, and ability to handle responsibility improved. She was placed at assembly tasks and eventually promoted to supervise a portion of one of the workshop's subcontract jobs. The selection of each assignment was made by the occupational therapist with specific consideration of Vivian's improving emotional status and work habits.

During the period of Vivian's work at the sheltered workshop, the occupational therapist collaborated closely with the vocational counselor assigned to Vivian's case and with the health center following her medical treatment.

Vivian is now living independently and is completing her first month of work in the packaging and shipping area of a small manufacturing firm. She goes regularly to the mental health center where she sees an occupational therapist who is helping her learn how to handle periods of stress.

Helen is now 48 years old and is seeing the occupational therapist in a rehabilitation center as an outpatient. Twelve years ago after a period of intense pain in her right wrist, her physician diagnosed rheumatoid arthritis and referred her for occupational therapy.

The occupational therapy program taught her how to perform her daily activities in ways that would be least stressful and deforming to her affected joints. Her entire weekly routine was analyzed, and suggestions made for maintaining the necessary strength and motion in her wrist and also for maintaining the proper balance between rest and activity that is so critical in the treatment of rheumatoid arthritis.

Since that first hospitalization Helen has returned to the hospital twice because of flare-ups of the disease. Each time the occupational therapist has reviewed Helen's activities and adjusted her level of exercise and work to ensure the greatest degree of comfort and to prevent deformities.

At various times over the years the therapist constructed hand splints to protect the affected joints of Helen's wrists and hands and showed Helen how to do her work in an energy-saving way.

As a result of this program Helen has avoided most of the characteristic joint deformities associated with her disease and has remained independently at home.

PERSONNEL AND EDUCATION

Registered occupational therapists (OTR) are professionally qualified graduates of occupational therapy programs that are accredited by the American Medical Association in collaboration with the American Occupational Therapy Association (AOTA). They have successfully completed a minimum of 6 months of full-time supervised field work and the national certifying examination. They maintain registered membership in the AOTA. The therapist functions at a level that may involve supervision, administration, and consultation in addition to the evaluation, planning, and execution of treatment programs. The roles assumed by individial therapists depend on their qualifications, areas of competence, and interests.

Educational requirements of occupational therapy curricula are geared to fulfilling the requirements for program accreditation. In addition to meeting certain specified minimum standards, each approved program must provide instruction in the basic human sciences, the human development process, specific life tasks and activities (their various implications and analysis), the health-illness-health continuum, and the theory and application of occupation therapy. In addition, each program must meet the requirements of the university in which it is offered and must provide a minimum of 6 months of field experience.

A person may become an OTR by one of two routes, academic or experiential. A qualified student may enter an accredited basic professional occupational therapy program at the baccalaureate, postbaccalaureate, or master's level. The latter two are for persons with undergraduate (BS or BA) degrees in fields related to occupational therapy, such as biology, sociology, or psychology. Each of these programs must meet the same standards of accreditation and prepare persons to enter the field at the professional level.

The experiential route permits a currently certified occupational therapy assistant (see below) to take the certification examination to become registered as a professional occupational therapist by showing evidence of at least 4 years of practice as a certified occupational therapy assistant and completion of the 6-month professional level field work requirement.

After qualification by one of these methods and successful completion of the professional certification examination, the individual may be admitted to the registry of therapists (OTR) maintained by the American Occupational Therapy Association.

There are an increasing number of graduate programs designed to permit registered occupational therapists to do advanced work in preparation for specialized clinical practice, research, or teaching in occupational therapy programs. These programs offer degrees at both the master's and doctoral levels.

Certified occupational therapy assistants (COTA) are technically trained and function under the supervision of an OTR in general activity, maintenance, and supportive programs of specific treatment. To become certified by the AOTA, it is necessary to complete an AOTA-approved technical training program and a minimum of 2 months of technical-level fieldwork.

These training programs include (1) studies of communication and interactional skills, (2) health and illness concepts, (3) knowledge of specific life tasks, (4) occupational therapy principles and practice, and (5) 2 months of supervised field work.

Programs may vary in length from 21 weeks to 2 years, depending on the type of program and its location. Two-year associate degree programs are offered by an increasing number of junior colleges. Graduates who meet the requirements may pass the examination and be employed as certified occupational therapy assistants, or they may receive some credit for transfer to a professional program at the baccalaureate level. Programs are also sponsored by the military services, vocational and technical schools, and public school departments of adult education.

Some programs may restrict admission to people from a particular geographical area or have an employment requirement for admission. Therefore those who are interested in becoming certified occupational therapy assistants should check the requirements of specific programs.

Occupational therapy aides are trained on the job to meet the requirements and standards of the occupational therapy departments in which they work. They are directed or supervised by a registered therapist or certified occupational therapy assistant and may perform clerical, maintenance, or patient-related duties.

PROFESSIONAL ORGANIZATION

The American Occupational Therapy Association is the national organization of occupational therapists, and participation involves the professional, technical, and student levels of personnel within the profession. It is composed of local organizations (usually at the state level) that are affiliated with it and have representation in its policy-making body. The AOTA establishes standards within the profession and provides means of communication within the profession through newsletters and journals. The AOTA's goal is to foster educational and professional growth in the practice of occupational therapy for the improvement of the public's health.

LICENSURE

Thirteen states now require those who provide occupational therapy services to be licensed and several additional states have such legislation pending, or proposed. These laws are designed to protect the public in need of health services from potentially dangerous or inadequate services provided by unqualified individuals. Each of these laws recognizes the AOTA certification process previously mentioned (OTR, COTA) as alternatives to their own licensure examination requirement. Persons who have qualified themselves by passing the AOTA certification examination are not required to take an additional examination in order to become licensed by the states but must furnish proof of their AOTA certification when applying for licensure.

PROFESSIONAL OPPORTUNITIES

There are not enough occupational therapists to fill all the positions available each year both in this country and abroad. In addition to direct contact with patients through treatment, therapists may be involved in research, teaching, consultation, and administration. The increasing national emphasis on health has opened many new frontiers of service, creating virtually limitless opportunities in this exciting and challenging profession.

In general, salary opportunities compare favorably with those of other health-related professions with comparable qualifying requirements. With specialty experience, experience in supervision or administration, or additional educational background, therapists may assume additional responsibilities and may receive appropriately higher salaries.

Suggested readings

American Journal of Occupational Therapy, published monthly by American Occupational Therapy Association.

Description of function in occupational therapy, New York (no date), American Occupational Therapy Association.

History of occupational therapy, Am. J. Occup. Ther. **31**(10): entire issue, 1977.

Hopkins, H. L., and Smith, H. D.: Willard and Spackman's occupational therapy, ed. 5, Philadelphia, 1978, J. B. Lippincott Co.

Lucci, A.: Occupational therapy case studies, Flushing, N.Y., 1977, Medical Examination Publishing Co. Inc.

Reference manual for occupational therapy educators, Rockville, Md., 1974, American Occupational Therapy Association.

Reilly, M.: Occupational therapy can be one of the great ideas of twentieth-century medicine. Am. J. Occup. Ther. **16**:1, 1962.

Yerxa, E.: Authentic occupational therapy, Am. J. Occup. Ther. **21**:1, 1967.

Professional organization where further information can be obtained

American Occupational Therapy Association
6000 Executive Blvd.
Rockville, Md. 20852

17

OPTOMETRY

James F. Noe

Optometry is the health profession specializing in the care of people's vision. Although modern optometry is a relatively young profession, its earliest foundations can be traced back to the Middle Ages. Like the other major health professions, optometry owes its present stature to a number of scientific discoveries and a series of contributing scientists.

PROFESSIONAL DEVELOPMENT

Visual care before 1300 AD was practically nonexistent. Spectacles had not been invented, and visual defects were merely tolerated. People suffering from "dimness of the eyes" were primarily thought to have an eye disease. They were considered to be useless members of society and were treated accordingly.

During the period between 1300 and 1900, astronomers, mathematicians, physicists, and other physical scientists made important contributions to the understanding of vision and the science of optics. Spectacle lenses were developed, and a limited number of people in the more technologically advanced nations were able to procure some primitive correction for their visual difficulties.

Additional optical knowledge and the development of modern physiological optics led to the era of "modern optometry." The first training school for optometrists in the United States was established in 1892, and in 1901 the first state optometry licensing law was passed. The remainder of the states passed licensing laws in rapid succession, and the profession continued to develop.

Formation of state and national professional organizations, the increased number and quality of optometric training institutions, and the growing demand for and acceptance of professional optometric services served to enhance the growth of optometry as a vital health care profession.

PROFESSIONAL FUNCTIONS

Optometrists today offer a variety of professional services. They provide comprehensive assistance to the public in maintaining and enhancing good vision and correcting vision defects. Their work involves much more than merely correcting blurred vision, although this is an extremely important function. A number of diagnostic tests are performed by the optometrist to determine how the eyes of the patient focus and adjust to critical near and far distances. (See Fig. 17-1.) The eyes are a complex system, and people require different types of visual abilities to read a textbook, drive an automobile, pilot an airplane, or enjoy a movie or television.

If often takes an optometrist many hours over a number of months to provide the necessary services demanded even in routine cases. This health care professional is much more than a mere provider of eyeglasses. The optometrist must provide basic optometric services for

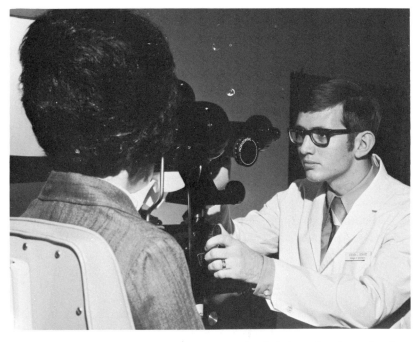

Fig. 17-1. One of a series of diagnostic tests is administered to determine the health and efficiency of the visual system.

every patient. The eyes must be carefully examined for possible disease conditions. This requires the expert use of a number of scientific instruments and an applied knowledge of anatomy, physiology, and pathology.

Vision must be scientifically measured and a determination made of the patient's ability to use his eyes to see, focus, and aim with accuracy and comfort. These measurements and findings must then be carefully analyzed to ensure the most efficient solution to any vision problem that has been detected.

An exact set of instructions has to be prepared so that the scientific and technical compounding of any corrective materials can be made by the laboratory. This finished prescription must then be carefully adjusted to the eyes of the individual patient to ensure maximum results as well as comfort.

More complex cases call for more complicated testing. Problems in color vision, image-size measurements, binocular (or two-eyed) coordination, fields of vision, and depth perception are some of the more involved areas that demand careful testing by trained optometrists. Each of these areas requires specialized training, techniques, and equipment to reach accurate solutions to the patient's problems.

Many times it will be determined that prescription glasses are not necessary to solve a particular problem. The optometrist may prescribe visual training or orthoptics to remedy the diagnosed visual defect. These eye exercises must be carefully planned and explained to the patient to maximize their effectiveness. Often the optometrist will assist the patient in this treatment, using special scientific apparatus over an extended period of time. Such conditions as crossed eyes in children often lend themselves to this type of corrective measure.

Older patients present a different type of challenge to the optometrist. Correction of their visual problems often requires more than a single lens prescription. Specially designed bifocals, trifocals, or quadrifocals must be carefully prescribed to deal effectively with the needs of these patients.

The specialty of fitting contact lenses occupies a large segment of many optometrists' practices. The intricate measurements and careful fitting techniques required by this optometric service are challenging and time consuming. Constant practice, study, and education are required to keep abreast of the latest developments. Ever-increasing numbers of people are selecting this type of visual correction, and the optometrist has the responsibility of keeping up-to-date in this rapidly changing area of specialization.

CAREERS IN OPTOMETRY

Most optometrists enter private practice. About 60% of the 21,000 licensed optometrists in the United States are engaged in solo practices. A majority of private practices have traditionally consisted of an individual optometrist assisted by one or more optometric aides. However, the present trend seems to be toward practices in which several optometrists with different areas of interest form a group practice, each contributing to a comprehensive optometric service.

There are various areas of specialization within optometry, in addition to the fitting of contact lenses. These include the examination and optical rehabilitation of aniseikonia, a discrepancy in the size of the images seen by each of the two eyes; the diagnosis and rehabilitation of problems involving binocular coordination and visual perception; the analysis and solution of visual problems associated with aviation, automobile driving, and other forms of transportation and with industry and schoolwork; and the correction of partial or subnormal vision. The goal is to help achieve clear, comfortable, safe, and efficient vision not only by optical means but also by making recommendations for enhancing the visual environment through better illumination, improved visibility of objects, and better design of equipment.

Optometrists are also employed by hospitals and clinics and by federal, state, and local agencies. A sizable number of optometrists serve as optometry officers in the Army, Navy, or Air Force or in the United States Public Health Service. Currently, graduate optometrists enter the Army and Air Force with the rank of captain and enter the Navy as lieutenants, junior grade.

Industry and government also employ optometrists in various research and development areas. For example, optometrists are involved in the National Aeronautics and Space Administration programs and in the work of major aviation companies as well as in the research projects of the larger optical manufacturing companies.

Optometrists are also needed to teach in colleges of optometry. Many of the colleges offer graduate programs in physiological optics for those optometrists interested in careers in education or research.

PERSONAL QUALITIES

Both men and women find optometry a rewarding career. An aptitude for and interest in science and mathematics coupled with a desire to be of service to people are the characteristics most important to an aspiring optometrist.

The personal satisfaction derived from rendering an important service combined with an adequate income make optometry an appealing health profession. Optometrists can determine their own office hours to best suit the requirements of patients and family. Women optometrists find this flexibility especially attractive in combining a career with marriage.

The income of optometrists depends on their professional skills and the services they provide. Their income should equal that of the other professionals in their chosen community. Recent reports cite an average net income in excess of $30,000 per year for the established practitioner.

EDUCATIONAL PREPARATION

Present educational requirements for the profession consist of a 4-year optometric curriculum preceded by a minimum of 2 years of specific preoptometry study. This preoptometry work can be completed at any accredited college or university, but the 4-year professional training can be pursued only at one of the institutions accredited by the Council on Optometric Education of the American Optometric Association (AOA). There are presently 13 accredited schools of optometry located in the population centers of the United States. Two additional schools are scheduled to begin admitting students in the near future.

Academic preparation for optometry should begin in high school with a college preparatory program in English, social studies, mathematics, science, and foreign language. Preoptometry curriculums include courses in chemistry, physics, biology, psychology, and mathematics. Professional curriculums embrace the various facets of the profession and include ocular anatomy, optics, psychology, pharmacology, physiology, and both the theory and practical application of optometric techniques. Students also spend a large part of their professional training in clinical settings. Under the supervision of the clinical staff, students work with patients to learn and refine the various skills so important in their future practices.

On successful completion of the professional curriculum, students receive the doctor of optometry (OD) degree, which makes them eligible to take the state board examination required in every state for licensure to practice optometry. Formal education for the optometrist does not end with the receipt of the professional degree and the successful passing of state board examinations. Most states (45) presently require optometrists to show evidence of approved continuing education to be eligible for license renewal.

PARAOPTOMETRICS

The optometrist's role has been refined in recent years by the addition of auxiliary personnel in the area of clinical practice. Although exact job descriptions vary according to the size of the optometric practice and the type of services provided by the optometrist, these assistants and technicians share certain general responsibilities.

Most optometrists employ an optometric office assistant who serves as receptionist, office manager, and housekeeper. An assistant's main tasks are scheduling daily appointments, preparing and filing patient examination records, billing, receiving fees, and attending to the details of operating an efficiently run professional office.

Most office assistants receive on-the-job training and their role is determined by their education and former experience. In addition, many optometrists encourage their assistants to attend periodic workshops and seminars sponsored by local and state optometric associations. These are often held in conjunction with state conventions and afford an opportunity for assistants to update their knowledge of optometric office management, meet other assistants, and exchange ideas and procedures with them.

As the practice grows, an optometrist may wish to employ an assistant to perform some of the more routine optometric tests. These assistants are referred to as optometric technicians, and their specific functions are determined by their education and experience in the area of optometry. The optometrist for whom the technician works carefully determines which diagnostic tests the technician can perform for a given patient to ensure an accurate vision analysis and diagnosis.

A more exacting description of the optometric technician's role is presently being evolved, and training programs for technicians are being developed at a number of optometry schools and other institutions of higher education that specialize in the preparation of health care technicians. With the growing demand for more efficient health care at all levels for a rapidly increasing population, the optometric technician seems to be one answer to the problem of the shortage of optometrists in the United States. For further information about a career in paraoptometry and a list of educational programs, write to the American Optometric Association.

FUTURE OUTLOOK

The complex demands made on vision by modern-day living create a steadily increasing demand for optometric services. Increasing numbers of employers are having vision care services added as fringe benefits. More people are becoming aware of the importance of early and frequent vision analysis as part of routine health care for themselves and their children.

Numerous studies indicate that at present the 21,000 optometrists in the United States are not able to meet even the current need for services. Estimates of future needs are as high as an additional 1,000 graduates per year. Even with the newer methods of health care delivery being planned, there remains a critical need in most health professions for well-qualified, highly motivated men and women.

SUMMARY

Optometry as a profession has had a short but dynamic history. With the various primary care services optometrists are now able to offer, the profession is beginning to realize its full potential as a part of the health care system. It is striving to meet the challenges of our growing population and the ever-increasing demand for quality health services. It offers a unique challenge to the student searching for a way to make a meaningful contribution to our complex society.

References

Gregg, J. R.: Your future in optometry, New York, 1968, Richards Rosen Press, Inc.

Hirsch, M. J., and Wick, R. E.. The optometric profession, Radnor, Pa., 1968, Chilton Book Co.

Kitchell, F.: Opportunities in an optometry career, New York, 1967, Universal Publishing and Distributing Co.

Professional organizations where further information can be obtained

American Optometric Association
Vocational Guidance Department
243 N. Lindbergh Blvd.
St. Louis, Mo. 63141

Association of Schools and Colleges of Optometry
1730 M St.
Washington, D.C. 20036

18

PHARMACY

David A. Knapp and James A. Visconti

Pharmacists are the most accessible of all American health workers. The pharmacy, their primary place of practice, may be found on almost any corner of any street in the country, and it has become a modern American institution. However, pharmacy is one of the most ancient of the professions. Since the dawn of history there have been those who have dedicated themselves to the development of drugs for healing and comforting the sick. Written prescriptions have been found that date from as early as 3600 BC, and the Ebers papyrus, written about 1550 BC, contains references to many chemicals, formulas, and cosmetics used at that time. In these years the professions of medicine and pharmacy were as one, and it was not until the Arabian period (700-1000 AD) that pharmacy was first delineated as a separate profession.

In America, pharmacists have always served as a necessary adjunct to the nation's physicians. Before the industrial revolution they personally compounded and prepared a large proportion of the remedies used in the practice of medicine. With the growth of pharmaceutical manufacturing, the technical work of compounding has been markedly reduced in the practice of the community pharmacist, being replaced by the even more complex duties associated with assuring the proper use of today's sophisticated medications.

Today, nearly everyone is familiar with the pharmacist's most frequent professional task—that of dispensing medications for individual patients. Not everyone is aware, however, of the knowledge and responsibility involved in performing this deceptively simple task. With the increasing number and sophistication of medicinal agents now available to combat and prevent disease, it has become even more important to have a highly trained health professional responsible for the safe and effective use of these products. The pharmacist is such a person.

There are presently about 140,000 pharmacists in the United States.

About 114,000 practice in community settings, another 15,000 work in hospitals, and about 11,000 are employed in academic or industrial settings. Enrollment in pharmacy schools increased dramatically during the 1970s primarily because of a large influx of federal funding for professional education. Thus, the enrollment in the last 3 years of the pharmacy program increased from about 15,000 students in 1970 to about 24,000 students in 1978. Enrollments have been stable at this level for the last few years. The result of this enrollment increase has been many more pharmacists going into practice each year than was previously the case. Although the vast majority of graduates can obtain employment with little difficulty, the job market is unquestionably tighter than it was in 1970. The increase in prescription volume and the tendency for modern pharmacists to become involved in a wide range of professional activities assure a continuing demand for pharmacists.

COMMUNITY PHARMACISTS AND PRESCRIPTION DRUGS

Most of today's pharmacists are employed in community or neighborhood pharmacies. They come into contact with literally hundreds of patients each week and dispense over 1.5 billion prescriptions a year. Each of those prescriptions represents an explicit order for a specific kind of drug for an individual patient. It is the responsibility of the pharmacist to determine whether the prescription includes the correct dosage, whether it will be compatible with other medications that the patient may be taking, and whether the directions for use are clear and complete. After selecting or preparing the proper drug and dosage form, the pharmacist must be sure that the medication is packaged in the right container and that the patient understands how to use it. For complete pharmaceutical service this usually requires a face-to-face discussion of the medication with the individual patient or his representative.

Obviously even the best of our modern drugs will be of no value if taken improperly or not at all. For example, many people think that a liquid antibiotic preparation for a baby's earache should be dripped directly into the ear rather than given orally. Some medications cause a patient's urine to change color, and unless he is told to expect this, a frantic call to the physician may result. A number of widely prescribed antibiotics are not absorbed properly if they are taken with milk. Since these products are often prescribed for children, a parent may give the child the product with a glass of milk, thus reducing the effectiveness of the therapy.

The pharmacist must also be alert to the possibility of drug interactions. With today's sophisticated drug therapy, it is not uncommon for a patient to be taking several drugs simultaneously, and some of these may interact with each other to the detriment of his health. Many patients today are under the care of several different physicians, and consequently a patient may receive prescriptions for the same drug from each. This is frequently the case with tranquilizers, since they are prescribed commonly by different kinds of specialists in medicine. Thus it is sometimes possible for a patient to be taking double or even triple the appropriate dosage of a particular drug, and this can sometimes result in dangerous overdoses. This type of problem is difficult to detect unless accurate drug histories of individual patients are kept. Many modern pharmacists are incorporating such patient prescription records into their practice. When new patients come to the pharmacist, they are asked to complete a patient record card, indicating any drug allergies or other problems that they may have. Other drugs that the patient may be taking are also recorded, so that every time a prescription is dispensed at that particular pharmacy, the patient's record card can be checked to see whether there are any possibilities of drug interactions or overdoses. The biggest drawback of this system is that patients must have all of their prescriptions dispensed at one pharmacy if all drugs are to be noted on the record card. Pharmacists are now experimenting with filing patient prescription records from many pharmacies in a computer in an effort to overcome this problem. Any cooperating pharmacy could then draw needed information from the computer file through a simple telephone call.

OTHER FUNCTIONS OF COMMUNITY PHARMACISTS

Pharmacists are in a strategic position to offer substantial professional services to the patient in connection with prescription drugs. However, this is by no means the only area in which they can make a contribution. The pharmacy is the largest source of self-medication products in the country, and the pharmacist is readily available to offer advice and counsel on the use of such agents. American families practice self-medication on a rather large basis; in fact, the typical family spends more than $40 each year on nonprescription drugs. Although pharmacists are not trained to diagnose and prescribe drugs for medical problems, they are qualified to make comparative judgments on the quality and effectiveness of the drugs that they dispense, and they are called on to do this quite frequently in everyday practice. Pharmacists may also provide professional services to the public by stocking and distributing surgical appliances and prescription accessories.

Some community pharmacists have expanded their professional services by acting as consultants to nursing homes and extended care facilities. Such facilities are usually not able to employ a full-time pharmacist and rely on the neighborhood pharmacist to meet their pharmaceutical needs.

HOSPITAL PHARMACIES

Another major area of employment for practicing pharmacists is the hospital. In contrast to their colleagues in the community, hospital

Fig. 18-1. A hospital pharmacist and physician discuss the choice of a patient's prescription drug.

pharmacists are generally most concerned with serving the needs of in-patients at the institution, although some outpatient dispensing may be offered. In the hospital setting, pharmacists may also be responsible for such tasks as bulk compounding, the development and implementation of intravenous admixture programs, and the control of drug use within the institution. (See Fig. 18-1.) The hospital pharmacy often serves as a drug information center for the hospital and in some instances for the entire community. Here pharmacists, generally those who have graduate training, analyze and compile information about drug products, including new drugs that may be available only for investigational use within the hospital.

Pharmacists in the hospital setting often come into contact with members of other health professions. For example, they may work in continuing education programs with physicians and other health workers. They may interact with the nursing staff in monitoring the drug therapy of inpatients and in attempting to minimize medication errors. They work with the medical dietitian, paying particular attention to food-drug interactions that may affect the well-being of the patient. For example, some foods may completely inactivate certain types of drugs, as in the case of the antibiotic-milk combination mentioned previously. In other cases, certain drug-food combinations may produce severe reactions in some patients.

Pharmacists may also be called on to consult in poisoning cases, and the poison prevention centers in many hospitals are staffed by pharmacists. Drug therapy can sometimes change the normal values to be expected from certain laboratory diagnostic procedures, and therefore pharmacists and medical technologists often work closely together. Thus it is apparent that the pharmacist contributes to the well-being of the patient in the hospital in many ways beyond the mere compounding and dispensing of pharmaceuticals.

OTHER CAREER OPPORTUNITIES

Although community and hospital practices employ the largest number of pharmacy graduates, opportunities exist for pharmacists in a variety of other settings. The armed forces need pharmacists for military service, and the United States Public Health Service has opportunities in Indian health programs and federal hospitals. Pharmacists engage in health planning and administration through various federal and state agencies such as the Food and Drug Administration and state boards of pharmacy. Positions are available in the drug industry for pharmacists interested in laboratory work, drug development, and sales. Advanced degrees are generally required for research positions in industry or for teaching positions in the nation's 71 accredited colleges of pharmacy. It is clear that the unique training of the pharmacist provides for great flexibility in career choice on graduation.

STARTING SALARIES

The pharmacy graduate of today commands perhaps the highest starting salary of any bachelor's degree graduate in the country. Positions in community pharmacy are financially rewarding, and especially attractive salaries are available in larger cities. Hospital salaries are somewhat lower, as are those paid for positions in government and industry. Pharmacists with advanced degrees may draw larger salaries.

WOMEN IN PHARMACY

The profession of pharmacy has become increasingly attractive to women. In addition to comprising about 15% of today's practicing pharmacists, over 38% of the pharmacy student population is female. Women make up a majority of students in eight of the nation's schools of pharmacy. Good salaries, flexible hours, and pleasant working conditions probably will continue to attract more women to the field.

MINORITIES IN PHARMACY

Pharmacy is similar to other health professions in that minority groups are greatly underrepresented in the field. Despite active recruitment and retention programs in the pharmacy schools, only 9.4% of total student enrollment is comprised of American students of minority-ethnic heritage. The largest group of minority students are Black Americans, who now comprise 4.2% of the student enrollment. These percentages, although low, represent a substantial increase over the last 10 years.

EDUCATIONAL AND PRACTICAL REQUIREMENTS

The professional program in pharmacy at most schools is 5 years in length, and graduates earn the degree of bachelor of science in pharmacy. A few schools offer the 6-year doctor of pharmacy degree as the first professional degree. The first 2 years of all programs consist of study in the basic sciences. These include general and organic chemistry, biology, anatomy and physiology, physics, and mathematics. These requirements can often be met at community colleges or branch campuses of universities. The last 3 or 4 years must be spent in a college of pharmacy. Areas of study include pharmacognosy (the study of drugs of plant or animal origin), medicinal chemistry (the study of drugs of synthetic origin and the relation of the chemical structure of drug products to their action on the body), pharmacology (the study of the action of drug products on living systems), pharmaceutics (the study of the effect of dosage forms on drug activity), the social and administrative sciences (studies of the social, psychological, public health, and administrative aspects of the practice of pharmacy), and the clinical or professional practice area (the integration of material from the basic sciences and its applications to the practice of pharmacy).

After graduation from an accredited college of pharmacy, the aspiring pharmacist must take a licensing examination administered by the state board of pharmacy. This examination usually requires 3 days and includes theoretical examinations concerning the separate disciplines of the curriculum plus a practical examination. Most states require the completion of 1 year of internship in a pharmacy before the board examination may be taken, although some states now recognize shorter periods of externship under the supervision of a school of pharmacy. After successfully passing the examination, the candidate becomes licensed to practice pharmacy. There is reciprocity concerning licensure in most states. In others, the candidate must be reexamined.

ADVANCED EDUCATION PROGRAMS

Students who wish to pursue graduate studies in pharmacy may choose either professionally oriented or research-oriented programs. Professional graduate degrees include the doctor of pharmacy and the master's degree in hospital pharmacy; both require 2 to 3 years of additional study, mainly in clinical areas. Some programs include residencies that offer practical experience in hospitals. Graduates assume positions of great responsibility in professional settings.

Research degrees at the master's and the doctor's level are offered in each of the pharmaceutical sciences. Doctoral programs require 3 to 5 years of additional study and include a dissertation. They prepare graduates for research positions in industry or for academic positions.

SUMMARY

There is a distinct need for properly educated pharmacists in a variety of positions. Pharmacists in all areas of practice and in every geographical location share the primary responsibility of contributing to the safe and effective use of drugs by all who need them.

Suggested readings

Pharmacists for the future; the report of the Study Commission on Pharmacy, Ann Arbor, Mich., 1975, Health Administration Press.

Smith, M. C., and Knapp, D. A.: Pharmacy, drugs, and medical care, ed. 2, Baltimore, 1976, The Williams & Wilkins Co.

Sonnedecker, G. L.: Kremers and Urdang's history of pharmacy, ed. 4, Philadelphia, 1976, J. B. Lippincott Co.

Professional organization where further information can be obtained

American Pharmaceutical Association
2215 Constitution Ave., N.W.
Washington, D.C. 20037

19

PHYSICAL THERAPY

Frank M. Pierson

Physical therapy is one of several health professions that has been developed and expanded to meet the needs of the citizens of the United States and the world. Physical therapy offers challenges to and provides stimulation for individuals who desire to satisfy societal and personal needs by working with people in a scientifically and medically oriented profession.

The evaluation and treatment of specific patient abilities and disabilities, both mental and physical, are two important functions of the physical therapist. (See Fig. 19-1.) Primary objectives of all treatment programs are to restore the individual to independent function, to maintain normal general health, and to prevent disability. Persons of all ages, economic levels, and cultural backgrounds are treated by the physical therapist in a variety of settings and environments. Treatment programs are developed and implemented on the basis of a knowledge of each patient's condition, the factors that have produced or caused it, and the factors that can correct, improve, or alleviate the problem.

A variety of exercise techniques and specific types of equipment are employed to obtain the results that will most effectively assist the patient. The selection and proper application of the most appropriate treatment procedures and equipment are also the responsibility of the physical therapist, following an evaluation or assessment of specific treatment needs and the identification of treatment goals by the physical therapist.

HISTORICAL REVIEW

The profession of physical therapy was founded during World War I by a group of women who functioned as "reconstruction aides" within the United States Army with the express purpose of promoting the physical restoration of injured service personnel. The first formally or-

158

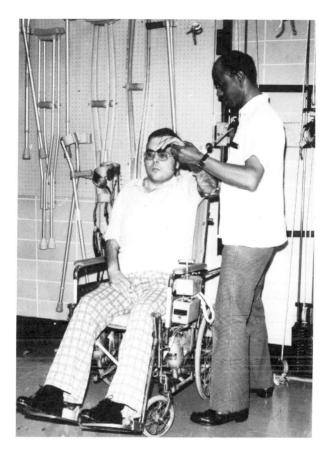

Fig. 19-1. A physical therapist and a man with paralysis resulting from an automobile accident work together to strengthen remaining shoulder function.

ganized physical therapy department was established by the United States Army at Walter Reed Hospital in Washington, D.C., in 1916.

After World War I these women continued to utilize their skills in civilian life, and by 1921 the American Women's Therapeutic Association had been organized. In 1922 the group became known as the American Physiotherapy Association. The present organizational title, the American Physical Therapy Association (APTA), was adopted in 1948.

The APTA maintains a paid and volunteer staff to assist its 27,000 members (all categories) with educational, legislative, public relations, financial, and related activities. There are 53 chapters of the Association located in the United States, the District of Columbia, Puerto Rico, and the Virgin Islands, and most chapters are subdivided into districts. Membership in the APTA is voluntary, and it is the only organization in the United States that directly attempts to protect the general welfare of physical therapists through legislative activities, continuing education programs, professional publications, and support for the economic well-being of its members.

EDUCATIONAL PROGRAMS

Four types of physical therapy educational programs are available: associate degree, baccalaureate degree, certificate, and graduate degree. Regardless of the type of program, each must be located in an accredited college or university and each program must be approved and accredited by the APTA.

The program that terminates in a baccalaureate degree requires 4 years of academic preparation in an institution of higher learning, including 1 to 2 years of preprofessional course work and 2 to 3 years of professionally oriented course work. The preprofessional requirements usually include courses in the basic sciences (mathematics, physics, chemistry, and so forth.), the humanities (English, philosophy, fine arts, and so forth), and the social sciences (psychology, sociology, history, and so forth). The professional courses include study in areas of advanced natural science (physiology and anatomy), specific physical therapy courses, general clinical and medical science courses, and clinical educational experiences.

Certificate programs are available in several institutions, and enrollment is usually limited to students who have previously completed a baccalaureate degree. Prerequisite requirements for admission may include: completion of specific natural and social science course work (chemistry, physics, physiology, anatomy, sociology, and psychology), evidence of satisfactory academic ability, and evidence of participation in some type of health care program. Twelve to 24 months may be required for completion of the academic and clinical phases of the certificate program.

In recent years, several graduate programs have been developed to provide an advanced degree in physical therapy or in allied health (medical) professions. Admission to these programs depends on the fulfillment of specific graduate school requirements and previous completion of a baccalaureate degree or certificate in physical therapy. Students occasionally are admitted as undergraduates, and on completion of an extensive academic and clinical education program, they are granted a graduate degree concurrent with the basic professional degree or certificate. Selection for admission into most physical therapy education curricula is very competitive and only the best qualified candidates are admitted. Early academic planning by the student is necessary to ensure fulfillment of the minimum criteria established for the review of the applicant's qualifications. Because the prerequisite requirements and criteria may differ among programs, requests for additional information about any of these programs should be submitted to the directors of specific programs. A listing of these programs can be obtained from the APTA and is also printed periodically in *Physical Therapy*, which is the official publication of the APTA.

Final entry into the profession is obtained on successful completion of the requirements for state licensure or registration. The primary criterion for licensure in most states is the successful completion of an examination that evaluates the applicant's knowledge in the categories of basic science, clinical science, and physical therapy procedures. If an individual has been licensed or registered in one state it may be possible through the process of endorsement to become licensed or registered in another state with reexamination.

SUPPORTIVE PERSONNEL

The APTA has developed two categories of supportive personnel to assist the physical therapist; these are the physical therapist assistant and the physical therapy aide.

The assistant's education consists of a 2-year educational program in an approved and accredited community, technical, or junior college. The program contains preprofessional and professional course work, some of which may be transferable for credit toward a degree in physical therapy. Completion of the physical therapist assistant program results in the granting of an associate degree. Although the assistant curriculum is not considered to be the most appropriate preparation for a baccalaureate program, it is sometimes possible for the assistant to be admitted to a baccalaureate program.

The assistant is employed to perform specific administrative and patient care activities under the supervision of the physical therapist. Primary evaluation procedures, preparation of entire treatment programs, or total departmental administration are not responsibilities assigned to the assistant. The assistant may be required to become licensed, registered, or certified in order to meet state requirements. The APTA has a membership category for assistants, and they have been granted many rights and privileges within the APTA. A list of existing programs for the physical therapy assistant can be obtained from the APTA and is also printed occasionally in *Physical Therapy*.

The physical therapy aide possesses a high school diploma and receives on-the-job training within the physical therapy department through in-service education programs under the supervision of a qualified physical therapist. The aide functions under the direct supervision of the therapist and is given responsibilities in equipment care and maintenance, supply requisition, housekeeping duties, department and patient preparation for treatment, and minor departmental administrative activities. Aides do not receive any formal recognition by the APTA on completion of the training program and cannot become APTA members. Licensure is not required of the physical therapy aide, but activities of the aide may be regulated by state statutes.

PERSONAL QUALITIES

Since physical therapists work directly with people to perform the majority of their professional activities, those considering the profession as a career should have an inherent desire to assist others. They should be aware of and sensitive to the physical, psychological, social, cultural, and personal needs of those with whom they work. The most effective therapists are people who are able to adjust and adapt to various patient personalities or disabilities while maintaining their own personal emotional stability. The therapist will be required to exhibit appropriate judgment, decision-making skills, common sense, and leadership in many routine and emergency situations. Reliability, dependability, conscientiousness, internal motivation, initiative, and creativity are attributes that enhance the physical therapist's ability to work effectively. (See Fig. 19-2.)

Age, sex, or stature are not limiting factors in the performance of professional activities, provided the individual maintains appropriate standards of physical and mental health. These include strength, endurance, and motor skills appropriate to the performance of sustained vigorous physical activity.

EMPLOYMENT OPPORTUNITIES

Physical therapists are employed in various types of facilities and environments, and the profession is an integral component of the health

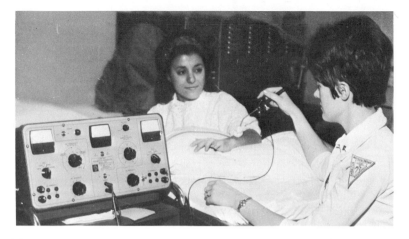

Fig. 19-2. The physical therapist uses electrical stimulation for both evaluation and muscle reeducation.

care delivery system. Many therapists are salaried employees of a hospital, but other employment opportunities include work in clinics, community agencies (for example, the Arthritis Foundation, Easter Seal Societies for Crippled Children and Adults, National Elks Foundation), local and state public health programs, physicians' offices, and federal and state agencies and institutions (including the armed services). The salary range for these positions is usually between $12,000 and $14,000 annually for the recent graduate who requires guidance from an experienced therapist. The experienced staff therapist may earn from $14,000 to $16,000 annually. A supervising therapist may earn from $16,000 to $18,000, and a departmental director may earn from $18,000 to $25,000. These ranges vary according to local economics, the demand for therapists, and similar factors.

Some experienced therapists serve as consultants to nursing homes, rural hospitals, and other types of facilities that offer a limited range of services. Their role may be to provide guidance in developing physical therapy in the facility through the education and training of personnel, or they may provide direct patient care.

It is also possible for the physical therapist to be an independent practitioner and treat clients in an office, in the client's home, or in a skilled nursing facility through the use of a physician's referral. Increased income for the self-employed therapist as compared with that of the salaried therapist is one advantage of this type of practice.

A limited number of therapists are active in sports medicine and serve as athletic trainers for high school, college, or university and professional sports activities. Although there is often a close relationship between physical therapy and athletic training, the two professions are separate and distinct from each other in didactic, clinical, student admission, and licensure or certification requirements. Both professions have an important role to fulfill in the preventive, acute treatment, and rehabilitation aspects of health care.

It is possible for a physical therapist to become certified as an athletic trainer by working with a certified athletic trainer for at least 2 years, either before, during, or after completion of an approved physical therapy educational program. Additional qualifications may be required by the National Athletic Trainers' Association (NATA) for certification as an athletic trainer by that association. However, an athletic trainer cannot become a physical therapist without attending an approved physical therapy education program. There are educational programs available for persons who wish to become athletic trainers without becoming a physical therapist, and information about them and career opportunities in athletic training can be obtained from the NATA.

Physical therapists with graduate degrees and extensive clinical experience are frequently employed as educators with the faculties of the physical therapy and physical therapist assistant programs. The need for teachers has increased recently due to the development of additional programs and an increased student enrollment within many of the existing programs.

Part-time employment is available to the physical therapist, since there is usually a greater demand for the service than can be provided by the available number of full-time therapists. Many therapists who are inactive have been encouraged to return to the profession to help fulfill the need for additional personnel and have been provided with "refresher courses" to update their skills, previous knowledge, and competence.

In 1978 there were approximately 20,000 active members of the APTA and 25,000 qualified physical therapists in the United States. The annual attrition rate due to retirement and other factors is about 20%, whereas the annual number of physical therapy graduates of all programs is approximately 1,900. It has been estimated that a 30% increase in the total number of employed therapists would be required to provide adequate delivery of physical therapy services in the United States.

The role of the physical therapist continues to expand because of the influence of recent revisions in federal health care legislation, the impact of the independent practitioner, and the need to provide the services requested by the consumers of health care services. Physical therapists are now expected to perform more sophisticated evaluative procedures, to use an interdisciplinary approach to improve total patient care, and to assume increased responsibilities for patient treatment, and program planning. They implement the treatment activities and evaluate the treatment results.

PROFESSIONAL CONTRIBUTIONS TO HEALTH CARE

The physical therapist as a member of the health care delivery group must actively participate in the direct and indirect treatment of a wide variety of patient problems. Specific treatment skills include the competent use of therapeutic exercise, massage, communication, and the use of physical agents (heat, cold, water, electricity, and sound). (See Fig. 19-3.) These skills are used to assist the person with musculoskeletal

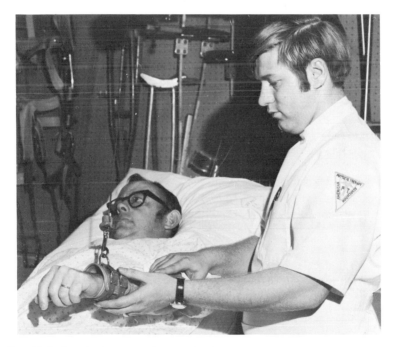

Fig. 19-3. Developing strength, coordination, and endurance of major muscle groups is part of rehabilitation.

(fractures, muscular strains, amputations, arthritis, and so forth), neurological (strokes, paralysis, spinal cord injuries, and so forth), and cardiopulmonary (emphysema, hypertension, asthma, postcardiac disease or surgery) problems as well as many other specific physical limitations. Additional skills required are those involved in the evaluation of patient problems, program development and implementation, general administrative activities, and patient-family education.

The physical therapist not only provides care to those persons who require treatment due to the results of an acute or chronic condition caused by illness, disease or trauma but also provides care to prevent disability or reduced function and to maintain proper health. Thus public and patient education activities and various exercise programs (prenatal and postpartum, cardiopulmonary, postural, and so forth) are frequently organized and directed by the physical therapist in conjunction with a physician's referral.

Therapists are also involved with patient and staff conferences, special clinics, and teaching activities. They have a responsibility to inform other members of the health care team of their professional knowledge of the patient and must be able to correlate the information received from other health professionals to their management of patients. Administratively, the therapist is required to complete various types of patient records, including status notes, attendance data, scheduling and census records, treatment procedures performed, patient data for billing purposes, budget planning, and professional care audit.

The following hypothetical case study has been designed to illustrate some of the responsibilities and activities in which the physical therapist engages while providing direct patient care.

J. D., a 20-year-old man, was admitted to the hospital following a motorcycle accident that caused irreparable damage to his spinal cord. This produced loss of motor and sensory function to the muscles, organs, and tissues below the level of his waist.

Two weeks after admission the physical therapist received a physician referral that requested an evaluation of J. D. and the development of a program to improve his functional independence.

Initial physical therapy treatments were performed in J. D.'s room and were designed to promote range of motion of the joints in his legs and hips and to strengthen the muscles of his arms and shoulders. Proper bed positioning and a schedule for turning were instituted with assistance from the nursing service to avoid muscular contractures and skin breakdown.

When he was able to be moved from his room, J. D. was treated in the rehabilitation unit of the physical therapy department. Arm strengthening activities were continued, while activities to develop sitting balance and wheelchair mobility were initiated. He was taught to protect his skin below the level of the spinal cord lesion from injury and pressure to avoid skin breakdown.

J. D. was eventually fitted with temporary leg splints to provide knee stability so that he could attempt standing and minimal ambulation exercises in the parallel bars. He also received additional instructions in wheelchair mobility skills that improved his independence.

The occupational therapist instructed J. D. in adapted techniques of dressing and personal hygiene. He was also evaluated for his manual dexterity and manipulative skills in preparation for educational and vocational counseling.

Through the combined efforts of the occupational therapist, physical therapist, and driving instructor, J. D. was taught how to transfer from his wheelchair into the car, place his wheelchair in the car, and drive with special hand controls to operate the brake and accelerator.

He became interested in wheelchair athletics and participated in basketball, track and field events, ping pong, archery, and swimming. He not only gained pleasure from these recreational activities but also improved his wheelchair skills, increased his endurance for physical activity, and gained a new self-confidence in his ability to interact with others.

At the time J. D. was discharged from the hospital, he was independent in all normal activities of feeding, dressing, personal hygiene, wheelchair mobility, and transfers. He was well aware of his physical abilities and was preparing to return to college.

SUMMARY

The primary activities of the physical therapist are those associated with direct patient care of persons of all ages (neonates to the elderly). The basic components of patient care for which the therapist is responsible are evaluation or assessment of the patient's functional capacities, development of objectives of treatment, program planning based on the predetermined objectives, implementation of the treatment program, and periodic reevaluation of the patient's functional capacities. The physical therapist must be able to work with the patient and the family to plan a program that will restore the patient to the highest possible level of independent functioning within the limits imposed by the patient's disability, whether it is the result of disease, trauma, or congenital factors. In addition to specific physical needs, concern is also given to the patient's social, economic, vocational, educational, and recreational needs.

The physical therapist works in cooperation with other health professionals, including nurses, occupational therapists, social workers, respiratory technologists, medical dietitians, and speech therapists. Guidance in the development of treatment programs is obtained from a licensed physician or dentist through written referrals or prescriptions and personal consultations.

Suggested readings

American Medical Association Council on Medical Education: Allied medical education directory, Chicago, 1974, American Medical Association.

Handbook for physical therapy teachers, Washington, D.C., 1967, American Physical Therapy Association.

Krumhansl, B.: Opportunities in physical therapy, Louisville, Ky., 1974, Vocational Guidance Manuals, Inc.

Physical Therapy, journal of the American Physical Therapy Association (published monthly).

Professional organizations where further information can be obtained

American Physical Therapy Association
1156 Fifteenth St., N.W.
Washington, D.C. 20005

National Athletic Trainers Association
P.O. Drawer 1865
Greenville, N.C. 27834

20

PHYSICIAN ASSISTANT

Martha Wilson Arrington

The physician assistant is medicine's newest and most challenging health care profession. The term "physician assistant" refers to the health practitioner qualified by academic and clinical training to perform, under the direction and supervision of a licensed physician, tasks ordinarily reserved for a physician. The physician assistant is trained to extend the physician's capabilities in the diagnostic and therapeutic management of patients while functioning within the parameters of the law.

Although the concept of assistants to physicians is not new, it was not until 1965 that formalized education and deployment of such health providers emerged in the United States. Dr. Eugene Stead at Duke University in Durham, North Carolina, is considered the father of the physician assistant concept. It was his belief that much of the service provided by primary care physicians could be rendered by persons less extensively educated in the biomedical sciences. The large numbers of former military corpsmen at that time provided an ideal source of students for the early physician assistant classes.

The physician assistant concept is unique in that it was conceived by and for physicians. The role of this new member of the health care team is to relieve the physician of the routine duties not requiring that level of expertise. Delegated tasks included patient histories, physical examinations, diagnostic and therapeutic procedures, follow-up care, and patient teaching and counseling. The physician assistant may be found in all types of medical settings, although the majority work in solo or group practices, hospitals, clinics, or extended care facilities such as nursing homes. Further, studies show most of these health practitioners deliver primary care under the supervision of family practitioners, pediatricians, or internists. They work predominately in rural and urban medically underserved areas.

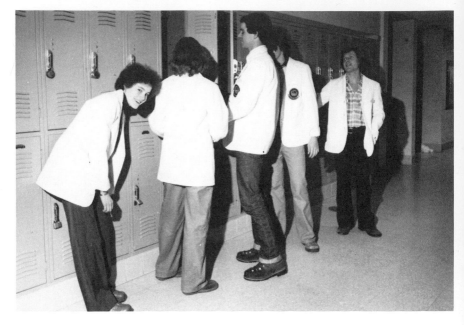

Fig. 20-1. Students gather before class.

Within 5 years after the establishment of the first physician assistant program at Duke University, 14 programs were offering training for the assistant to the primary care physician. Today approximately 60 programs exist for the physician assistant. They carry such titles as Child Health Associate, Community Health Medic, Family Nurse Practitioner, MEDEX,* Physician Assistant, Physician Associate, and Surgeon's Assistants. These programs are found in medical school, junior college, and public health and allied health school settings. (See Fig. 20-1.)

To ensure these educational programs met minimal standards of quality, the American Medical Association in collaboration with six other major medical associations, including the American Academy of Physician Assistants, developed and adopted the Essentials of an

---

*"Medex" is derived from the French term *"medicin extension,"* meaning physician's extension. Reference is made to the training program when the word appears in capital letters; lowercase letters refer to the student or certified assistant.

Accredited Educational Program for both the assistant to the primary care physician and the surgeon's assistant. These standards are used as a guide for the development and self-evaluation of physician assistant programs. More than 50 such programs are now accredited through a review process conducted by representatives of six medical specialty organizations.

EDUCATION

Each year nearly 1,500 students enroll in physician assistant programs throughout the country. Although admission requirements vary among the programs, generally a high school diploma or its equivalent (GED), a minimum of 2 years college course work and/or related health experience, scores from ACT or SAT examinations, and three character references are requisite. Competition for the available seats in physician assistant program classes is keen. Recent studies have shown that entering students typically have a baccalaureate degree plus 2 to 5 years of patient or other health care experience.

Physician assistant programs average 24 months in length. The first 9 months of the program are usually devoted to preclinical subjects and study of the basic sciences. Included in this portion of the curriculum are such subjects as anatomy, physiology, microbiology, pharmacology, and medical ethics. The second phase of instruction is a clinical practicum comprised of structured clinical learning experiences in medical specialities ranging from general and internal medicine to surgery and psychiatry. On completion of the program the physician assistant may be awarded a certificate or an associate, baccalaureate, or master's degree, depending on the policy of the institution and the qualifications of the student.

CERTIFICATION

In December 1973, the National Board of Medical Examiners administered the first tests for national certification of physician assistants. Graduates of accredited physician assistant programs as well as those informally trained physician assistants who qualify may take the national certification examination. In 1974 the National Commission on Certification of Physician Assistants was organized and assumed the responsibility for certifying physician assistants. The certification examination is given in the fall of each year and includes written and physical assessment sections. After passing the national certifying examination, the physician assistant must earn 100 hours of approved continuing medical education credit every 2 years to reregister the certificate and must be recertified by reexamination every 6 years. In this manner the physician, patient, and general public are assured of the competency of these midlevel providers of health care.

The physician assistant profession has enjoyed widespread acceptance as a member of the health care team since its beginning. Forty-five states have now enacted enabling legislation for these health professionals (the remaining five states are currently considering such legislation), and more than 12 states have extended limited prescribing authority to physician assistants.

The outlook for the profession is bright since physician assistants have proved to be accessible and cost effective providers of health care. It is projected that the demand for these health professionals will continue to increase as they assume a vital role in the health delivery system.

Suggested readings

National health practitioner program profile, Arlington, Va., 1978, Association of Physician Assistant Programs.

Sadler, A. M., Sadler, B. L., and Bliss, A. A.: The physician assistant today and tomorrow, Cambridge, Mass., 1975, Ballinger Publishing Co.

Professional organizations where further information may be obtained

American Academy of Physician Assistants
Suite 700
2341 Jefferson Davis Highway
Arlington, Va. 22202
Association of Physician Assistant Programs
Suite 700
2341 Jefferson Davis Highway
Arlington, Va. 22202

National Commission on Certification of Physician Assistants
Suite 560
3384 Peachtree Rd., N.E.
Atlanta, Ga. 30326

21

PODIATRY

William F. Munsey

Podiatry is the health science profession dealing with the examination, diagnosis, treatment, prevention, and care of conditions and functions of the human foot. This care is realized through the utilization of medical, surgical, mechanical, or physical means.

HISTORY OF THE PROFESSION

The profession of podiatric medicine is one of the oldest medical arts. Perhaps the earliest podiatric care began with cavemen who wrapped their feet with animal skins as protection from the elements and rough ground. There is also evidence of rudimentary foot care in ancient times, especially in ancient Egypt. The first recorded references to foot problems were made by the Greeks in the fourth century BC. The modern specialty of podiatric medicine, however, can trace its beginnings to medieval times when the guilds of barber-surgeons—itinerant practitioners of primitive surgery, dentistry, and other pseudoscientific procedures—attempted to work their "skills" for beautification as well as healing.

Gradually podiatric medicine underwent its metamorphosis, and today it is a profession that forms a separate, distinct, and complementary division of the healing arts.

The term "chiropodist" was introduced in England in 1774. It was coined by David Low, who had authored a book entitled *Chiropodologia*. The word originates from the Latin *chirugen,* or surgeon, and *pod,* or foot; thus a chiropodist was a surgeon of the foot. In 1917 the profession adopted the term "podiatrist," and both chiropody and podiatry were used interchangeably until World War II. Today, podiatry is the accepted term.

Among the earliest foot specialists in the United States were Julius Davidson, who opened an office in Philadelphia in 1841, and Dr.

Nehemiah Kenison, who started in Boston in 1846 and soon had branch offices in many eastern cities.

At the time of the Civil War, Dr. Isacher Zacharie wrote the first text on chiropody published in the United States. As President Lincoln's personal chiropodist, Dr. Zacharie served on several occasions as an emissary for the President, who is reputed to have recommended him for the commission "Chiropodist-General of the United States Army."

The maturation of the profession begin in earnest in 1911 with the establishment of the first school of podiatry in New York City. One year later the National Association of Chiropodists was established. In 1912 the Illinois College of Chiropody and Orthopedics began offering a course in surgical chiropody and mechanical foot orthopedics. In 1916 the Ohio College of Chiropody began training foot specialists.

The national professional organization is now called the American Podiatry Association (APA). There are now five colleges of podiatric medicine in the United States accredited by the Council on Podiatry Education of the APA and recognized by the United States Office of Education and the National Commission on Accrediting. The newest college began accepting students in the fall of 1975.

CAREERS IN PODIATRY

Of the approximately 8,500 podiatrists in the United States, nearly 85% are engaged in private practice. Although podiatrists have traditionally been engaged in solo practice, the trend is now changing and group practices are more common.

The average podiatrist practices the full scope of the profession, ranging from the routine care of chronic problems such as corns, calluses, warts, ingrown toenails, and injuries, to extensive foot surgery. (See Fig. 21-1.)

In addition to private practice, podiatrists serve on the staffs of nursing homes, hospitals, and extended care facilities accredited by the Joint Commission on Accreditation of Hospitals and the American Osteopathic Association. Podiatrists also serve on the faculties of the colleges of podiatric medicine, medical schools and nursing schools, in the Armed Forces, and in municipal health departments.

Podiatrists are often the first to diagnose systemic diseases, including arthritis, heart disease, kidney ailments, and arteriosclerosis. Whenever such symptoms are detected, the foot specialist consults with the patient's medical doctor concerning continuing treatment.

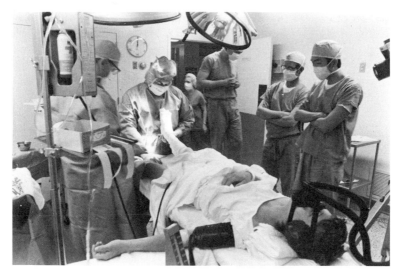

Fig. 21-1. The podiatrist inspects dressings following completion of foot surgery. (Courtesy American Podiatry Association, Washington, D.C.)

PERSONAL QUALITIES

Podiatry offers a rewarding career for both men and women who sincerely care for people and wish to devote their lives to the relief of human suffering. It is also a unique profession in that the majority of patients seen daily leave the office with immediate relief from the symptoms with which they entered.

It is also an uncrowded profession, with approximately 3.4 podiatrists for every 100,000 population, a figure that falls far short of providing services to the millions of people who have some type of foot disorder.

Recent surveys indicate that most podiatrists practice by appointment, working 48 to 50 weeks per year. The average net income after 3 years of practice is in excess of $42,000 annually.

EDUCATIONAL PREPARATION

Published minimum standards for admission to a college of podiatric medicine are 60 semester hours or 90 quarter hours of accredited undergraduate study. More than 90% of the students in professional training, however, have baccalaureate degrees at the time of entrance. The remainder of the successful candidates have 3 or more years of accredited college work.

Each applicant's preprofessional college credits must include a 1-year course or the equivalent in each of the following subjects: English, general chemistry, and general biology or zoology, and one semester of organic chemistry and physics. These standards are nearly universal at all colleges of podiatric medicine, but it would be well to inquire at a specific college for complete requirements. In addition, a satisfactory score on the New Medical Colleges Admission Test is a preadmission requirement.

The professional training, a 4-year course, is very similar to that of a medical college. Students in their junior and senior years receive extensive clinical training. Graduates are awarded the degree of doctor of podiatric medicine, and may apply for residency programs that are 1, 2, or 3 years in length. As a general rule, the first-year residency is a general program, and the 2- and 3-year programs specialize in foot surgery. These programs are conducted at the colleges of podiatric medicine and in Joint Commission–accredited hospitals, as well as in those accredited by the American Osteopathic Association.

Graduates are required to take a state board examination in order to practice in a particular state. The profession also has a National Podiatry Board examination that is accepted in many states.

SUPPORTING PERSONNEL

Podiatry assistants play an important role, and there are several formal training programs. Addresses may be obtained from the organization listed below.

SUMMARY

Podiatry is a relatively new profession that has rapidly earned the acceptance of the general public and the other health professions. Current podiatry education is comparable to training offered in other schools for health professionals, and the field today offers unique opportunities for its practitioners, including women and members of all ethnic groups.

References

Approved podiatric residency programs 1974-75, Washington, D.C., 1974, Council on Podiatry Education, American Podiatry Association.

Characteristics of patients treated by podiatrists, D.H.E.W. Publication No. (HRA) 751809, Rockville, Md., 1974, U.S. Department of Health, Education, and Welfare,

Public Health Service, Health Resources Administration, National Center for Health Statistics.

Podiatry manpower; characteristics of clinical practice, United States, 1970, Rockville, Md., 1973, U.S. Department of Health, Education, and Welfare, Public Health Service, Health Resources Administration.

Suggested readings

Feinberg, H.: Podiatric medicine; professional profile, J. Am. Opt. Assoc. **41:**454, 1970.

Shangold, J., and Greenberg, F.: Opportunities in a podiatry career, New York, 1971, Universal Publishing and Distributing Co.

Professional organization where further information can be obtained

American Association of Colleges of
Podiatric Medicine
20 Chevy Chase Circle, N.W.
Washington, D.C. 20015

22

RADIOLOGIC TECHNOLOGY

Philip W. Ballinger and J. Robert Bullock

Almost every patient admitted to a hospital requires some type of x-ray examination. This service may vary from a routine chest film to an elaborate study of one of the body systems that involves tremendously complicated and expensive equipment. Whether the examination is simple or complex, the final results represent the combined efforts of the radiologist (a physician whose specialty is the use of x-rays and other radiation in diagnosis and treatment) and a radiologic technologist.

DEVELOPMENT OF THE PROFESSION

Few events have had as great an impact on the medical world as the discovery of x-rays in 1895. Physicians immediately realized the potential of this new energy that would allow them to see inside the patient. Therefore those with the necessary mechanical and technical abilities worked with physicists and other scientists, and within a year significant x-ray studies were being performed on patients.

The first radiographs (x-ray photographs) resulted from the combined efforts of physicians and physicists. At this stage the physicists operated crude x-ray generating equipment while the physician positioned the patient and evaluated the image on the finished glass plate. Soon x-ray equipment was being manufactured commercially, and more refined equipment became available.

As the practices of radiologists began to expand, they developed an increasing need for competent people who could assume responsibility for much of the technical work involved in performing radiographic studies, allowing the radiologist to focus his efforts on the interpretation of films and other professional duties that must be performed by a physician.

While physicians were developing the field of radiology as a medical specialty, x-ray technicians were being trained in the technical as-

178

pects of obtaining a radiograph. The introduction of radioactivity and the increased sophistication of therapeutic and diagnostic procedures required expanded educational programs. Through more demanding educational requirements and added responsibilities, these technical people were accumulating the knowledge and skills that distinguish today's radiologic technologists.

Since its inception, the field of radiology has developed with remarkable rapidity. This progress has resulted from the development of new techniques by clinicians, mechanical and electronic contributions by the x-ray industry, and the continuing development and refinement of radiopaque contrast materials by the pharmaceutical industry.

The radiologist of the 1920s and 1930s studied images on a fluoroscopic screen—images so dim they could be seen only in a room that was totally dark. By the late 1950s, image intensifiers capable of increasing the brightness of the fluoroscopic image 6,000 times had become available. This image intensifier now permits the use of television, motion picture cameras, and videotape to transmit or record studies of organs where motion is involved. This system can demonstrate the valves and blood vessels of the heart with great clarity, and it can also be used to great advantage for the more traditional studies of the gastrointestinal tract.

In certain respects the radiologic technologist is a representative of, as well as an assistant to, the radiologist. Radiologic examinations may be divided into two general categories: those performed by a radiologist because medical judgments are involved in the performance of the study and those in which the technologist produces radiographs that are later interpreted by a radiologist. In the latter case the patient will frequently be seen only by the technologist. This situation is particularly common in rural or small community hospitals where a radiologist may consult only on a part-time basis. Under these circumstances technologists must function with greater independence, judgment, and responsibility because they are often the only members of the health care team with any expertise in the field.

DIAGNOSTIC RADIOLOGY

When a patient is directed to the radiology department for a diagnostic study, the patient is greeted by the technologist, who prepares him for the examination. Preparation usually includes an explanation of the procedure to allay the patient's anxiety and elicit cooperation.

In order to obtain a radiograph, technologists must position the patient precisely to project the desired anatomical structures onto the film. To accomplish this they must relate external body landmarks to internal structures. (See Fig. 22-1.) The technologist must evaluate the patient's weight, age, and physical condition in order to select the proper x-ray exposure values. The film will then be exposed and sent to the darkroom to be processed by personnel under the technologist's supervision. Finished films are prepared for the radiologist's interpretation, and reports are given to the patient's attending physician.

Radiologic technologists are responsible for patients during their stay in the radiology department, and some patients require considerable supportive care. In addition to working directly with patients, technologists must supervise the maintenance of equipment to ensure dependable function, test new products, and maintain an appropriate inventory of expendable supplies. In some institutions they may be called on to participate in developing new techniques to assist in research programs.

Radiologic technology can be thought of as an art, and in this respect it can be highly rewarding. A well-composed and properly exposed radiograph that clearly reveals the anatomy in question can ap-

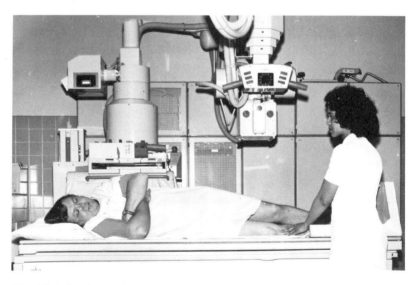

Fig. 22-1. Precise positioning of the patient is essential to project the desired anatomical structure on the radiograph or x-ray film.

propriately be compared to an example of any of the graphic arts. In addition, technologists have the satisfaction of knowing that the information revealed will be essential to the patient's care and treatment. Personal satisfaction is also derived from performing difficult radiographic studies without causing additional discomfort to a patient who is already in pain. Radiographic examinations may range from relatively routine films to those urgently required in the emergency room or during surgery. In some cases, portable radiographic equipment is taken to the patient whose condition does not allow him to be moved to the radiology department.

The following case study illustrates the radiologic technologist's role in the care of one patient.

Mrs. H. fell down the front steps of her home and was taken to the hospital emergency room, where she was examined by her physician. He detected a probable hip injury and directed a request for a hip study to the radiology department. Mrs. H. was taken to an x-ray room and carefully moved onto the radiographic table.

The technologist placed film in a tray under the radiographic table and moved the x-ray tube above the patient, centering it over her injured hip. The technologist was careful not to cause her further injury. After the initial exposure was made, the technologist moved the equipment so that a second projection could be made without moving the patient and risking additional pain and injury. Special devices were required to hold the second film at the patient's side, with the x-ray tube placed at right angles to the hip joint. Care was taken to move only the uninjured leg so that the injured area remained stationary. After the films were processed, the physician interpreted them and confirmed that Mrs. H's hip was fractured. Her physician informed her of the diagnosis; she was admitted to the orthopedic service and scheduled for surgery.

Immediately before the surgical repair of Mrs. H's hip was begun, the radiologic technologist joined the other members of the surgical team in the operating room to take preliminary films. The information provided by these radiographs permitted the surgeon to correctly adjust the injured hip and initiate surgery. When the incision revealed bony structure, the surgeon placed a guide wire into the fractured hip and the technologist took additional films. When the films indicated that the wire was satisfactorily located and did not require additional manipulation, the surgeon attached the repair device to the fractured hip by sliding it over the guide wire. After the permanent pin or plate was installed, the guide wire was removed and another series of radiographs were taken. When the films showed satisfactory placement, the surgeon closed the incision. Mrs. H was kept under close observation immediately following surgery and subsequent films were taken to monitor her recovery.

THERAPEUTIC RADIOLOGY

The therapeutic application of x-rays parallels the development of diagnostic radiology. The first therapeutic use of x-rays was reported in 1896. Since that time there has been an increased understanding of radiobiology and continuous development of higher energy generators and radioactive treatment sources with different and more effective modalities.

Technologists in radiotherapy work under the direction of a radiologist. They assist in checking calculations involving the treatment and position the patient so that the radiation source and the area to be irradiated are in proper alignment. They regulate the controls of the radiation source to deliver the exact amount of radiation to be administered and observe the patient continually during the treatment period either through a television monitoring system or directly through lead glass windows. Technologists also assist the physician in regular examinations of patients to chart their progress. Assisting the radiologist in planning treatment programs is an interesting and challenging part of their activities. Many technologists prefer to work in therapeutic radiology because the longer association with a patient provides opportunities for technologists to see the results of their contributions to patient care.

NUCLEAR MEDICINE

Nuclear medicine is a product of the atomic age. In this medical specialty, radionuclides (radioactive pharmaceuticals) are administered to the patient, whose body is then scanned with a device that detects radiation emitted from organs or areas where the nuclide may have collected. An imaging device records the patterns of radioactivity on a film that the physician can use to diagnose tumors or other disease entities. In addition, tests of various biochemical and physiological functions are performed. Because the nuclides that are used are active for only a limited time, patients commonly experience no ill aftereffects.

Nuclear medicine technologists may prepare the selected nuclide and administer it to a patient under the direction of a physician. They also operate the imaging device and produce the resultant scan film. People with a special interest in physics who enjoy precise laboratory work and complex instrumentation find this aspect of radiology especially attractive.

RELATED IMAGING MODALITIES

Recent technological advances have made possible the development of sophisticated equipment that allows more accurate diagnosis with less patient discomfort and risk. Much of the specialized equipment is operated by radiologic technologists because they have both a knowledge of the physical principles involved and the essential skills in identifying recorded anatomic images. These new modalities include diagnostic medical sonography (also called ultrasound), computerized tomography (CT), and thermography.

Diagnostic medical sonography is similar to sonor (*so*und *n*avigation *a*nd *r*anging) used for marine navigation. In this procedure high-frequency sound waves are directed into the patient by a device called a "transducer." This instrument also detects the "echos" that are reflected back from organs and other anatomic structures. The echos are converted to electrical impulses, which in turn produce an image (of the anatomy) on a tube much like a television picture. (See Fig. 22-2.) This image is studied for diagnostic purposes. The quality of the image is totally dependent on the technologists' knowledge of anatomy and their skill in manipulating the transducer. A major advantage of sonography is that no significant undesirable biological effects have been identified. Sonography is most useful in evaluating abdominal, cardiac, and obstetrical conditions.

The first CT scanner, which was introduced in 1972, combined a computer and a specialized x-ray machine. Conventional radiography is based on the fact that the x-rays that pass through a patient make an image on film. With the CT system, the x-rays create a signal in electronic detectors. These signals are evaluated and stored by a computer. This information can be recalled to appear as an image on a television monitor. Because these images can be electronically manipulated, images that would normally be obscure can be enhanced to improve clarity. Today, CT scanners make possible accurate diagnosis of many abnormalities in the chest and abdomen. This technique is particularly valuable in revealing pathology in the skull and brain.

Thermography, as the name implies, produces an image based on heat emitted from the body. After the patient is prepared for the procedure, a sensing device receives infrared rays emitted from his skin and produces a photograph of the patient in which areas of increased skin temperature appear lighter than the surrounding tissue. (An increase in the normal blood supply, such as a tumor might produce, causes an increased temperature in the affected area.) Thermography is a totally safe procedure for the patient and is useful in screening patients for breast cancer as well as detecting blood vessel abnormalities and other disease processes.

Of the three related modalities, only medical sonography has an es-

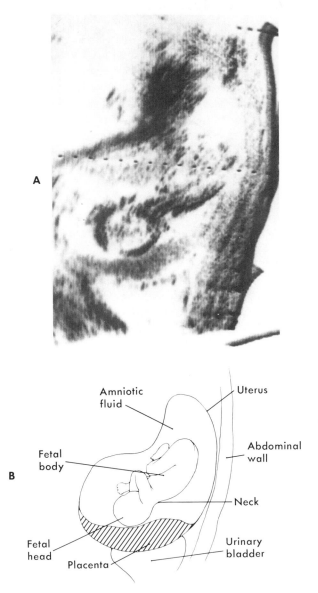

Fig. 22-2. A, Sonograph or ultrasound scan of a developing fetus in utero. **B,** An artist's line drawing of **A.**

tablished professional certifying organization (the American Registry of Diagnostic Medical Sonographers) and has identified 1-year educational programs. Registered radiologic technologists as well as other allied health professionals are admitted to these programs. CT scanning is an area of specialization in diagnostic radiology. Because the equipment is highly sophisticated, well-qualified registered radiologic technologists are selected for the advanced instruction necessary to perform these procedures. Thermography equipment is often operated by radiologic technologists but is operated by other allied health professionals as well. Instructional courses will certainly be established as the field of thermography achieves wider use in patient diagnosis.

EDUCATIONAL PREPARATION

The American Association of Radiological Technicians, the first professional organization for allied health personnel in radiology, was founded in 1920. This organization whose official title is now the American Society of Radiologic Technologists (ASRT), has worked continuously to develop and improve curriculums in schools of radiologic technology. The American Registry of Radiologic Technologists (ARRT), sponsored by the American College of Radiology and the ASRT, examines and certifies graduate technologists. Successful candidates earn the title of registered technologist and use the abbreviation RT following their names. As the field of radiology continued to expand, the ARRT recognized the need for additional education and certification for radiation therapy and nuclear medicine technologists.

Today there are well over 1,000 AMA-approved programs in diagnostic radiography, and approximately 100 each in the specialties of radiation therapy and nuclear medicine technology in the United States. Although there is an increasing trend toward 2-year associate degree and 4-year baccalaureate programs, the majority of schools are hospital-based certificate programs. The objective of most baccalaureate programs is to produce technically competent professionals with the additional preparation needed to assume administrative or teaching positions. All AMA-approved programs include didactic instruction in conjunction with extensive clinical instruction. The total length of an educational program must be at least 24 months, and graduates of all AMA-approved programs are eligible to apply for certification by the ARRT. To qualify for admission to a diagnostic radiologic technology program, one must be a high school graduate with preparation in mathematics and science.

Schools following the curriculum suggested by the ASRT offer courses in the following areas:

Radiation protection
Radiologic physics
Anatomy and physiology
Principles of radiographic exposure
Radiation biology
Radiographic processing technique
Radiographic film evaluation
Pathology
Orientation to the operating room
Nursing procedures
Standard and special radiographic procedures
Medical ethics
Medical terminology

Candidates for admission to programs that offer instruction in radiation therapy technology may be either graduates of approved schools of radiologic technology or registered nurses who have successfully completed a course in radiation physics. Students who are accepted into these programs spend a minimum of 12 months to become eligible to take a registry examination in radiation therapy technology. Some radiation therapy programs offer 2 years of concentrated studies. Applicants must be high school graduates. Those who achieve satisfactory scores on the registry examination become registered radiation therapy technologists.

Accredited schools of nuclear medicine technology consider candidates who are registered medical laboratory technologists, registered radiologic technologists, registered nurses, or individuals with a baccalaureate degree from an accredited college with a major in the biological or physical sciences. On completion of the 1-year program of combined instruction and clinical experience, graduates are eligible to apply for the registry examination in nuclear medicine technology.

Technologists who have earned certification following a minimum of 24 months of education but who do not have professional work experience will find that starting salaries vary according to geographical area, size of the community, and availability of registered technologists. Radiologic technologists' salaries in general are comparable to those offered to similarly educated allied health professionals.

SUMMARY

Approved schools graduate approximately 7,000 students each year, but far greater numbers are needed to supply technologists for the more than 7,000 hospitals, 5,000 clinics, and several thousand laboratories in private offices. Opportunities exist in rural areas as well as in urban centers.

Those considering careers in radiologic technology must have compassion for the sick and injured. Emotional maturity is essential if the technologist is to work effectively in the hospital environment.

Reference

Grigg, E. R. N.: The trail of the invisible light, Springfield, Ill., 1965, Charles C Thomas, Publisher.

Suggested readings

Allied health educational directory, Monroe, Wis., 1978, American Medical Association.
The challenge—radiologic technology. The future—yours, New York, 1968, E. R. Squibb & Sons, Inc.
Donizetti, P.: Shadow and substance, Elmsford, N.W., 1967, Pergamon Press, Inc.
Grigg, E. R. N.: The new history of radiology, Radiol. Technol. **36:**229, 1965.
Horizons unlimited, ed. 8, Chicago, 1970, American Medical Association
Roth, C. J., and Weimer, L.: Hospital health services, New York, 1964, Henry Z. Walck, Inc.
X-rays and you, Rochester, N. Y. 1965, Eastman Kodak Co.

Professional organizations where further information can be obtained

American Registry of Diagnostic Medical Sonographers
Division of Cardiology
Children's Hospital
Cincinnati, Ohio 45229
American Society of Radiologic Technologists
Suite 1820
55 E. Jackson Blvd.
Chicago, Ill. 60604

American Registry of Radiologic Technologists
2600 Wayzata Blvd.
Minneapolis, Minn. 55405

23

RESPIRATORY THERAPY

F. Herbert Douce

The field of respiratory therapy exemplifies the accelerated growth and development of the allied health professions. Respiratory therapy procedures are most often prescribed for patients with disorders of the cardiopulmonary system, such as pneumonia, asthma, or heart failure. It is because of the growing incidence of these disorders that respiratory therapists are being called on to expand their numbers and services.

Although most commonly practiced in the general acute-care hospital, respiratory therapy is also practiced in outpatient clinics, extended care facilities, and patients' homes. Respiratory therapy is both a diagnostic and therapeutic specialty using specialized equipment and technological procedures. Services benefit patients of all age groups, from the prematurely born to the elderly. (See Fig. 23-1.) In the hospital setting, respiratory therapy services have no geographical boundaries. Some service is often rendered on every patient unit and is commonly required by critical patients in the intensive care units. Most respiratory therapy departments provide valuable services 24 hours a day, 7 days a week.

The continuing development of the profession has created significant variability in the levels of practice from one hospital to another. In general, the practice of respiratory therapy includes the administration of oxygen and oxygen mixtures by various devices and appliances, the application of mechanical ventilators to assist or control breathing, the maintenance of clear airways by humidification, suction or physical manipulation, the administration of drugs by inhalation, the assistance with cardiopulmonary resuscitation (Fig. 23-2), the monitoring of heart and lung function of critically ill patients in the intensive care unit, the evaluation of patients in the pulmonary laboratory, and the education of patients in the rehabilitation clinic. In some hospitals, the respiratory therapist's role extends beyond this scope; transporting the critically ill

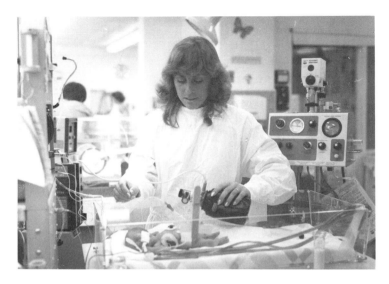

Fig. 23-1. The therapist prepares to manually ventilate an infant who was born with immature lungs.

to the hospital or providing extracorporeal oxygenation are such examples. Some common respiratory therapy activities are discussed in detail later in the chapter.

PROFESSIONAL HISTORY AND DEVELOPMENT

Although the biblical prophet Elisha possibly used mouth-to-mouth resuscitation in reviving the widow's son (II Kings 4:34), and Dr. Thomas Beddoes initiated the use of therapeutic gases at eighteenth century England's Pneumatic Institute, the development of an entire profession dedicated to the prevention and treatment of respiratory disorders was not actually begun until a meeting in Chicago during the mid 1940s. Following the development of the clinical use of oxygen and inhalation pressures between 1926 and 1946, a group of interested physicians and oxygen technicians from Chicago organized a series of meetings to discuss these therapeutic modalities and methods of improving the care of patients requiring the administration of medical gases. One outcome of this series of meetings was the formation of the Inhalational Therapy Association (ITA) in 1947 and the formal birth of a new profession.

From the onset, the pace of professional growth and development

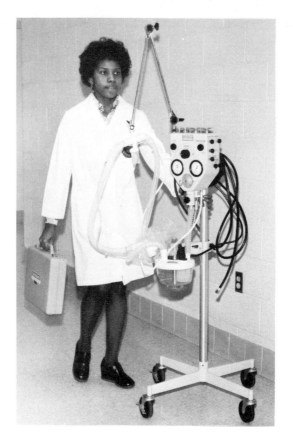

Fig. 23-2. The respiratory therapist responds promptly to assist with cardiopulmonary resuscitation (CPR).

has been rapid. Following a name change in 1948, the new Inhalation Therapy Association began to publish a quarterly newsletter in 1950. Thirty-one certificates were awarded for participation in the annual series of educational meetings that year. In 1953, the American College of Chest Physicians (ACCP) became an official sponsor of the ITA, signaling the commencement of the profession's close relationships with physician groups. The American Society of Anesthesiologists (ASA) and the American Thoracic Society (ATS) subsequently became early sponsors. By 1954, the scope of the profession had broadened and had become nationwide. Many practitioners who were once termed "oxygen technicians" were commonly referred to as "inhalation therapists." The ITA responded by initiating state and local chapters and by changing its name to the American Association of Inhalation Therapists (AAIT).

Minimum standards for schools of inhalation therapy were proposed to the American Medical Association in 1957, and the first school enrolled its first student that year. The initial curricula were of 1-year duration. *Essentials,* the word implying minimum standards and the title of the document published by the American Medical Association, were later approved by the AMA and adopted for inhalation therapists in 1962.

A second organization, the American Registry of Inhalation Therapists (ARIT), was incorporated in 1960. One purpose of the ARIT was to establish standards of competency and to evaluate the understanding and competency of therapists on a voluntary basis. This beginning of professional credentialling registered 12 examinees in 1961. The critical need for qualified entry-level personnel led to the formation of a second credentialing body under the auspices of the AAIT. The technician-level credential and the curricular guidelines that could be used to initiate technician level training programs were adopted by the AAIT in 1969.

Respiratory therapy entered the 1970s with the major constituents of a profession, but the young and vigorous profession did not stop changing and developing. The names of the association, the practitioners, and the hospital departments changed during the early 1970s to encompass exhalation as well as inhalation. The American Association for Respiratory Therapy (AART) adopted its new name in 1972, and today nearly all practitioners and services have adopted "respiratory" in their titles. The journal has assumed a scientific orientation and has published monthly since 1972. *Essentials* for technician-level training programs were adopted by the AMA in 1972 when the therapist *Essentials* were revised, increasing the minimum program length to 18 months. A new organization, the National Board for Respiratory Therapy (NBRT), incorporated both the therapist and the technician credentialing systems in 1975. The medical sponsors now include American Academy of Pediatrics and the American College of Allergists as well as the original groups.

Today, there are over 50,000 respiratory therapy practitioners of which approximately 5,000 are Registered Respiratory Therapists (RRT), and 15,000 are Certified Respiratory Therapy Technicians (CRTT). In 1978, over 5,000 persons attended the annual educational meeting and exhibition. From a series of local meetings in Chicago 30 years ago, respiratory therapy has become a vigorous allied health profession, and the respiratory therapist and technician have emerged as trusted and contributory members of the health care team.

SCOPE OF PROFESSIONAL SERVICES

The scope of a contemporary respiratory therapy department is described in the introduction. Services that began with oxygen delivery systems and with the use of devices that provided respiratory assistance under pressure as well as medications have grown. They now include new technology as well as some services formerly performed by other health team members. In an attempt to more closely coordinate a patient's total respiratory care, many respiratory therapy departments have assumed responsibility from physicians, nurses, and physical therapists for analyzing arterial blood gases, inserting a tube into the trachea to maintain a passage for air, caring for the airway, and inducing drainage from bronchi by postural and percussive means. Since respiratory therapy departments normally provide services 24 hours a day, 7 days a week, the additional responsibilities guarantee the continuous availability of these essential services. The variability in practice from one hospital to another is primarily due to the degree to which the department has been able to assume total respiratory care. The services of a modern respiratory therapy department may be better understood by considering what respiratory therapy has been able to offer the members of one hypothetical family, the Johnsons.

Ricky Johnson was born prematurely at the Community Hospital. Because he weighed only 2 pounds, he was placed in an incubator, an apparatus permitting control of the temperature, humidity, and oxygen concentration of Ricky's environment. The respiratory therapist obtained and analyzed a sample of Ricky's blood in order to assure that the apparatus was meeting the infant's physiological needs. Later that night, the nurse and therapist observed that Ricky's breathing had become labored and irregular and that his color had changed. After checking the oxygen concentration of the incubator and obtaining and analyzing another blood sample, the therapist reported to the physician that Ricky needed more oxygen but that his carbon dioxide level remained within normal limits. Being aware of the toxic effects of breathing high concentrations of oxygen, the physician prescribed breathing the same concentration, but under pressure. The therapist prepared an apparatus to provide pressurized oxygen breathing and applied it to Ricky's nose. It worked, for awhile. Ricky's breathing and color improved, and another blood sample revealed that Ricky's oxygen level was improved, but now his carbon dioxide level was increased. Suddenly the therapist was called because Ricky stopped breathing, a common occurrence for premature infants. Since the therapist realized that a premature infant's problems are often temporary, a form of stimulus was indicated to keep Ricky breathing. The therapist connected a ventilator to an air mattress under Ricky. Every 5 seconds the ventilator would inflate the mattress; this movement kept Ricky stimulated and breathing. Another blood sample revealed that Ricky's environment was now effective; the incubator kept him warm; the device attached to Ricky's nose provided enough oxygen, humidity, and pressure; and the ventilator kept him stimulated. Ricky required constant monitoring and attention by the therapist, nurse, and physician that night. The next day Ricky began to improve, and the therapist systematically removed the respiratory supports. Ricky had survived a life-threatening crisis partly because of his respiratory therapy.

The Johnsons were accustomed to breathing difficulties; Ricky's older sister, Karen, was born with cystic fibrosis, a disease that produces very thick secretions in the lungs that often cause pneumonia. Karen must visit the hospital regularly for chest x ray films to be taken by the radiologic technologists and for pulmonary function tests to be given by the respiratory therapist. If Karen begins to develop an infection, her physicians wants to know immediately because pneumonia is a devestating complication for children with cystic fibrosis. Last year Karen was hospitalized with a pneumonia and required intensive respiratory care. Karen inhaled medications to relax her bronchial muscles and to thin and liquefy her secretions. Following this aerosol treatment, Karen was placed in a dozen different positions in order to take advantage of gravity to drain her lungs. While in each position, the therapist clapped Karen's chest, coached her in coughing, monitored her comfort, and assured that her vital signs remained stable. Although Karen received similar treatments at home each day, her pneumonia required treatment every 2 hours. Following 10 days of intensive respiratory care, fluids administered intravenously, and antibiotics, Karen had recovered. At home, her family again resumed treating Karen, using the same techniques that the respiratory therapist taught them in the hospital.

Several years ago, James Johnson, Ricky's and Karen's father, was in an automobile accident. The emergency medical technicians (EMT) responded with an ambulance and transported Mr. Johnson to the hospital's emergency room (ER). As they arrived in the ER, Mr. Johnson vomited and aspirated his stomach contents into his lungs. Suddenly his respiration stopped, and his heart stopped beating. A "code blue" was called, and the resuscitation team arrived to assist the ER nurses and the EMTs. As the nurses recorded the events, prepared medications, and connected him to a monitor, the respiratory therapist ventilated him manually with oxygen using a bag and mask, intermittently suctioning the airway. The physicians administered chest compressions and drained blood from his chest cavity. Since Mr. Johnson had not responded, the therapist placed a tube in his throat, which provided a secure airway. Luckily the EMTs had already inserted an intravenous tube. After a few minutes, his heartbeat returned, but his breathing remained irregular and ineffective. After Mr. Johnson was stabilized, he was transported to the intensive care unit. All along the way, the respiratory therapist provided manual ventilation. When they arrived, the therapist connected him to a mechanical ventilator that assisted his breathing. The therapist obtained and analyzed Mr. Johnson's arterial blood and adjusted the ventilator according to the results. Mr. Johnson was safe for the night, although he required the ventilator for several days. The therapist's job was to maintain the ventilator, keep it and all its tubing clean and aseptic, and adjust it according to the changes in his blood gas values. Once the ventilator was discontinued and the tube removed from his trachea, the therapist continued to provide oxygen but now with cold water aerosol to soothe his sore throat. Mr. Johnson was lucky. When he aspirated, his vomitus did not go very far into his lungs and cause complications. As a result, after 2 weeks he was able to leave the intensive care unit and went home 1 month after his accident.

John Johnson, James' father, has been smoking for most of his 60 years. After the senior Mr. Johnson complained repeatedly of being short of breath while walking up some stairs, and after James noticed that his father coughed daily, James convinced his father to quit smoking and to participate in the community's pulmonary screening program sponsored by the local lung association in cooperation with the local chapters of the American Association for Respiratory Therapy and of the chest physicians' society. At the local shopping center, a respiratory therapist administered some breathing tests on a device called a spirometer. From the tests, the physician suspected that he had an obstructive-type lung disorder and advised the senior Mr. Johnson to schedule more sophisticated tests at the community hospital.

At the hospital, the respiratory therapist was able to test Mr. Johnson's lung function more precisely and obtain an arterial blood sample for blood gas analysis. Indeed, the first test at the mall was confirmed. Mr. Johnson had significant emphysema and chronic bronchitis. Although there are no known cures for these conditions, respiratory therapy was prescribed to minimize the symptoms and make him more comfortable. The respiratory therapist instructed him in the use and effects of the inhaled medications that the physician prescribed, taught him the drainage positions and techniques of bronchopulmonary hygiene that Karen used, and some exercises to

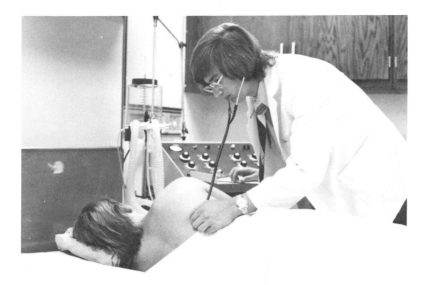

Fig. 23-3. The respiratory therapist monitors the ventilatory status of a drug overdose patient whose ventilation is being assisted by a mechanical ventilator.

strengthen his chest muscles. Although his lungs will never regain their original function, the techniques learned from the respiratory therapist will enable him to lead a more active and pleasant life.

These patient examples illustrate several routine activities of respiratory therapy. If Ricky, Karen, or James Johnson had not received prompt and accurate respiratory care, each might have died, and John Johnson would have continued in his pulmonary decline to a premature death. The nature of respiratory therapy often involves the breath-to-breath care of critically ill patients. (See Fig. 23-3.) The resultant stress is responsible for the periodic reassignment of therapists to noncritical care areas. The diversity of services provided by a respiratory therapy department enables therapists and technicians to routinely work on different patient units at a variety of tasks.

PROFESSIONAL LEVELS AND EDUCATION

Two levels of professional education are currently identified by the Council on Allied Health Education and Accreditation (CAHEA), an agency of the American Medical Association: the respiratory therapist and the respiratory therapy technician. There are approximately 200 accredited technician schools and 200 accredited therapist schools. Only Alaska, Hawaii, and Vermont do not have at least one training program. Most states have one at each level.

Technician schools are generally of 12 months' duration and are housed in large hospitals or community colleges. In 1978, the technician *Essentials* were revised, and upon reaccreditation each hospital-based school must include some college-level credit in its curriculum. The future trend should be for all technician programs to be in alliance with the community college. Eligibility for admission is partly based on completion of high school or its equivalent. Most programs include basic science, math, technical theory, and clinical practice components.

Educational programs for respiratory therapists are either of 18 months' duration at a community college or 4 years at a baccalaureate college or university. The 18-month curriculum expands the technician level training by placing more emphasis on technical theory. Pulmonary medicine and the clinical skills are generally expanded to include puncturing arteries to remove blood for gas analysis and testing for pulmonary function. The 4-year baccalaureate programs build on a liberal arts base and expand the 2-year curriculum with study of subspecialties such as rehabilitation, pulmonary laboratory, pediatrics, critical care, or cardiopulmonary bypass. Some emphasize management, education, and research principles. Most community colleges maintain an open door policy on admissions; students are often accepted with a high school diploma and a good science background. Admission to 4-year programs is often partly based on 2 years of college level work in the basic sciences. Over the last 5 years, baccalaureate level education has expanded to comprise 15% of therapist programs.

Only graduates of AMA-accredited technician and therapist schools are eligible for the CRTT and RRT examinations, respectfully. A few states have implemented state licensure exams as well.

EMPLOYMENT OPPORTUNITIES

Demand for respiratory therapists and technicians has not been met by the schools. As a result, some hospitals utilize in-service education and on-the-job training to upgrade their staff. Where therapists are available, their responsibilities commonly include critical respiratory care or supervision of technicians in the intensive care unit. Technicians form the backbone of the work force on the general patient units, whereas instructors, pulmonary laboratory supervisors, and directors of hospital departments are generally respiratory therapists. The baccalaureate degree programs have not been able to supply the profession with enough leaders. As a result, many leadership opportunities continue to be available for associate degree therapists as well as for exemplary technicians. As the profession continues to grow, services are expanded outside the traditional hospital environment, and hospitals continue to develop departments, the demand for trained practitioners will continue to exhaust the supply. Although the demand in some metropolitan areas has diminished, employment opportunities continue to be readily available throughout the country. Although salaries vary from region to region, they are usually based on education, level of responsibility, and availability of qualified personnel. Newly graduated therapists may initially earn more than $11,000, technicians somewhat less. The therapist who has successfully completed the national board examinations may receive $13,000 for clinical work. The salaries of supervisory personnel, instructors, and hospital department directors range from $13,000 to $20,000.

SUMMARY

Respiratory therapy is a young and vigorous allied health profession. As expected in a developing profession, the roles and responsibilities of the practitioners vary from one hospital to another. The nature of the work often involves interaction with critically ill and terminal patients in addition to orientation to various kinds of respiratory equipment. Professional education exists at three levels, and employment opportunities are abundant. As air pollution, smoking, and environmental insults continue to plague our society, the respiratory therapist and technician will continue to find a challenging and rewarding position on the health care team.

Suggested readings

A career for now and the future, Dallas, 1978, American Association for Respiratory Therapy.

Burch, D.: Spotlighting the profession, A.A.R. Times **2**:12, 1978.

Egan, D. F.: Inhalation therapy department; staffing and services, Hospitals **42**:40, 1968.

Eisenberg, L.: History of inhalation therapy equipment, Int. Anesthesiol. Clin. **4**:549, 1966.

Ford, C. W., and Morgan, M. K., editors: The great debate—technician training; to be or not to be, Resp. Care **22**:184, 1977.

Krumholz, R. A., and Hayward, D. R.: Respiratory therapy utilization in a general hospital, Inhal. Ther. vol. 13, 1968.

McKnight, C., and Watson, T.: A new respiratory care center; model for planning and design, Respir. Care **22:**1304, 1977.

Miller, W. F.: Respiratory therapy; what does it offer? Anesth. Analg. **47:**599, 1968.

Respiratory therapy educational programs, Dallas, Joint Review Committee for Respiratory Therapy Education (published annually).

Professional organization where further information can be obtained

**American Association for Respiratory
Therapy**
1720 Regal Row
Dallas, Tex. 75235

24

SOCIAL WORK

Elizabeth J. Laschinger

Professional social workers help people in many different settings. They work with people of all ages, with all sorts of stresses, challenges, and problems of social functioning. They work with people who are economically poor as well as with those who are rich. They work with juvenile delinquents and adult criminals. They work with parents who have difficulties raising their children and with the children of those parents. They may choose to work with couples who are not getting along with each other. They may work with people who are physically ill or with those who are mentally and emotionally unable to cope; those who work with the last mentioned groups work in health care settings.

"Health care" is our society's attempt to deal with pain. Pain is defined as suffering or distress, the opposite of pleasure, or the sensation that one feels when hurt. Pain occurs when bodies are damaged or malfunctioning because of disease or injury. It occurs when minds are ill at ease. It can be caused by feelings alone. "That was a cutting remark" and "you hurt my feelings" identify emotional pain.

"Health care settings" are those places where individual health professionals or a group of health professionals apply their knowledge and skills toward alleviating pain, such as hospitals, clinics, community health centers, health maintenance organizations, or private offices. A health care setting is usually viewed as a place where either the body or the mind and emotion is treated; however, bodies and feelings cannot be separated. We take our relationships with our family, friends, school, employment, church, social clubs, and so forth with us whether we go to a physician's office or a clinic or are admitted to a hospital. In many of these places, there are social workers whose professional purpose is that of helping the patient-client to (1) meet the challenge of his life's events (in this case, illness), (2) solve the problem of living with himself and other people in a way that is satisfying to all, and (3) strengthen him

199

and those close to him so that he and they are more likely to be able to handle future stresses and problems without professional help.

PROFESSIONAL FUNCTIONS

Social workers in health care settings are concerned primarily with the stresses and problems created by illness. People, when they are ill, worry not only about their own condition but also about how it will affect others. "Who will care for my children while I am in the hospital? How will my wife and children manage if I cannot work for a year or two? How will my associates react when they know I am in a mental hospital? Can I ever manage to make anything of my life if I can never walk or run or play tennis?" Patients who are not overburdened with social, financial, and emotional stresses are likely to respond best to medical treatment. Social workers help patients deal with these stresses in two kinds of health care settings, medical and mental health.

In *medical settings,* social workers help not only the individual who is sick or injured but also his family. The social worker is responsible for being certain that the community resources needed are provided to the patient-family. (See Fig. 24-1.)

> Mr. H., a 43-year-old man, has had his leg amputated recently. His wife, with three children to care for, is distraught with worry about her husband. "Will he get well? What does he feel about the loss of his leg? Will he ever be able to work again? At what? Surely not the factory job where he was hurt. What about money? Maybe I shall have to go to work. Who will care for the children?" And the children; they are upset. "What happened to Dad? Why is Mother so cross, so different? I miss my Dad." And Mr. H., lying in a hospital bed, silently grieves his loss. "I'm different; everybody else has two good legs." He too worries about his family, his job, his future and, yes, the bowling team. While physicians, nurses, physical therapists are concerned with helping Mr. H heal his leg wound, his social worker, with highly disciplined skill in observing behavior and listening, assesses the abilities of this family to deal with their problems and sets priorities for the solution. Mr. and Mrs. H. will be assisted with the complexities of applying for Workman's Compensation so that the family may have money to maintain them during the long period of unemployment. The social worker may help Mrs. H. budget her time, energy, and financial resources as she struggles to be both father and mother. Mrs. H. may be confused about how she will interpret Mr. H.'s limited abilities to the children when he returns home. Meanwhile the social worker is helping Mr. H. to express his feelings of sadness and anger about his loss, to understand these feelings, and to work them through to a realistic optimism about his future, his

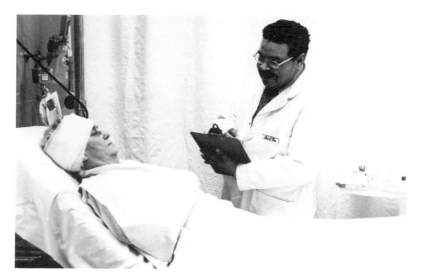

Fig. 24-1. A woman treated in the emergency room for multiple injuries resulting from a car accident discusses with a medical social worker the need for planning care for her aged mother who will be alone at home.

manhood, and his abilities to be father and breadwinner again. The employer may be contacted about Mr. H's eventual return to work either in his old job or in some other capacity where he might need retraining. In time the couple may be assisted with planning for the arrangement of their home life so that Mr. H. may take an active but different role in the family instead of being isolated as a "cripple" by family members and friends. By helping this family deal with the feelings of grief and anger that are always associated with a loss, the social worker (1) assists the patient in meeting the challenge of his disability, (2) helps the family as a social unit solve the many problems such an accident creates, and (3) promotes their confidence that by dealing with these problems, they can face and master other problems that life will bring.

In *mental health settings,* social workers work with individuals or groups of persons who are suffering from "the pain that feelings cause," feelings of rejection by family, friends, or society, feelings of isolation and the inability to make daily decisions. In these settings, social workers are often called on to contribute their skills in assessing the patient's social environment (both past and present) so that others who work with the patient may understand how the people in the patient's world view him, how he relates to them, what they have expected him to be, how they have expected him to act, and in what ways he has been unable to meet their expectations. The other members of the therapeutic team became aware of the patient's feelings about himself and the people in his world. The social worker's report frequently contributes to a greater understanding of the patient's past and present situations and involves the family in the treatment of the patient. The social worker is frequently requested to develop with the distressed person a different social environment. Upon leaving the hospital or during treatment at a community mental health center, a patient may need help in locating a place to live that provides him with either the independence or the support he needs. He may function better in his "own place," in a family other than his own, or in a home with a group of his peers. He may need the services of other community resources. Very frequently a social worker with extensive knowledge of health and social agencies is called on to gain the consent of the patient for a referral. In this way, the linkage between the patient and the service provider is completed, and the professional liaison between the therapeutic team and other helping persons is maintained.

In the past, what was accepted as treatment of the seriously disturbed adult offered few alternatives to months or years of custodial care in a mental hospital. The professional social worker's responsibilities were limited frequently to making arrangements for food, clothing, and shelter for those comparatively few patients who could leave the hospital. Gradually new knowledge about mental illness and how to treat it emerged, and by the 1940s professional social workers were being asked to engage in intensive counseling. This required that social workers gain greater knowledge and deeper understanding of the reasons for and causes of mental illness and emotional pain. Because professional social workers use themselves as instruments of helping, it was necessary that they gain a greater understanding of their "use of self"—how their beliefs, biases, values, and attitudes about people help or hinder them in their work of helping people effect change in themselves.

By the 1960s, a number of psychotherapeutic medicines were available and aided many of those who were mentally ill and emotionally disturbed to feel better about themselves and enabled them to act responsibly and more effectively in the complex world outside the hospital. At the same time, community mental health centers were being established not only to keep people from getting so sick that hospitalization would be required but also to help others who were feeling overwhelmed by the pain that feelings can cause.

For years, professional social workers had been serving families in other social work settings, such as public and private family and children's agencies. Their acquired knowledge and experience had developed ways of helping whole families rather than just one member when the family was falling apart. As social workers moved to the community mental health centers, their knowledge and skills in family therapy were employed in these new settings.

EDUCATION FOR SOCIAL WORK

The National Association of Social Workers, Inc., the professional organization serving social workers, published in 1973 *Standards for Social Services Manpower,* which established the following six-level classification.

Preprofessional

Social service aide: No educational requirements, entry based on individual's personal qualifications and employment in a social agency.

Social service technician: Completion of a 2-year junior or community college education in one of the social services with an associate arts or baccalaureate degree in another field. *

Professional

Social worker: A baccalaureate degree from an accredited program.

Graduate social worker: A master's degree from an accredited graduate school of social work.

Certified social worker: Certification by the Academy of Social Workers (ACSW) as being capable of the autonomous, self-directed practice of social work.

Social work fellow: Completion of a doctoral degree or substantial practice in the field of specialization following certification by ACSW.

More information about social work and these classifications may be obtained from the National Association of Social Workers. Inquiries about the work opportunities for social work aides and technicians in health settings should be sought from social workers in hospitals and clinics and from the area junior college faculty.

The Council on Social Work Education is responsible for setting

---

*A comparable mental health technician curriculum exists in a number of community colleges. Persons interested in preprofessional work in the fields of mental health and mental retardation should inquire using this title as well as social service technician.

standards and accrediting social work educational programs at both the undergraduate and graduate levels. Each year the council publishes a list of the undergraduate and graduate schools that meet their standards. Both lists may be obtained free by writing to the council.

CAREER OPPORTUNITIES IN HEALTH SETTINGS

Increasing numbers of well-educated social workers are being employed in both public and private health care settings for a number of reasons.

1. A greater number of people, both health care providers and patient-families, are recognizing that social stresses caused by physical or mental illness involve many people other than the patient and that all must plan and work together if the stresses are to be reduced and social dysfunctioning minimized. Coordinating this planning is one of the major responsibilities of the social work profession. (See Fig. 24-2.)

2. Provision of the services needed to reduce these stresses requires knowledge of and skill in blending these services for the patient-family benefit. One of the professional responsibilities of social work in health care settings is that of understanding how these agencies and services

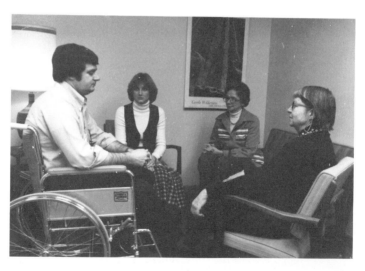

Fig. 24-2. The social worker helps the family overcome stresses and make new plans as a result of a physical disability.

can be organized so that the needs of the patient-family are met most effectively.

3. In response to the American goal of providing adequate health care to all of its people, health care providers are making their services more available to racial and cultural minorities. One part of social work education centers on the development of an appreciation of cultural and racial differences and teaches the skills in working with people different from oneself. Attitudes about health and illness vary from group to group, family to family. Social workers knowledgeable about these differences can be helpful to patients and their families. They can also interpret the significance of these attitudes to the other members of the health team.

Career opportunities for social workers knowledgeable about the impact of physical illness are many and varied. Some are hospital-based social workers. Others work in clinics, children's and family services, adoption services, mental health programs, rehabilitation, government welfare programs, and services to the aged, blind, crippled, and disabled. Many volunteer organizations such as the Epilepsy Association, American Cancer Society, American Heart Association, Kidney Foundation, Arthritis Foundation, and their state and local auxiliary organizations also employ medical social workers.

Social workers at all professional levels are also employed in mental hospitals and community mental health centers. Mental health aides and technicians perform helping tasks. Professional social workers with a bachelor's degree may counsel individuals, families, and small groups of distressed people, often as co-therapist with another professional person. Social workers with more education and skill may work as more skilled counselors; as educators and supervisors to less experienced staff members; as consultants in mental health to schools, businesses, and other health and social agencies; as researchers in mental health and community problems; and as administrators of the centers' services.

Mental health services for children through the years have made extensive use of professional social workers in hospitals and institutions for disturbed children and in child guidance clinics. Mental health services to children are not presently as widely available as those for adults, but such programs as Head Start (educational opportunities for the underprivileged preschool child), private family agency programs, and federal, state, and county programs in child welfare do provide the knowledgeable help of social workers to many distressed children and their families.

Salaries within the health care system differ depending on the skill and responsibilities required to perform the work. The National Association of Social Workers through its Committee on Professional Standards has established recommended salary ranges based on education and experience. Social workers with sound education, proved skills, and appropriate work experience command higher salaries than those less qualified. Also, the geographic area, the availability of money for the health care setting, and the value placed on social work services by the employer influence salaries.

In 1978, professionally qualified social workers graduating with a baccalaureate degree in social work from an accredited curriculum received salaries ranging from $9,000 to $10,500 annually. Salaries for those with master's degrees ranged from $11,000 to $15,000.

SUMMARY

Social work is predicated on the profession's firm belief that individuals have a right to their own self-hood and dignity and a right to make decisions for themselves as long as they do not hurt others or society.

To be effective, social workers must understand themselves, be able to handle their own life problems with competence, and be able to ask for help when it is needed. They should bring to their professional education an interest in the great diversity of people, few strong prejudices, and sensitivity to individual's feelings, attitudes, and beliefs. They must be noncondemning and have the ability to think conceptually.

Social work education provides a core of knowledge in the basic techniques of helping people with problems of social functioning and in understanding how to use oneself to effect change. It extends one's knowledge about people, their common needs, and the multiplicity of their attempts to meet their needs. In addition, it will increase a student's knowledge and understanding of community resources to meet people's needs and wants, and heighten his or her ability to assess the troubled situation, make sound professional judgment, and bring about constructive change.

Before one decides on social work as a profession, it is advisable to volunteer in a number of different social work settings, such as assisting a group leader at a community center, working as a "candy striper" at a local hospital, joining a group that visits nursing home patients or shut-ins regularly, or becoming a "big brother" or "big sister" to a ward of a local children's agency. Many more opportunities to serve exist; a varicty of volunteer experiences will aid greatly in helping one decide that one likes being associated with all kinds of people. The acquisition of knowledge of why people act as they do and the sharpening of helping skills come with further education.

References

Encyclopedia of social work, Washington D.C., 1977, National Association of Social Workers, Inc. See the following chapters: Disability and physical handicap—services for the chronically ill, pp. 252-260; Mental health services—social workers in, pp. 897-905; Health services—social workers in, pp. 615-625.

Ferguson, E. A.: Social work; an introduction, ed. 3. Philadelphia, 1975, J. B. Lippincott Co.

Professional organizations where further information can be obtained

Council on Social Work Education
345 E. Forty-sixth
New York, N.Y. 10017

National Association of Social Workers, Inc.
Suite 600, Southern Building
1425 H St., N.W.
Washington, D.C. 20005

25

SPEECH AND HEARING SCIENCE

John W. Black

WHAT IS SPEECH AND HEARING SCIENCE?

Speech and hearing science is neither new nor narrow in scope. It deals with the system people use for verbal communication. Conversation, public speeches, acting, or reading aloud are all means of communicating, whether the parties are face to face or use electronic equipment. It is acoustic, involving talking and listening. These systems are so important that persons with defective speech or hearing are often treated at public expense. Moses lamented, "I am slow of speech," and commonly special reference is made to a person's speech skills. For example, letters of recommendation often include comments on the manner in which a person communicates and refer to the quality of voice, articulation, pronunciation, and vocabulary. (See Fig. 25-1.)

Specialists in speech and hearing science may be referred to as speech and hearing therapists, speech pathologists and audiologists, logopedists, or phoniatrists. They have studied such topics as (1) speech and hearing disorders; (2) the development of language; (3) the development of language processes in children; (4) language and speech for the deaf; (5) vocal pitch, loudness, and quality; (6) the physics (acoustics) of speech; (7) the anatomy and physiology of the head and neck and the process of respiration; (8) the theories and measurement of hearing; (9) semantics; and (10) phonetics.

Speech and hearing scientists do not work alone. They are part of a team whose members vary according to the special needs of each patient or client. Team members may be teachers, medical specialists (pediatricians, surgeons, otologists, neurologists, physiatrists, and psychiatrists), dental specialists, psychologists, nurses, and social workers. The typical specialist in speech and hearing works with other professional people and serves individuals of all ages.

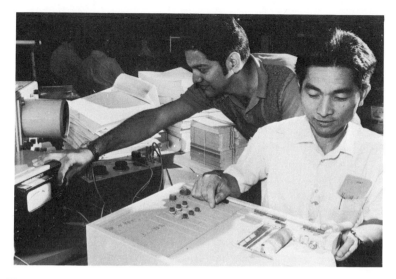

Fig. 25-1. Speech and hearing scientists are studying the intonation patterns of some well-known speakers for research purposes.

In hospital settings, speech and hearing specialists see patients recovering from laryngectomies or surgical repair of cleft palates. They may also work with those who are considering an operation on the middle ear as well as those who have Parkinson's disease or who have suffered a stroke. In schools they often work with children who talk with obvious misarticulations, stutter, have voice disorders or a loss of hearing, or are slow in developing language skills. In clinics, speech and hearing specialists deal with all of these types of disorders in addition to working with persons who seek assistance in learning to communicate more effectively. In industry they may assess the hearing of employees who work in an environment where there are high noise levels. They may work in laboratories to improve hearing aids and telephones or design electronic devices that people can use for self-instruction.

WHAT IS THE HISTORY OF SPEECH AND HEARING SCIENCE?

Speech and hearing science has been the subject of much study. In 1779 the annual prize of the Russian Academy of Science was awarded for an explanation and successful simulation of vowel sounds. Although

Alexander Graham Bell is best known for his work on the telephone, this invention evolved from his achievements as a phonetician (a student of speech sounds) and his work in teaching deaf persons to communicate. His interest in the field had been spurred by his wife's acute hearing loss. Sir Richard Paget, an Englishman with interests similar to Bell's, served as president of the British Deaf and Dumb Association and wrote an especially scholarly account of a theory of the origin of language, a work that contrasts sharply with Bell's phonetics books and inventions with their practical applications. Professor Edward Scripture was absorbed with the same core of facts that intrigued Bell and Paget. He worked first as an experimental psychologist and subsequently as a theoretical and practical speech pathologist. Scripture's works related primarily to talking rather than hearing and illustrate the diversity among speech and language pathologists and audiologists, or speech and hearing scientists. Harvey Fletcher began his career in speech and hearing science as a physicist in a university. His interests expanded in many directions as he coped with the topics of telephony in the Bell Telephone Laboratories. The insights of this distinguished researcher extended the horizons of speech and hearing science. Herman Helmholtz, an eminent German psychologist and physicist, maintained an active interest in hearing. His monumental volume, *The Sensation of Tone,* is available to students of speech and hearing science in a highly readable English translation by the dedicated phonetician Alexander J. Ellis, who studied and translated the epoch-making work of Helmholtz in his own search for a rationale for the perception of speech.

These examples illustrate the many phases of speech and hearing science, or speech and language pathology and audiology. They may clarify why the term ''speech and hearing scientist'' is used in this chapter to represent the fully trained practitioner-teacher-researcher, the product of sustained undergraduate, graduate, and professional specialization.

WHAT ARE THE CRITERIA OF ADEQUATE VOICE COMMUNICATION?

From the point of view of speech and hearing science, the following principal criteria are used to evaluate the communication system: (1) intelligibility both in talking and in hearing, (2) pleasantness of voice and minimal distraction in the production of speech, and (3) an adequate vocabulary and use of correct syntax.

Intelligibility can be graded, that is, given a numerical score. Intelligibility depends on the speaker, the listener, the acoustics of the room in which the speaking takes place, and the unit at a person's ear; for example, a telephone receiver or a hearing aid.

Pleasantness in speech is first an absence of certain readily identifiable vocal qualities, rhythms, and patterns of pitch that are identified with speech disorders. Reducing the distracting movements and mannerisms that may accompany abnormal talking has more than just cosmetic value.

The language that is used in talking is evaluated at all ages. Is this child developing normally? Can this patient make sense? Can either one of them understand me? Here the topic is normal versus abnormal speech and language. The professional worker must also be interested in the adequacy of speech skills for special uses. For example, a person who is employing a sales clerk, receptionist, or telephone operator needs people whose speech will be effective in those situations.

WHAT ARE THE NEEDS FOR PROFESSIONAL SPEECH AND HEARING SCIENTISTS?

Because speech and hearing skills affect our public as well as our private lives, the shortage of people who are trained to work with speech and hearing is especially critical. This shortage affects universities, state and local health agencies, and schools, and accordingly there is an increasing use of supportive personnel such as hospital corpsmen trained in audiology who work with speech pathologists and audiologists.

Training programs for supportive personnel are only now being developed. The laws in some states permit agencies to sponsor in-service programs to train high school graduates as audiometrists. Some universities are also experimenting with brief courses of study to train aides who will work routinely with isolated segments of speech therapy.

HOW DOES ONE STUDY SPEECH AND HEARING SCIENCE?

Speech and hearing science may be taught in university or college departments established to deal with these areas, or relevant courses may be offered in a number of departments involved with different subjects related to speech and hearing.

Undergraduate students majoring in speech and hearing science study voice and diction, acoustics, phonetics, speech development in children, anatomy and physiology of the ear and vocal mechanisms, and introductory speech pathology and audiology. They study psychology and should include courses in languages, linguistics, anthropology, mathematics, and biology in their undergraduate programs. This course work constitutes preprofessional study.

It is important that graduate students clearly keep in mind the professional requirements of the American Speech-Language-Hearing Association. To qualify for a certificate of clinical competence in either speech pathology or audiology, candidates must meet the following qualifications*:

1. *General background education.* As stipulated below, applicants for a certificate should have completed specialized academic training and preparatory professional experience that provides an in-depth knowledge of normal communication processes, development and disorders thereof, evaluation procedures to assess the bases of such disorders, and clinical techniques that have been shown to improve or eradicate them. It is expected that the applicant will have obtained a broad general education to serve as a background prior to such study and experience. The specific content of this general background education is left to the discretion of the applicant and to the training program which he attends. However, it is highly desirable that it include study in the areas of human psychology, sociology, psychological and physical development, the physical sciences (especially those that pertain to acoustic and biological phenomena) and human anatomy and physiology, including neuroanatomy and neurophysiology.

2. *Required education.* A total of 60 semester hours of academic credit must have been accumulated from accredited colleges or universities that demonstrate that the applicant has obtained a well-integrated program of course study dealing with the normal aspects of human communication, development thereof, disorders thereof, and clinical techniques for evaluation and management of such disorders.

Twelve (12) of these 60 semester hours must be obtained in courses that provide information that pertains to normal development and use of speech, language, and hearing.

Thirty (30) of these 60 semester hours must be in courses that provide (1) information relative to communication disorders, and (2) information about and training in evaluation and management of speech, language, and hearing disorders . . .

Thirty (30) of the total 60 semester hours that are required for a cer-

---

*From Directory, Danville, Ill., 1979, American Speech-Language-Hearing Association.

tificate must be in courses that are acceptable toward a graduate degree by the college or university in which they are taken . . .

3. *Academic clinical practicum*. The applicant must have completed a minimum of 300 clock hours of supervised clinical experience with individuals who present a variety of communication disorders . . .

4. *The Clinical Fellowship Year*. The applicant must have obtained the equivalent of nine (9) months of full-time professional experience (the Clinical Fellowship Year) in which bona fide clinical work has been accomplished in the major professional area (speech-language pathology or audiology) in which the certificate is being sought . . .

5. *The National Examinations in Speech Pathology and Audiology*. The applicant must have passed one of the National Examinations in Speech Pathology and Audiology, either the National Examination in Speech Pathology or the National Examination in Audiology.

Simultaneously with their professional study, prospective specialists master the tools of research and independent study to enable them to approach a client in the spirit of inquiry rather than prescription. They read the professional literature with understanding and seek to make their own contributions to it.

Much of the student's practical experience is gained through work in a speech and hearing clinic. Typical university clinics offer four types of interrelated services.

1. They provide opportunities for prospective professionals in public schools, colleges, hospitals, community agencies, private clinics, or private practice to work with and observe clinical cases.
2. They provide clinical cases for original study and research in speech and hearing disorders.
3. They extend free services to university students who have impaired hearing or speech deviations.
4. They render services in speech correction and hearing disorders to members of the general community. (See Fig. 25-2.)

The typical university clinic is coordinated by a director or supervisor, who accepts cases for examination and therapy in keeping with the four purposes of the clinic and according to its best interest. The director maintains and preserves a record on each person who is accepted for examination or therapy. Such clinics handle a variety of cases such as the following.

1. *Speech:* Each client is given a speech evaluation, and recommendations are made. Most therapy is individual. When there

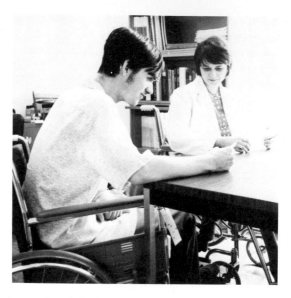

Fig. 25-2. A speech pathologist in a rehabilitation center helps a client relearn language skills.

are a sufficient number of persons with a similar defect, supplemental clinics are organized for corrective group instruction. The following types of groups may be formed:

a. Children 3 to 4 years of age (preschoolers) with delayed language development
b. Children 5 to 8 years of age with delayed speech or language problems
c. Children 5 to 8 years of age with articulation difficulties
d. Children who stutter
e. Children with repaired palates
f. Stutterers 10 to 16 years of age
g. Adult stutterers
h. Patients with brain injuries, for example, aphasics
i. Individuals who have undergone laryngectomies
j. Persons who speak with foreign dialects
k. Adults with voice problems.

2. *Hearing:* The services include audiometric testing, lipreading (speech reading) instruction, auditory training, speech correction

for the articulatory and voice disorders that occur in many instances with a loss of hearing, and hearing aid evaluations.
All services are coordinated with those offered by other members of the
allied health professions.

Current salary scales for speech pathologists and audiologists relate
closely to the different levels of training and are further contingent on
regional cost-of-living indexes.

Level of training	Median (beginning) salary (first 9 to 10 months)
Doctoral degree	$13,500
Master's degree	$11,000

• • •

The following case study illustrates the various contributions that
speech and hearing scientists can make in evaluating client problems
and helping clients to achieve improvements.

Mrs. Burns brought her 7-year-old son Tommy to the University
Speech and Hearing Clinic. She explained that Tommy had difficulty
in forming "s" sounds, that he was unable to make himself understood, and that he stuttered at times. According to his mother, Tommy's early motor and speech development had been normal. He had
just completed the first grade, and he reportedly enjoyed it very
much. However, his teacher reported that he confused many words
because of his inability to differentiate between many of the sounds
in the English language. He therefore was to attend summer school
five mornings a week, because his teacher felt this additional stimulation and training period would give him better preparation for the
second grade. Tommy has a brother Steven who is 5 years of age.
The brothers are quite close and usually play harmoniously together,
according to their mother.

Mrs. Burns is divorced and works as a clerk in a department store.
While she is at work, her mother baby-sits with the children. When he
stays with his grandmother, Tommy does not receive much stimulation even from children's television programs, because he is permitted to watch only his grandmother's favorite programs. For
example, he has never seen "Sesame Street" or any of the shows
designed especially to interest youngsters.

Mrs. Burns was 30 years of age when Tommy was born. She reported that hemorrhaging had occurred approximately 24 hours before his birth, which was 2 weeks premature. Although Tommy
weighed 8 pounds when he was born, he was placed in an incubator
for 2 weeks.

Mrs. Burns appeared to be an interested, intelligent parent. She realized that Tommy could benefit from greater environmental stimulation and was receptive to the examiner's recommendations for improvements in this area.

A specialized articulation test was administered and Tommy was found to make the following errors:

1. At the beginning of words he would substitute *s* for "ch" and say *soo* for "chew"; substitute *w* for "r" and say *wed* for "red"; substitute *g* for "j," saying *gill* for "jill"; substitute *d* for "th," saying *dough* for "though"; and substitute *d* for "z," saying *dip* for "zip."

2. In the middle of words, Tommy would substitute *k* for "t," saying *kiken* for "kitten"; substitute *s* for "sh," saying *fasin* for "fashion"; substitute *d* for "r," saying *tidesome* for "tiresome"; substitute *h* for "th," say *gaher* for "gather"; and substitute *g* for "z" saying *regen* for "reason."

3. At the end of some words, Tommy would substitute *d* for "r," saying *load* for "lower."

When asked to do so, Tommy was successful in pronouncing *sh, t, ch, z,* and *th* in nonsense syllables such as "sha," "ta," "cha," "za," and "tha"; and there did not seem to be anything wrong with his articulatory mechanism. He could move his tongue at will and had intact teeth, palate, and lips. Pure-tone audiometry tests indicated that his hearing was within normal limits. However, when he was asked to repeat words as he heard them, he made more mistakes than would be expected, missing five of the thirteen items on the Boston University Short Discrimination Test. On a standard test of intelligence, Tommy attained the raw score of 60, a mental age of 6 years and 10 months, and an IQ of 89. On the geometric form copying task of this test, Tommy successfully copied the circle, cross, square, and triangle—a performance level appropriate for a child 6 years of age. On the Goodenough Draw-A-Man Test, Tommy's drawing was characteristic of a child 5 years and 9 months of age.

Tommy is right-handed. His performance in hopping on one foot, throwing a ball, running, and rail walking indicated normal gross motor coordination. His manipulation of the pencil for drawing demonstrated normal fine motor coordination. No dysfluencies were noted during the diagnostic evaluation, nor could they be precipitated by increasing communicative stress.

On the basis of these tests and observations, it was concluded that Tommy had a moderate functional articulation problem and poor auditory discrimination skills. It was therefore recommended that he be enrolled for speech therapy, with special emphasis to be placed on building his auditory awareness in general and his auditory discrimination skill in particular. His progress or improvement was to be measured after 3 months of therapy through administration of the Peabody Picture Vocabulary Test, Form A. Mrs. Burns was advised to check the public library for reading material on speech and language acquisition. Her permission was requested to send the results to Tommy's teacher together with recommendations.

The low level of Tommy's environmental stimulation appears to be a strong etiological factor in his general lack of awareness of sounds and existing differences between sounds. Although he is stimulable for many of his error phonemes, prognosis is only fair due to his distinct deficiency in auditory discrimination.

Suggested readings

Davis, H., and Silverman, S. R.: Hearing and deafness, ed. 4, New York, 1978, Holt, Rinehart & Winston.

Denes, P. B., and Pinson, E. N.: The speech chain, Baltimore, 1963, The Williams & Wilkins Co.

Singh, S., and Singh, K.: Phonetics; principles and practices, Baltimore, 1976, University Park Press.

Van Riper, C.: Speech correction: principles and methods, ed. 6, Englewood Cliffs, N.J., 1978, Prentice-Hall, Inc.

Professional organization where further information can be obtained

American Speech-Language-Hearing Association
1801 Rockville Pike
Rockville, Md. 20852

26

VETERINARY MEDICINE

Clarence R. Cole

Veterinary medicine is concerned with the health and well-being of animals and human beings, the control of diseases transmissible from animals to human beings, and the discovery of new knowledge in comparative medicine. It has existed as one of the healing arts since prehistoric people perceived that the health of their animals was nearly as important as their own health. Records of ancient civilizations show some attempt to describe and treat illnesses of animals. Four thousand years ago an Egyptian papyrus recorded prescriptions for diseases of dogs and cows.

HISTORY OF THE PROFESSION

Nearly 200 years ago Benjamin Rush, physician and veterinarian, signer of the Declaration of Independence, and member of the Continental Congress and the medical faculty of the University of Pennsylvania, spoke of there being only one medicine. He was pleading for one of the many causes he championed—the establishment of veterinary medical colleges in the United States. His plea went unanswered for nearly half a century, until the truth of his arguments became all too evident. Disease acquired from animals caused widespread human illness and death, and food shortages resulted from epidemics among food-producing animals. It was a truth that has been demonstrated throughout history. Tuberculosis, rabies, typhus, and many other diseases, some of the most dreaded health threats, are passed from animals to people.

VETERINARY MEDICINE TODAY

Historically, veterinary medicine has come to the rescue of a disappearing food supply. Doctors of veterinary medicine, from those who guard the health of protein-producing farm animals to those who set and enforce standards for pure food from animal sources, monitor the food-

218

processing industry. Safeguarding our food supply by ensuring livestock health and the wholesomeness of foods of animal origin is one of the veterinarian's important functions. Through this work the whole population is served directly.

Modern veterinarians, however, are responsible for a host of other safeguards—both to human and animal health—that are often simply taken for granted as part of the blessings of modern life. The control of rabies is a classical case in point. Anyone who has undergone the painful series of antirabies inoculations and knows that because of them he has been spared far greater suffering and certain death is not likely to dismiss lightly the veterinarian's contribution in this field. Fortunately, few of us fall into this category, thanks to the work of veterinarians. In 1945 over 10,000 cases of rabies in animals were reported, and thousands of people were treated with antirabies serum. There have been only nine reported human deaths from rabies in the United States between 1951 and 1974; only one person contracted rabies in 1977. Its incidence has been decreased by 76% in the last 15 years. Yet because rabies still persists in wild animals, veterinarians have the responsibility for vaccinating pets so that they cannot become a link in transmitting the disease from wild animals to human beings.

Because of their special knowledge of diseases that affect both animals and people, the work of veterinarians is essential to the control of zoonoses, one of the greatest concerns in the field of public health. Zoonoses are diseases transmissible from animals to human beings. Rabies is one of the zoonoses that no longer threatens human health because veterinarians have brought it under control in domesticated animals.

In 1893 Dr. Theobald Smith, who was chief pathologist of the United States Bureau of Animal Industry in Washington, D.C., and Dr. F. L. Kilbourne, a veterinarian and director of the Veterinary Experimental Station of the Bureau from 1885 to 1894, published a paper, *Investigations in the Nature, Cause, and Prevention of Texas or Southern Cattle Fever*. In the paper the two doctors furnished the first proof that diseases can be transmitted by insects, something that had not been suspected until shortly before the turn of the century. Their discovery not only led to the eradication of Texas fever but provided the basis for Walter Reed's breakthrough regarding yellow fever in 1900. Other researchers went on to discover the insect links, or "vectors," responsible for transmitting malaria, typhus, African sleeping sickness, and Rocky Mountain Spotted fever from their wild animal reservoirs to man.

The list of diseases controlled through the work of veterinarians is impressive and may lull us into thinking that zoonotic study is a closed chapter in medical history. The facts are less reassuring. According to the World Health Organization, 30 of the more than 175 known zoonoses occur with some frequency in the United States. And these may shift insidiously because mutations in microorganisms can cause them to adapt to new hosts, possibly creating new zoonoses. Continual vigilance and alertness are needed to prevent them from becoming threats to human health.

In addition to old enemies in new disguises, diseases that were formerly found only in remote regions are being spread by the increasing convenience, speed, and volume of trade and travel and now are a worldwide threat to animal and human health.

Far from being exclusively concerned with animals, the veterinary medical profession today is oriented toward comparative medicine and the biomedical sciences. The veterinarian is in the forefront of space medicine and marine research, comparative pathology, and efforts to discover new and safe treatments for human and animal diseases.

Nearly all members of the veterinary profession, regardless of the branch of medicine in which they work, encounter disease conditions in animals that can contribute to an understanding of human medical problems. Since veterinary medical training involves many animal species, it provides a particularly good background for studies in comparative medicine.

There are many ways in which veterinarians combat both human and animal illnesses. Animal models of human diseases can be used for experimentation by veterinarians, who are familiar with both the animal and human forms of the disease. For example, swine, pigeons, and monkeys spontaneously develop arteriosclerosis, a disease that affects a high percentage of human beings and frequently results in heart attacks and strokes. Veterinarians are currently investigating leukemia in cats, pulmonary emphysema in horses, rheumatoid arthritis in swine, and aortic aneurysms in turkeys and are conducting experimentation vital to overcoming these diseases in human beings.

The veterinarian is responsible for research using laboratory animals, the indispensable bridge between theoretical chemistry and the use of new drugs on human beings. The laboratory animal industry is valued at nearly $500 million annually, and millions of dollars, for example, may be invested in a single stage of a research project involving germfree animals of a given genetic type. But the expense and the effort are wasted if the animals carry a latent disease or a genetic factor that can distort the investigator's findings. Veterinary and other medical researchers depend on veterinarians in laboratory animal medicine to conduct investigations using high-quality standardized animals such as those that are germ free. The development of the Sabin vaccine alone required 15 years of research on 30,000 Indian and Phillippine monkeys. Since this vaccine prevents poliomyelitis, we no longer need to close restaurants, swimming pools, and theaters during the summer in vain attempts to prevent the spread of this dread disease that killed and crippled thousands of people every year.

Veterinarians have played an important part in putting people into space by studying the reactions of animal subjects to high altitudes, acceleration, and deceleration. Their space research using monkeys and chimpanzees preceded manned space flight. In the manned space program a veterinarian heads the food and nutrition section that supplies the specialized space flight food, and another heads the radiological health team that is responsible for planning the evasion of radiation belts on space flights. A veterinarian was the first biological scientist to use lunar material in toxicological experiments.

Veterinarians are also working with marine mammals such as sea lions and dolphins to determine the effects of pressure and stress under water. Their findings will aid human aquanauts working at great depths in the sea exploring marine resources to help with the task of feeding the world's people.

Veterinary medical research is essential to determine the effects of radiation on animals, ultimately to protect human welfare. Veterinarians study the effects of both industrial nuclear energy and emergency radiation degree dosage to see how they affect the animal systems that we use for food. Animal tests can also establish safe dosage levels for human beings.

We depend on veterinary toxicologists to determine the toxic potential of many chemicals, discover how they accumulate or dissipate in the environment, and evaluate their potential threat to people and animals. The present severe shortage of these specialists could have alarming repercussions, since over 3 million chemicals are known and new substances are being synthesized at the rate of over 7,000 a year. Veterinarians conduct research using animals to determine whether newly synthesized compounds are useful for the treatment or prevention of disease in human beings. If a drug has therapeutic value, the verterinarians pursue their investigation to determine the dosage that can be safely administered.

Dr. Luther Terry, former vice president for medical affairs of the

University of Pennsylvania and surgeon general of the United States Public Health Service, has referred to veterinary medicine as being at a stage of scientific maturity to make its greatest contribution to human health and welfare. Some of the programs now being conducted by veterinarians have enormous implications for human health. Germ-free isolators and technology developed by veterinarians are now being used for burn patients. Some of the most promising investigative work on viruses as a possible cause of cancer is being done by veterinarians using germ-free technology. A new technique for repairing heart defects in animals may mean survival for human babies born with this defect. Research using germ-free animals has enabled veterinarians to make discoveries related to virus-induced cancer and infectious diseases in animals. The Stader splint, a metal bar with a steel pin at each end for insertion into the bone on either side of a fracture, was first demonstrated in early 1937. It is the invention of Dr. Otto Stader, a veterinarian from Ardmore, Pennsylvania. Spinal anesthesia was first developed by veterinarians, who were also the first to perform open heart surgery and organ transplants.

In the field of animal health itself, veterinary medicine is responding to the huge growth in popularity of all types of animals kept as pets for companionship and pleasure. It has been recognized that pets make very definite psychological contributions to the mental health and well-being of urban dwellers. There are an estimated 125 million dogs, cats, birds, fish, and other companion animals owned by families in the United States now, and a projected estimate using a ratio of animals owned by the present population indicates that there may be more than 135 million by 1980.

Horse racing is a billion-dollar business, and the number of pleasure horses is on the increase in every part of the country. Zoos now have more types of exotic animals, and more scientific attention is being paid to keeping them healthy and making it possible for them to reproduce in captivity. Doctors of veterinary medicine each year provide hospital medical services for many thousands of small and large animals, in addition to making many "house calls" through ambulatory services and caring for innumerable zoo animals.

In the field of animal health care, techniques and facilities are highly advanced. Since new surgical and medical techniques are discovered in animal research, veterinarians naturally use them on animal patients before they are made available to physicians for the treatment of human beings. (See Fig. 26-1.)

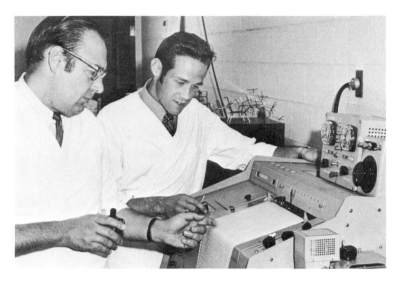

Fig. 26-1. The modern veterinary hospital provides health services comparable to those available in the human hospital. Two veterinarians use a spectrophotometer to check the blood chemistry of an animal with a heart impairment.

EDUCATIONAL REQUIREMENTS

The study of veterinary medicine requires 3 to 4 years of preveterinary college study in areas such as biology, mathematics, chemistry, physics, animal science, English, and the humanities and social sciences. The first 2 years of most veterinary curricula involve students in-depth studies of those basic sciences that are required before they can go on to the study of clinical veterinary medicine. During the first year they study the anatomy of the dog, cat, horse, cow, and other representative species as well as the principles of physiology, microbiology, and biochemistry. The second year is spent expanding their knowledge of physiology and introducing them to pharmacology in addition to the pathology of animal disease.

The third and fourth years of the typical veterinary medical curriculum plunge students into the practice of veterinary medicine through clinical studies in such areas as medicine, surgery, radiology, receiving, outpatient practice, farm practice, clinical pathology, public health, and preventive medicine. Many veterinary colleges are working toward improvements in their curriculums, and several have adopted variations of the core-elective program.

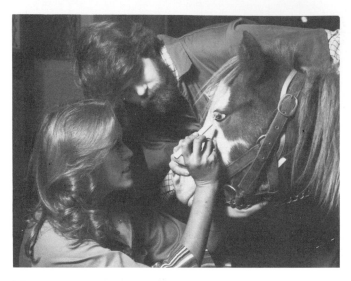

Fig. 26-2. Veterinary students are examining the reflexes and response of the iris of the eye to light. (Courtesy The Ohio State University.)

In the core-elective curriculum the principles of comparative medical science are taught in the first two quarters. From the third quarter to the end of the third year, the core requirements for clinical medicine is taught by interdisciplinary teams, presenting an intensive study of animal disease on an organ system basis. Time is allowed for electives, since the faculty recognizes that knowledge acquired through individual choice and effort has the greatest value and the most permanence. During the fourth year, seniors study clinical veterinary medicine. They concentrate on specific clinical subject matter in preparation for a career in one of the various areas of clinical veterinary medicine.

The curriculum reduces the time necessary for the core courses and allows more time for electives. It also provides for an interdisciplinary approach to all subjects and offers maximum opportunities for independent study to permit the most effective possible use of student time. (See Fig. 26-2.)

REQUIREMENTS FOR LICENSURE

The doctor of veterinary medicine (DVM) degree is the only educational requirement for eligibility to take the national board examination for a license to practice veterinary medicine, dentistry, and surgery. Some states do not require those with sufficiently high scores on the national boards to take the state board examinations.

JOB OPPORTUNITIES

Arthur D. Little, Inc., of Cambridge, Massachusetts, completed a study of veterinary medical manpower needs for 1978-1990. Based on a state-by-state analysis, it was concluded that there will be a surplus of about 3,900 veterinarians by 1985 and a surplus of at least 8,300 veterinarians by 1990. The report recommended that steps be taken to minimize the oversupply of veterinarians. Opportunities will be better for veterinarians with post-DVM education leading to PhD degrees and/or board certification than for veterinarians with only a DVM degree.

Veterinarians may prepare for careers in research by completing the MS and PhD degrees in the basic veterinary medical sciences such as anatomy, physiology, pharmacology, and pathology.

The American Veterinary Medical Association recognizes veterinary medical specialties in the preventive medicine, laboratory animal medicine, pathology, surgery, radiology, toxicology, ophthalmology, theriogenology, internal medicine, cardiology, neurology, urology, and microbiology. Specialty areas require 3 to 6 additional years of study beyond the DVM degree. For example, to specialize in surgery, it is necessary to complete an internship of 12 to 15 months at a veterinary college or at a large private institution plus 2 years of residency training and 2 years of surgical practice for certification. (See Fig. 26-3.) The American College of Veterinary Surgeons, an arm of the American Veterinary Medical Association, is the certifying agency. There is a great deal of competition for the available internships. Recently there were 60 applicants for the ten positions open at the Animal Medical Center in New York.

Veterinary pathologists are certified on passing an examination given by the American College of Veterinary Pathologists. They may take the examination not sooner than 5 years after receiving their DVM degree. Three of those years must have been spent in studying pathology and 2 of the 3 years in work with a board-approved pathologist.

Nearly half of today's veterinarians who are not self-employed work in the pharmaceutical, biological, and food industries or in government agencies. They conduct research to discover new drugs, vaccines, and food additives and to test their safety and efficacy. Veterinarians in the

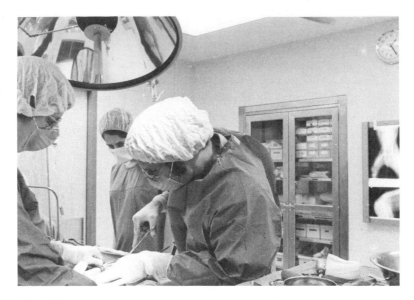

Fig. 26-3. Veterinary surgery involving an orthopedic surgeon, the animal patient, a surgical resident, and a veterinary student.

military are responsible for the quality and safety of all foods served to the armed forces. Veterinarians supervise the inspection of all animals and animal products imported into the United States, and their vigilance has kept this country free of epidemics of serious foreign diseases for over 50 years. The importance of this activity is illustrated by the outbreak of the foot-and-mouth disease in 1967 and 1968 in Great Britain that resulted in the loss of 415,800 animals. Government veterinarians at both the state and federal levels work in wildlife, ecology, space, and nuclear medicine programs. Veterinary researchers work for hospitals, universities, or drug and pharmaceutical corporations to discover new treatments and surgical techniques applicable to both people and animals. Several veterinarians hold high posts in drug and pharmaceutical corporations.

The profession offers low financial rewards. The average annual salary received by graduating veterinarians in 1978 was $15,800.

For private practitioners the initial investment in instruments and facilities is very great. Practitioners usually begin their career as associates with an established veterinarian at an average salary of $1,321 per month. In 1978 the average monthly salary paid to MS-degree graduates in the six disciplines and to BS-degrée graduates in several fields other than veterinary medicine exceeded the $1,321 paid to new DVM graduates from Purdue University. After a period of experience and accumulation of capital, many young veterinarians will build their own animal hospitals and employ several veterinarians as associates.

Obviously, to call any of the many careers in veterinary medicine typical is an oversimplification, but since private practitioners are still in the majority, the daily routine of a veterinarian in a small-animal practice is described below.

On arriving at the hospital, the veterinarian might first make the rounds of patients and then perform surgery until noon. In the afternoon office hours, the veterinarian decides whether the animals brought in for treatment should be hospitalized or handled on an outpatient basis. Evening ward checks and office hours are required. The veterinarian probably employs a receptionist who keeps patient records, a book-keeper, a medical technician to help with laboratory work and surgical preparation, and one or more assistants on the wards of the hospital.

Veterinarians in small-animal practice perform nearly all their work in their hospitals and offices, whereas their counterparts in large-animal medicine are likely to use their laboratories and offices primarily as headquarters, maintaining radio contact while they drive from patient to patient. As with all professions, veterinary medicine demands a dedication to performing a needed service without regard for a fixed schedule. This is particularly true of the private practitioner who must be available 7 days and nights a week.

Much of veterinary medical practice is devoted to preventing rather than curing disease. Pets receive immunizations in much the same manner as human babies and against as many diseases. The greater part of the large-animal practitioner's work involves diagnosis, vaccination, and consulting with animal owners as to nutrition, vaccination schedules, breeding programs, and all other aspects of herd management.

SUPPORTIVE PERSONNEL

The profession of veterinary medicine requires many types of supportive personnel. Colleges of veterinary medicine employ nurses, medical technologists, and medical illustrators as well as technicians who specialize in radiology, cardiology, electroencephalography, pulmonary function, and ophthalmology. They also hire medical librarians, medical record librarians, computer programmers, medical record administrators, and laboratory animal technologists. Private practitioners employ assistants in one or more of these technical and supportive areas. The size of the staff maintained by private practitioners will depend on the size of the veterinary hospital. All supportive personnel have two factors in common: they are greatly needed by the veterinary medical profession, and they are allied health professionals working under the direction and supervision of licensed veterinarians.

Veterinary medicine is in constant need of supportive personnel. The demands made on the veterinary medical profession, especially in the areas of research and animal care, exceed the available numbers of such personnel. Therefore opportunities for graduates in the allied health professions continue to increase. Among the various fields the greatest demand is for animal technicians.

Animal technicians

An animal technician is defined by the American Veterinary Medical Association as "a person knowledgeable in the care and handling of animals, in the basic principles of normal and abnormal life processes, and in routine laboratory and clinical procedures. The person is primarily an assistant to veterinarians, biological research workers, and scientists."

Animal technicians are engaged in a rapidly expanding health profession that offers a rewarding career for individuals who wish to combine scientific and medical knowledge with an interest in working with animals and people.

According to the Institute of Laboratory Animal Resources, National Academy of Sciences, there were 14,000 people employed in laboratory animal care in 1970. Fifteen of the available positions in the field were vacant at the time of the survey in 1970.

This field involves a diversity of functions, including clinical laboratory procedures, radiology techniques, medical records, preparation of animal patients for surgery, and nursing care.

As employees of veterinarians, animal technicians work in all of these areas of veterinary hospitals and in veterinary research and service laboratories.

To become a qualified animal technician one must have successfully completed an approved course of study. Prospective students may select one of 42 schools whose programs have been accredited by the American Veterinary Medical Association. Other schools are presently involved in the accrediting process. Two to 4 years of education are required before an individual can qualify for registration as an animal technologist.

References

Committee on Animal Technicians: Standards for the future, J. Am. Vet. Med. Assoc. **156:**396, 1970.

Rapport, S., and Wright, R., editors: Great adventure in medicine, New York, 1958, Dial Press.

Smithcors, J. F.: The American veterinary profession, its background and development, Ames, 1963, Iowa State University Press.

Summary of U.S. veterinary medical needs, 1978-1990; report of research conducted by Arthur D. Little, Inc., Cambridge, Mass., J. Am. Vet. Med. Assoc. **173:** 369, 1978.

U.S. Department of Health, Education, and Welfare: Morbidity and Mortality **23:**267, 1974.

Professional organization where further information can be obtained

American Veterinary Medical Association
930 N. Meacham Rd.
Schaumburg, Ill. 60172

CALENDAR OF HEALTH CAREERS*

The calendar on the following pages gives you a quick check on how many years of education after high school you should count on for the representative health occupations listed here. The lines and symbols show what is customary—some people take only minimum required training; many take more. The symbols used in the calendar are explained below.

● This kind of work requires no special training beyond what you can usually get in high school.

●--- After starting, you serve an apprenticeship or get similar organized on-the-job training.

▬▬▬ Lines and symbols used with them indicate full years. To start requires special training either in college, in a hospital or special school, or in a professional school after 1-4 years of college.

⌐ Special training is required, but you have a choice, each type of training taking a different number of years.

□ First symbol means you can get beginner's job after college but will usually need more study as well as experience for advancement. Graduate training ordinarily goes to or beyond master's or doctor's degree.

→ Your planning should look beyond minimum requirements; continuing study, after entering professional practice, is important to further advancement.

○ Although the line shows the minimum to qualify, more preprofessional years in college often lengthen the total training time.

(9 m) Special course or on-the-job training is shown in number of months.

*From the National Health Council and the United States Employment Service: Health careers guidebook, Washington, D.C., 1968, U.S. Government Printing Office. Revised according to the Occupational Outlook Handbook 1974-75, Washington, D.C., 1974. U.S. Department of Labor, Bureau of Labor Statistics.

230

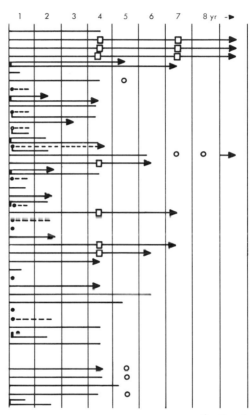

	1	2	3	4	5	6	7	8 yr -▶

Administrative assistant
Biochemist
Biomathematician
Biophysicist
Blood bank specialist
Certified laboratory assistant
Circulation technologist
Computer operator
Computer programmer
Corrective therapist
Credit manager
Cytotechnologist
Dental assistant
Dental hygienist
Dental laboratory technician
Dentist
Dietitian
Director of volunteer services
Electrocardiograph technician
Electroencephalograph technician
Electronics technician
Executive housekeeper
Food and drug inspector and analyst
Food service supervisor
Food service worker
Food technician
Food technologist
Health economist
Health information specialist
Histologic technician
Home health aid and homemaker
Homemaking rehabilitation consultant
Hospital administrator
Hospital librarian
Hospital service worker
Laundry manager
Manual arts therapist
Medical assistant
Medical communicator
(media specialist
scientific writer)
Medical engineer
Medical illustrator
Medical librarian
Medical record administrator
Medical record technician

Continued.

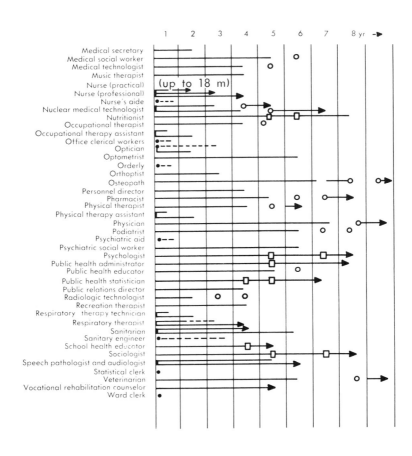

SUPPLY OF ACTIVE FORMALLY TRAINED SELECTED HEALTH PERSONNEL*

Occupation	1970	1980†	1990†
Certified laboratory assistants	6,700	22,260	41,160
Cytotechnologists	2,400	4,670	7,400
Dental assistants	9,200	39,110	71,530
Dental hygienists	15,100	34,190	57,650
Dental laboratory technicians	1,600	7,070	14,290
Dentists	102,220	126,170	154,910
Dietitians	15,300	18,170	22,340
Licensed practical nurses	400,000	565,890	819,790
Medical record administrators	4,200	5,140	6,430
Medical record technicians	3,800	4,900	6,460
Medical technologists	45,000	80,620	123,520
Occupational therapists	7,300	11,760	16,880
Occupational therapy assistants	600	4,360	8,820
Optometrists	18,400	21,800	28,000
Pharmacists	129,300	146,100	179,900
Physical therapists	11,550	23,030	36,570
Physicians (MD and DO)	323,200	446,800	593,800
Podiatrists	7,100	8,500	13,000
Radiologic technologists	41,000	93,560	161,280
Registered nurses	723,000	1,099,600	1,466,700
Respiratory therapists	3,850	10,510	18,810
Speech pathologists and audiologists	13,300	37,070	70,930
Veterinarians	25,900	36,400	48,100

---

*Modified from The supply of health manpower 1970, profiles and projections to 1990, Washington, D.C., 1974, U.S. Department of Health, Education, and Welfare.
†Figures in these columns are projected data.

PROFESSIONAL ORGANIZATIONS WHERE FURTHER INFORMATION MAY BE OBTAINED

American Academy of Physician Assistants
2341 Jefferson Davis Highway
Arlington, Va. 22202

American Association of Colleges of Podiatric Medicine
20 Chevy Chase Circle, N.W.
Washington, D.C. 20015

American Association of Dental Schools
1625 Massachusetts Ave., N.W.
Washington, D.C. 20036

American Association for Health, Physical Education, and Recreation
1201 Sixteenth St., N.W.
Washington, D.C. 20036

American Association of Nurse Anesthetists
Suite 929
111 E. Wacker Dr.
Chicago, Ill. 60601

American Association for Respiratory Therapy
1720 Regal Row
Dallas, Tex. 75235

American Board of Cardiovascular Perfusion
P.O. Box 20345
Houston, Tex. 77025

American College of Emergency Physicians
3900 Capitol City Blvd.
Lansing, Mich. 48906

American College Health Association
Health Education Section
2807 Central St.
Evanston, Ill. 60201

American College of Hospital Administrators
840 N. Lake Shore Dr.
Chicago, Ill. 60611

American College of Nurse Midwives
1000 Vermont Ave., N.W.
Washington, D.C. 20005

American Dental Association
211 E. Chicago Ave.
Chicago, Ill. 60611

American Dental Hygienists' Association
211 E. Chicago Ave.
Chicago, Ill. 60611

American Dietetic Association
430 N. Michigan Ave.
Chicago, Ill. 60611

American Medical Association
535 N. Dearborn St.
Chicago, Ill. 60610

234

American Medical Record Association
875 N. Michigan Ave.
Suite 1850, John Hancock Center
Chicago, Ill. 60611

American Nurses' Association
2420 Pershing Rd.
Kansas City, Mo. 64108

American Occupational Therapy
Association
6000 Executive Blvd.
Rockville, Md. 20852

American Optometric Association
243 N. Lindbergh Blvd.
St. Louis, Mo. 63141

American Osteopathic Association
212 E. Ohio St.
Chicago, Ill. 60611

American Pharmaceutical Association
2215 Constitution Ave., N.W.
Washington, D.C. 20037

American Physical Therapy
Association
1156 Fifteenth St., N.W.
Washington, D.C. 20005

American Public Health Association
1015 Eighteenth St., N.W.
Washington, D.C. 20036

American Registry of Diagnostic
Medical Sonographers
Division of Cardiology
Children's Hospital
Cincinnati, Ohio 45229

American Registry of Radiologic
Technologists
2600 Wayzata Blvd.
Minneapolis, Minn. 55405

American School Health Association
P.O. Box 708
Kent, Ohio 44240

American Society of Allied Health
Professions
Suite 300
#1 Dupont Circle, N.W.
Washington, D.C. 20036

American Society of Clinical
Pathologists
2100 W. Harrison St.
Chicago, Ill. 60612

American Society of Extracorporeal
Technology
Reston International Center
11800 Sunrise Valley Dr.
Reston, Va. 22091

American Society for Medical
Technology
Suite 200
5555 West Loop South
Bellaire, Tex. 77401

American Society of Radiologic
Technologists
Suite 1820
55 E. Jackson Blvd.
Chicago, Ill. 60604

American Speech-Language-
Hearing Association
1801 Rockville Pike
Rockville, Md. 20852

American Veterinary Medical
Association
930 N. Meacham Rd.
Schaumberg, Ill. 60172

Association of Medical Illustrators
6022 W. Toby St.
Chicago, Ill. 60648

Association of Physician Assistant
Programs
2341 Jefferson Davis Highway
Arlington, Va. 22202

Association of Schools and Colleges of
Optometry
1730 M St., N.W.
Washington, D.C. 20036

Association of University Programs in Health Administration
Suite 420
#1 Dupont Circle, N.W.
Washington, D.C. 20036

Council on Social Work Education
345 E. Forty-sixth St.
New York, N.Y. 10017

Emergency Department Nurses' Association
Suite 1729
666 N. Lakeshore Dr.
Chicago, Ill. 60611

Health Education Media Association
P.O. Box 5744
Bethesda, Md. 20014

Health Sciences Communication Association
P.O. Box 79
Millbrae, Calif. 94030

National Accreditation Council for Environmental Health Curricula
Suite 704
1200 Lincoln St.
Denver, Colo. 80203

National Accrediting Agency for Clinical Laboratory Services
Suite 1512
222 S. Riverside Plaza
Chicago, Ill. 60606

National Association of Emergency Medical Technicians
P.O. Box 334
Newton Highlands, Mass. 02161

National Association of Social Workers, Inc.
600 Southern Building
1425 H. St., N.W.
Washington, D.C. 20005

National Athletic Trainers' Association
P.O. Drawer 1865
Greenville, N.C. 27834

National Certification Agency for Clinical Laboratory Personnel
Suite 726
1625 Eye St.
Washington, D.C. 20006

National Commission on Certification of Physician Assistants
3384 Peachtree Rd., N.E.
Atlanta, Ga. 30326

National Environmental Health Association
Suite 704
1200 Lincoln St.
Denver, Colo. 80203

National League for Nursing
10 Columbus Circle
New York, N.Y. 10019

Registry of Medical Technologists of ASCP
2100 W. Harrison St.
Chicago, Ill. 60612

Society for Public Health Education
655 Sutter St.
San Francisco, Calif. 94102

INDEX

n indicates footnote.

237